EARTHSHIPS IN EUROPE

Earthship France, Normandy © Kevin Telfer

EARTHSHIPS IN EUROPE
Second edition

Mischa Hewitt and Kevin Telfer

Published by IHS BRE Press

IHS BRE Press publications are available from
www.brebookshop.com
or
IHS BRE Press
Willoughby Road
Bracknell RG12 8FB
Tel: 01344 328038
Fax: 01344 328005
Email: brepress@ihs.com

Printed on paper sourced from responsibly managed
forests

Front cover image: The Groundhouse, Brittany
© Daren Howarth

Back cover image: Earthship France, Normandy
© Kevin Telfer

Index compiled by Margaret Binns
www.binnsindexing.co.uk

Requests to copy any part of this publication should
be made to the publisher:
IHS BRE Press
Garston, Watford WD25 9XX
Tel: 01923 664761
Email: brepress@ihs.com

EP 102
© Mischa Hewitt and Kevin Telfer 2007, 2012
First published 2007 (ref. EP 78)
Second edition published 2012
ISBN 978-1-84806-236-8

For Gilbert and Mia

CONTENTS

Oscar Briz levels rammed tyres at Earthship Valencia, 2005 © Lisa-Jane Roberts and Oscar Briz

PREFACE

This new edition sets out to be rather different to the first edition. To begin with, we have widened the scope of the book to include the whole of Europe, rather than just the UK. Second, we have told the stories of the people who have built earthships in Europe in order to gain both practical insights and to learn more about them, their motivation and experiences. Third, we have interrogated in much more detail whether the US-developed earthship paradigm has been translated into genuinely effective building performance in built European examples. We aimed to be as objective as possible in doing this: no sacred cows. Fourth, we have been more comprehensive and detailed across the board with the information and analysis we present, especially after studying the thermal performance of Earthship Brighton. Only in this way could we come to any meaningful conclusions. And, last of all, this has been an ideal opportunity to evaluate a more general 'ten years of earthships in Europe' (when we started work on this new edition – in 2010 – precisely a decade had passed since Mike Reynolds first spoke in Brighton and kick-started the European earthship movement).

TV presenter, architectural pundit and self-build guru Kevin McCloud wrote the foreword for the first edition and there is an element of *Grand Designs* in this one too – one of the buildings featured herein was also on the 2009 series of the Channel 4 show, and the review of earthship projects are also case studies focusing on people's personal self-build stories.

Grand Designs is all about individual aspiration (collective, at a stretch, in the sense of most of the participants are couples). But is it possible to find a housing model that satisfies intensely personal dreams and desires while at the same time delivering outcomes that benefit the wider population and environment by being genuinely sustainable? After all, legislation and planning from governments can only go so far in countries with market economies where people are as commonly referred to as consumers as they are citizens. People need to want to live in sustainable buildings as well as being told that they should. But choice is restricted by what is available in the marketplace and, so far, very few low carbon homes have been built, and certainly not in a way that reflects the complexity of what different people want from a house. It means that, for most people, the aspiration remains out of reach. Self-builders, though, are people who decide to take matters into their own hands: 'forget about what the government wants us to do; forget about the rubbish that housebuilders are putting up: we're going to do it ourselves.' Earthships are entirely representative of this independent attitude.

Earthships are generally individualistic buildings, even if their construction often involves a great deal of communal effort; yet they claim to deliver benefits for the wider environment. In some cases, as we demonstrate in this book, people's motivation for building their own earthship is not at all about environmental sustainability, but for other reasons, like long-term financial security. These things *are* linked but this is not always obvious and most people would accept that doing something for money or doing it to save the planet should be regarded as different types of rationale. Although this in itself is a way of thinking that needs to change: earthships suggest that people can both be more financially free and more socially responsible at the same time. And this in turn suggests that certain forms of sustainable housing are not, in fact, part of some illusory, wishy-washy left-wing dream in the way they are often portrayed to be by critics.

But whatever the motivation for building an earthship, you need, to begin with, a building that works, or you'll waste tonnes of money and burn carbon like it's going out of fashion (which, of course, it is). This book is not a campaigning screed: 'build an earthship; they're the future.' Nor does it aim to be a glossy consumer pitch, saying 'look how cool you could be if you lived in one of these tyre homes'; nor is it a coffee table book nonchalantly surveying the scene. Instead, we explore – as objectively as possible – the pioneers' stories to examine whether the first generation of earthships built in Europe do work, and if not, then what can be done to make the next generation work better. Buildings that function effectively can dramatically improve people's lives in many different ways. Nice ideas that don't work are a waste of everybody's time. We – the authors – passionately believe in many of the visionary ideas that have gone into creating earthships. And we hope that this book helps to develop the vision of what earthships can achieve so that more people in Europe – and the environment as a whole – can benefit from them.

Mischa Hewitt and Kevin Telfer,
July, 2012

ACKNOWLEDGEMENTS

The authors would like to thank:

Laura Davies and David Buchanan; Lisa-Jane Roberts, Oscar Briz and their daughter Carla; Gillian and Kevan Trott; and Daren Howarth and Rick Lander for sharing their stories.

Clive Humphries and Scarlett Elsworthy at the Environment Agency.

Members of the European Earthships Builders United (EEBU): Willy Raets, Marcus Lewitzki and Kevin Schott.

All the members, board and volunteers of Low Carbon Trust who have worked on the Earthship Brighton project over the years.

All the funders, sponsors and philanthropists who made the Earthship Brighton project happen.

Professor Andrew Miller, Dr Kenneth Ip and their team at the University of Brighton for their work installing the monitoring equipment and downloading and archiving the data at Earthship Brighton.

The Centre for Alternative Technology (CAT) Graduate School for the Environment, especially Blanche Cameron and Damian Randle as tutors. The Arts Humanities Research Council for providing funding to turn the Architecture: Advanced Environmental and Energy Studies Masters degree at CAT from a dream to reality.

All of the people and organisations who have kindly supplied images.

Hybrid earthship hut at night (Taos, New Mexico)
© Kirsten Jacobsen

ABOUT THE AUTHORS

MISCHA HEWITT is a sustainability consultant and project manager. He has MSc Architecture: Advanced Energy & Environment Studies from the Centre for Alternative Technology/University of East London and is also a Certified Passivhaus Designer. He is also director of Low Carbon Trust (www.lowcarbon.co.uk) where he project managed the award winning Earthship Brighton project, and runs a range of sustainable construction courses.

Mischa runs the sustainable building company Earthwise Construction (www.earthwiseconstruction.org) based in Sussex and in recent years has organised many environmental events, including the 'Eco Open Houses' weekends in Brighton & Hove and several conferences. He is also a trustee of the AECB – the Sustainable Building Association (www.aecb.net).

In his spare time he plays the piano and composes classical music.

KEVIN TELFER is an author and journalist. He first found out about earthships when he interviewed Mike Reynolds at Earthship Brighton on an assignment for *The Architects' Journal* in 2003. He has been fascinated by them ever since. He has also written about earthships for *The Guardian* and *The Idler* and was the co-author of *Earthships: Building a Zero Carbon Future for Homes* published in 2007 with Mischa Hewitt.

He is the author of *Peter Pan's First XI*, nominated as one of the 2010 books of the year in *The Guardian*, *The Telegraph* and *The Sunday Times* and shortlisted for the Independent Booksellers book of the year award in 2011. He also co-wrote *Grand Designs Abroad* with Kevin McCloud and *The Remarkable Story of Great Ormond Street Hospital*. As a journalist he has written for *Green Building Magazine*, *Grand Designs* magazine, and *Green Futures*, among others.

He is married and lives in the New Forest.

Entrance to Earthship France, Normandy
© Kevan and Gillian Trott

1   INTRODUCTION

BACKGROUND

The first edition of this book was written when the construction industry and legislators in the UK were, for the first time, having to engage seriously with sustainable building and the challenges of a low-carbon economy. The 2006 UK government-commissioned Stern Review, *The Economics of Climate Change*, was one of the main catalysts for this engagement. It recommended that early action to try to both minimise and mitigate the damaging impacts of climate change was economically far preferable to inaction. In terms of housing, the report stated that 'It is vital that homes and other buildings are as sustainable and eco-friendly as possible. Further tough action is still needed to deliver significant energy use reductions in existing homes, but within a decade [we] want every new home to be zero carbon'. Policy initiatives such as the Code for Sustainable Homes[1] and the Climate Change Act[2] soon followed. The first edition of this book published in 2007 argued that there were difficulties in using earthships as the prototype for the required new wave of zero-carbon, sustainable mass housing in the UK. But, nonetheless, we suggested that many aspects of earthship design could inform architects, legislators, housebuilders and others on the road to achieving this goal.

The prophecy that earthships would not become an integral part of plans for sustainable housing has so far been fulfilled. A small number of earthships, though, have been successfully completed across Europe. And it is these European builds that form the focus of this book – they essentially remain prototypes of a building approach that was first developed in the arid, high-altitude desert of New Mexico, and has now been translated to a variety

Figure 1: Hut House kitchen (Taos, New Mexico) with bananas growing in greywater planter © Kirsten Jacobsen

of European climates. The key question is whether or not this transition has been successful, and if the future of earthships in Europe can now extend beyond a few high-profile projects.

THE EARTHSHIP DREAM

The people who have undertaken builds so far are pioneers – what Kevin McCloud, in his foreword to the first edition of this book, called 'first adopters and adventurers'[3]. Their experiences offer a fascinating insight into whether the earthship dream can actually be realised in Europe.

In the first edition, the earthship dream was defined by the writers of this book as being something like this[4]:

'Envisage a building that is, without exaggeration, a passport to freedom, where it is not necessary to work to pay utility bills, because you have none. Your home effortlessly heats itself in winter and cools itself in summer, harvests water every time it rains and recycles that same water for multiple uses. Whenever the sun shines and the wind blows electrical energy is pumped into your house and stored for your use.

'The water recycling system allows for the cultivation of numerous edible plants within the building itself, and you are able to live happy in the knowledge that your footprint on the earth produces a negligible level of carbon emissions and uses only bountiful and renewable resources that are flowing freely from nature to sustain your life.

'The building you live in looks after you and cares for your needs. Ecological living through earthships is not about privation but about an improvement of the quality of life for its inhabitants and descendants.'

This second edition follows the stories of a number of European builds to see whether this dream has materialised for those who have reached for it. In some ways this is a qualitative rather than a quantitative assessment – a question of people's experience rather than anything that can be nailed down with facts and figures. Anecdotal reports based on real-life experience are important – and the reality of what it is like to build, and then live, in an earthship in Europe is exactly the kind of insight that was lacking in the first edition of this book and one of the main reasons for this second edition. But interviews are also not the whole story either; more than two years of detailed thermal monitoring and other data taken at Earthship Brighton has been analysed to provide an in-depth study of the performance of an earthship in a temperate climate for the very first time. This analysis has

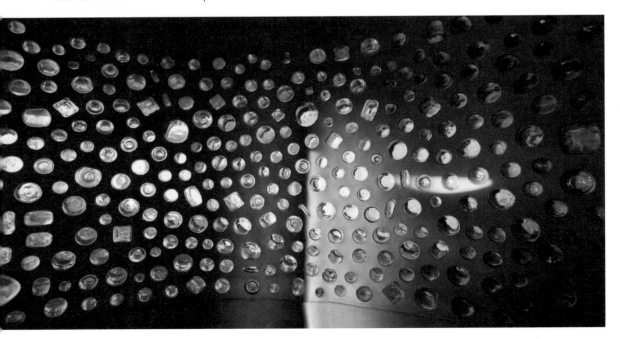

Figure 2: Reusing bottles in walls can create a beautiful visual effect (Taos, New Mexico) © Kirsten Jacobsen

Figure 3: The Groundhouse (Brittany) in the snow © Daren Howarth

been used as the basis to inform a series of design recommendations for future projects.

'GREEN DREAM' OR 'AUTONOMOUS SURVIVALISM'?

Earthships retain their appeal more than 10 years after their introduction to Europe, and more than 30 years after they were first built, because their implicit critique of wasteful, inefficient houses in a society powered by expensive, polluting and vulnerable energy infrastructure remains as relevant now as it was then. In the recent economic climate of instability across Europe and fear of even more widespread economic meltdown, against a background of fuel prices continuing to rise beyond the rate of inflation in some countries, the dream of no utility bills is a doubly attractive one[5]. And it is the economic factor that has proved to be as appealing, if not more so, than any environmental concerns with a number of earthship builders. Lisa-Jane Roberts and Oscar Briz built their earthship near Valencia in Spain, completing construction in 2009. Oscar said, when he was asked why they decided to build one in the first place, that: 'We found [the idea] inspirational and challenging. We like challenges. And also, the economic side

of it. The possibility of building our own house by ourselves … trying to get away from mortgages … it's a question of freedom'[6].

The idea that people are drawn to earthships not because they represent an opportunity for low-carbon living, but for completely different reasons, is interesting. This is especially the case when earthships are predominantly represented as ecological housing. So it raises the question about the design rationale of the buildings in the first place. Were earthships designed as environmentally-friendly structures, or was this an incidental by-product? Were they, in fact, developed merely to fulfil an inexpensive and independent off-grid lifestyle – autonomous survivalism in the high desert mesa of New Mexico for Mad Max-style refugees fleeing from the dying cities to live in post-industrial, tyre-walled enclaves?

Perhaps it does not matter. After all, if earthships offer successful strategies for environmentally-friendly living, then surely the origin and motivation behind the design of the building is irrelevant. And there is also a clear link between low-cost living and low-energy living; energy is not just environmentally damaging, it is also expensive.

Mike Reynolds, the American architect who invented earthships, claimed that his original inspiration came from news stories. He said that he was 'basically responding to the news' when he had the idea to design a radically new type of structure[7]. He was already critical of existing housing, calling it a 'dependent trap'[8]. By this, he meant that housing is non-functional without expensive centralised utilities for space and water heating, water, cooking and electricity being piped into the building. Those systems are not only costly, but potentially vulnerable as well. The news in the early 1970s told him that the USA was facing huge environmental problems, along with a 'major energy crunch'[7]. His solution was to design a building made largely from waste materials – initially cans and bottles, but later principally old car tyres – that aimed to take full advantage of natural resources: earth, sun, wind and rain. He realised that what most people regarded as rubbish could easily be reused in construction and he described certain types of waste as 'indigenous building materials' that could be used alongside other materials that people had built with for centuries[9].

He chose a challenging environment in which to design and test his buildings – the high mountain desert mesa of Taos county in New Mexico, about 2000 m (approximately 7000 ft) above sea level, with extremes of temperature varying between 40°C (104°F) in the summer and -10°C (14°F) in the winter, and with an annual precipitation of only approximately 200 mm (compared with over 1200 mm in New York City, for example)[10]. In the preface to his book *A Coming of Wizards*, Reynolds wrote:

'Immediately after graduating from architecture school in 1969, I moved to Taos, New Mexico, because I had been there on vacation and loved it. … Since I moved here I have never wanted to leave. Something happened to me here. I felt so at home that I think I must have stumbled onto my own energy.' Mike Reynolds[11]

But New Mexico also had two great attributes for budding architects – a lot of space, and low land prices. The building that Reynolds has developed over almost 40 years of trial and error in the unforgiving environment of New Mexico is a totally off-grid construction, unconnected to electricity, gas, water mains or sewage systems. In essence it has had to look after itself out there in the big, bad desert. And, according to anecdotal reports at least, it does it extremely well, maintaining an interior ambient temperature throughout all seasons – and without any kind of heating input or electrical air-

Figure 4: Jacobsen earthship at sunset (Taos, New Mexico) © Kirsten Jacobsen

conditioning system – of between 18°C and 23°C. Reynolds, on a trip to the UK in 2006, told a story about some visitors he had taken to one of his earthships:

'I took some people from Colorado into this room last week and it was 100°F (38°C) outside and they were sweltering getting out of their cars to walk to the building and in the room they thought we had an air conditioning system. When they found out we didn't, they wanted an earthship!' Mike Reynolds[12]

Sustainable space heating and passive ventilation are not the only features of earthships – earthships attempt to offer a holistic version of sustainability rather than just reduce emissions from space heating and cooling. The building also harvests its own water, which is then recycled to make it fulfil as many uses as possible, and generates its own electricity from micro-renewable sources. The greywater planters that form the basis of the water-recycling process also offer the opportunity to grow food, including bananas, grapes, tomatoes and herbs – even in the harsh winters of New Mexico. In essence, then, the earthship is an almost wholly autonomous, self-reliant building that uses waste materials in its construction, and has a negligible carbon footprint in its day-to-day running, being cheap to run with virtually no utility bills to pay and relatively little maintenance. Although the earthship design evolved in a very particular set of climatic conditions in the New Mexican desert, their creator has always believed that they should be able to adapt successfully to any other climate across the planet – 'it can be taken anywhere,' he wrote in *Earthship*, Volume 1[13]. More detail both on Mike Reynolds and the evolution of the earthship design are provided in chapter 2.

THE CREDIBILITY GAP

For all the fantastic promise of what earthships can deliver, there remains what might be called a credibility gap. Earthships have remained on the fringe of not just the construction industry at large but also that part of the construction industry that regards itself as at the leading edge of sustainable design. 'Earthships are not whacky, "way-out" or extremist buildings from the lunatic fringe,' was how the first edition of this book began, yet they have remained tarred with this image, perhaps even more so now than then. This is also despite the fact that they have been popularised in several different ways in recent years. Daren Howarth's Groundhouse (a building featured in this book, based on an earthship design, although also with significant differences, such as the fact that it is connected to the electrical grid and mains water) was on the UK Channel 4 TV show *Grand Designs*, a programme that regularly achieves viewing figures in the millions. A YouTube video of the episode has at the time of writing had over 100,000 views[14]. Mike Reynolds was also the subject of a feature documentary by Oliver Hodge, called *Garbage Warrior*, which was shown in cinemas around the world[15]. The film, though, may provide a clue as to why earthships remain so marginalised.

Figure 5: Tyre walls at Earthship Almeria, Spain © Laura Davies and Dave Buchanan – earthship.es

Reynolds has been described as a 'missionary, maverick, revolutionary bad boy of architecture' and an 'outlaw' by one British journalist[16]. In *Garbage Warrior* he is seen battling the authorities to try to get legislative approval for his own architectural test sites. He has a long history of battling the authorities. He was forced to give up his architect's licence after becoming embroiled in various lawsuits with clients and falling out with the New Mexico State Architects' Board. His licence has since been reinstated, but he remains an outlaw counter-culture figure and his buildings embody the same ethos, and arguably come with lashings of his charisma attached.

Sustainable building in general used to be regarded in the common lexicon as synonymous with 'alternative living', a preserve for a minority of do-gooders. It was code for hair-shirts, dreadlocks, sandals, hippies and idealistic dreams. Since about 2007, in the UK at least, and earlier in other parts of Europe, that is no longer the case. Sustainability has become part of mainstream language, used by businesses everywhere as shorthand to their customers that they have a conscience, care about the planet and offer quality products. Construction companies have had to embrace the new nomenclature as well. This is partly for PR and marketing reasons (so-called 'greenwash'), but also because legislation and programmes such as the Code for Sustainable Homes in the UK have forced housebuilders and other construction firms to start building more responsibly – or at least *appear* to be building more responsibly.

Anyone who has been going to the annual London Ecobuild conference for the past five years will have noticed how the cob wall and straw bale demonstrations given by people in jeans and muddy boots have given way to men in black suits and shiny ties showcasing their products in brightly lit corporate booths. Sustainable building has been sanitised, corporatised and professionalised. It has been made high-tech for the 21st century. The interior of the new type of sustainable home should be furnished with furniture from an out-of-town megastore rather than reclaimed wood from a skip. Sustainable homes are not off-grid in remote locations; they are being built in urban and suburban streets and housing estates, and connected with utilities. In this way they have been trying to fit in

with mainstream aspiration – after all, most house-buyers do not want to live in a house with mud walls in the middle of nowhere. Other than agriculture, there are relatively few jobs in the countryside across Europe and mud walls do not fit in with the existing construction supply chain and skills set.

This may sound like nostalgia, a longing for a time when sustainable building was supposed to represent an alternative lifestyle. But for anybody who is concerned about achieving lower carbon emissions from buildings (which represent more than 40% of total emissions in the UK) – as well as the other benefits to the environment that genuinely sustainable housing provides – the journey into the mainstream should surely be welcomed[17]. Those people are right to be sceptical about greenwash from companies selling 'magic paint' and other wondrous low-carbon panaceas, coupled with weak legislation that allows housebuilders to claim their products are environmentally friendly when they are not. In the UK, Building Regulations still represent a lowest common denominator standard instead of a tough benchmark for achieving genuinely high-performing buildings. But, at the same time, incorporating higher standards into mainstream housebuilding, using technology to solve problems of airtightness, heat recovery and insulation, and professionalising the construction process so that detailing is adequate to provide excellent performance is surely better than a bunch of hippies standing around in a muddy field making it up as they go along. Isn't it?

PASSIVHAUS AND ONE PLANET LIVING

Passivhaus is a standard that has been developed over the last 20 years to help produce successful, 'mainstream', energy-efficient buildings. The Passivhaus Planning Package is used as a design tool to achieve the standard in a variety of different climates. Several strategies are used to minimise space heating, including high levels of insulation, high performance building components and an exceptionally airtight building envelope. Passivhaus is gaining in popularity and according to BRE it is 'the fastest growing energy performance standard in the world'[18]. The approach is scientific, rigorous and relies on careful detailing to ensure that there are no draughts or thermal bridges (joins of external elements where additional heat escapes from the building). Most importantly it is proven, is quality-assured, and has an admirable track record all around the world. This is as far away from amateur, off-the-cuff design as it is possible to get. To date, around 30,000 buildings have been built to the Passivhaus standard around the world[18].

In comparison, earthship design, for all its extensive evolution over the last 40 years, lacks the same kind of rigour, analysis and attention to detail in precisely those areas identified by the Passivhaus standard as representing poor building performance. This is looked at in more detail in chapter 8 of this book, and it provides a clear example of how earthships are struggling to keep up with the new, computerised, professionalised approach to sustainable building.

This may actually be a point in favour of earthships for some people who reject a main-stream, design-by-numbers approach in preference to a more intuitive style, or who just want to live in a self-built, off-grid rural home. But that judgement is not necessarily made on environmental criteria. The 'green dream', if it is actually dedicated to reducing emissions and other forms of harmful consumption, might not be about what it is commonly conceived to be: living in an off-grid rural home and relying on a car to get to amenities such as shops and transport links. Instead, the more widely accepted version of the 'green dream' may well consist of a compact lifestyle in a city in a Passivhaus, using public transport, cycling and walking to access amenities.

The BioRegional/WWF One Planet Living initiative is based on ecological footprinting – a sustainability assessment tool based on 10 overarching principles[19]. Crucially, though, it is not just based wholly on the actual dwelling itself, but on an entire lifestyle, including food, transport and biodiversity. Earthships score well on most of the 10 principles. However, most earthship sites are in rural areas where there is little or no public transport or amenities, and the inhabitants are dependent on car use. This is at odds with the One Planet Living principle of sustainable transport and is certainly the case with most of the earthships in New Mexico, many of which are a considerable distance from major population centres. It is also

the case with all but two of the European builds featured in this book.

The point is that tools for designing and evaluating sustainable buildings are becoming increasingly varied and sophisticated. Construction practices are also developing in line with these standards. And this provides an opportunity for earthships to continue to evolve. It is clear that earthships offer their inhabitants more than just low-carbon living – they can also provide self-empowerment, self-sufficiency and low-cost living as well as meaningful connections with other people that often rise out of community-based building projects. They are inspiring and provoking. But improved efficiency and effectiveness need not compromise these things. If anything, they should enhance them. As Hunter S. Thompson once said, 'When the going gets weird, the weird get pro'[20]. And he should know.

EUROPEAN EARTHSHIPS

The aim of this book is to take an objective look at earthships in general and, in particular, at how the earthship paradigm has translated into a European setting.

The book began to take shape in 2010, 10 years after Mike Reynolds first gave a major speech in Brighton in 2000. That visit spawned the first two European earthship projects – in Fife (completed in 2004) and Brighton (completed in 2006). Two other builds also sprang out of the Brighton project: Gillian and Kevan Trott, who had both been to Reynolds' talk, built their earthship in Normandy (completed in 2008); and Daren Howarth, who played a leading role in getting the Brighton Earthship off the ground, built his Groundhouse in Brittany (completed in 2010).

Lisa-Jane Roberts and her partner Oscar Briz began building the first part of their earthship in 2002, and completed the whole build in 2009. Also completed in 2009 was the Zwolle Earthship in Holland, which was built as a community cafe in a park. Reynolds has been involved in various ways with several of these buildings and a European branch of his Earthship Biotecture company was founded in 2005 to advance European projects; in particular, plans for a multi-earthship community in

Figure 6: Earthship France, Normandy © Kevin Telfer

Brighton Marina, which gained planning permission but to date has not been realised. However, Earthship Biotecture Europe no longer exists as a trading entity.

A variety of other earthship buildings are in various stages of completion across Europe, including builds in Sweden, Belgium, Estonia and Spain. Several other buildings have been heavily influenced by earthships and the most notable of these are described in chapter 8.

There has also been the development of a grassroots, not-for-profit movement called European Earthship Builders United (EEBU), which at the time of writing has 85 members across Europe, and is growing. Its stated aim is to be 'the place where volunteers can find earthship projects and project owners can find volunteers. But it is more. It is about building a new way of living based on taking back control, sharing and helping each other making it become reality for all involved'[21].

SUMMARY OF CHAPTERS

Chapter 2: What is an earthship?
This chapter identifies the main elements that combine to make up an earthship, and how it is different from other buildings. It also looks at how new variations and hybrid ideas are stretching the fundamental design concept in different ways.

Chapter 3: Construction methods
A step-by-step account of how an earthship is built, with tips on everything from site selection to material choices that will be especially useful for self-builders.

Chapter 4: Building with waste
A look at the reasoning behind building with waste, the legislative position across Europe, and a specific analysis of risk assessment concerns with tyres.

Chapter 5: Renewable energy and power systems
An examination of the history, effectiveness and financial implications of off-grid living, and a review of micro-generation in Earthship Brighton and other European builds.

Figure 7: Home page for European Earthship Builders United website

Chapter 6: Water

A discussion of whether fully off-grid water strategies are genuinely sustainable or desirable. This chapter looks at the earthship's water systems from the first drip to the last drop, and the differences between the projects in Europe. It also considers the quality of water that the earthship supplies.

Chapter 7: European builds

Chapter 7 reports on European builds in the form of data and case study interviews that provide background on each earthship's construction and, in those builds that have been completed, what it is actually like to live in them.

Chapter 8: Passive solar design and monitored thermal performance

This chapter looks at the history of passive solar design, reports the findings of how people feel about living in earthships, and considers several academic papers written about earthships. It presents the findings of the Brighton earthship-monitoring programme, and analyses the results in terms of thermal comfort.

Chapter 9: Conclusion: the future of earthships in Europe

This concluding chapter synthesises all the information provided in the book and provides design recommendations for future European earthships. It also speculates about what will happen with earthships in Europe over the next 10 years.

Earthship France © Kevin Telfer

2   WHAT IS AN EARTHSHIP?

INTRODUCTION

The question of what an earthship is has not fundamentally changed since the first edition of this book, published in 2007[3]. And a higher media profile through television, cinema and the internet, as well as through architectural and home-building magazines and books such as this one, has meant that many more people now know exactly what earthships are. Nonetheless, there are still endless variations of the rather tiresome 'earthships have landed' headline that frequent the media, such as the recent 'Eco-friendly "Earthship" homes are out of this world'[22].

It may be an unconventional name for an unconventional building, but earthships are not frivolous or theatrically 'whacky' structures. Instead, they are a serious architectural response to many of the most pressing challenges faced by home-builders in the 21st century. The word 'earthship' is not just about one aspect of construction – 'buildings made from old car tyres', for example – but describes a holistic and practical approach to sustainable architecture, an introduction to which follows.'

Figure 8: Hybrid earthship at night (Taos, New Mexico) © Kirsten Jacobsen

TWO DEFINITIONS

The title of this section is a direct question that deserves a direct answer. In his first book on the subject, Mike Reynolds, the inventor of earthships, dedicated a chapter to explaining the concept behind the buildings. In a sentence, he defined earthships as 'independent vessels – to sail on the seas of tomorrow'[23]. He explained an independent vessel as being 'a self-contained vessel capable of sustaining an environment for human habitat on its own, through its own interfacing with natural phenomena' as opposed to a 'dependent trap' – a compartment that on its own is not able to adequately sustain human life[24]. As for the 'seas of tomorrow', he explained that 'considering the condition of the planet (due to years and years of abuse), our vessels must now be self-contained. Our numbers are too great for us to continue taking from the planet – we must now stand with it'[25].

Arguably, this is not so much a definition of an earthship as a definition of the concept behind it. In more practical terms, an earthship can be defined in a single sentence as a heavyweight, earth-sheltered, passive solar building with tyre walls, renewable power, water harvesting and recycling and sewerage systems.

THE EVOLUTION OF THE EARTHSHIP IDEA

The unmediated connection that earthships have with nature was in many ways not a true choice for Reynolds, who began building in a remote area of New Mexico where there was no available infrastructure (see Box 1 for a biographical sketch of Mike Reynolds). So the buildings he designed had to be self-sufficient or else they would fail to be habitable. But the initial impulse for Reynolds' design did not come out of the same type of sustainability agenda that appears to be the driving force behind eco-building today.

His first buildings from 1970 were made out of steel cans, in a bid to try to recycle some of the massive amounts of waste being generated by society. So, even at the very beginning, he was already experimenting with waste materials as the building blocks for structures.

'We patented a brick made out of beer cans, the old steel beer cans before they started making aluminium ones. That's what put us in the frame of mind to be thinking of bottles and tyres and other things as well. So it did start with that, we still use cans, bottles and plastic bottles we're using a lot of, the Third World countries have tonnes of them. We're using these materials, the bottles and cans were used as little bricks basically, for non-bearing interior walls and the basic structure is made from the earth rammed tyres.' Mike Reynolds[26]

The progression to using recycled tyres as building materials took place a few years later. Reynolds says that:

'In the mid-seventies we began looking for ways to build thermal mass into buildings for the purpose of stabilising temperatures. Because we were already building with cans, we found ourselves in the frame of mind to see [about] the possibility of using tyres for buildings.' Mike Reynolds[27]

This was partially motivated by unfolding energy crises at the time, such as that of 1973, and by concerns about the long-term security of fossil fuel supplies, which established the idea of self-sufficiency from the perspective of energy security, as much as from an ecological viewpoint. Medium- to long-term security of supply remains a critical issue in the fossil fuel energy industry today[28].

On building with car tyres, Reynolds has said that 'we don't desperately need tyres, but they're growing as fast as trees, if not faster!'[29].

The experiment of building with tyres was a successful one in a number of different ways; for example, both structurally and in terms of thermal mass. It started a process of experimentation and evolution that has continued over the past 30 years.

In the USA, earthships have been built in Arizona, Colorado, Ohio and many other states, but most of them are located in three communities located near Taos, New Mexico: the Greater World, STAR and REACH[30]. The Greater World was created in 1994, and is spread over 256 ha of desert mesa located at an altitude of 2120 m. It became a legal subdivision in 1998, and has a code in place to restrict all development to earthships[31]. Social Transformation Alternative Republic (STAR) was founded in 1992, is situated west of Taos, and is spread over 260 ha. Rural Earthship Alternative

MIKE REYNOLDS: A BIOGRAPHICAL SKETCH

Mike Reynolds is a wide-eyed visionary from the desert, a modern-day William Blake, full of uncompromising wisdom, aphorisms and poetry; a rugged outlaw American individualist like Henry David Thoreau or Ken Kesey. In short, he's not what you'd call a conventional architect. His first book, before he published a whole series of books on earthships, was called *A Coming of Wizards*[a]. It contains a mixture of autobiographical material, visions and writing on architecture, psychology, physics, religion and energy. It is copiously illustrated with his own drawings. This is how Reynolds introduces it:

'This book centers around and was inspired by an experience with four wizards. From this experience I have developed a way of thinking and living that is vividly expressed in my architectural work.'[a]

This may sound like pretty far-out stuff to some readers but the object of this sketch is not to hold Reynolds up to ridicule but to try to understand a little more of the background behind how earthships came into being.

He arrived in Taos, New Mexico in 1969 after graduating from architecture school and has remained there ever since. He writes in *The Coming of Wizards* that when he moved to New Mexico he was interested in pyramids. He built his own pyramid on top of his house and used it as a space to sleep and relax in. He began to have 'intense experiences, dreams, instances of automatic writing, and outright visions.'[b] He points out that he was not under the influence of any drugs. He explains that:

'My work as an architect/builder began to reflect what was happening to me. The earth became a sacred place that I wanted human life to embrace rather than exploit. I set about trying to achieve this for myself and others. I became focused on developing self-sufficient housing made from recycled materials using energy from the sun and wind.'[a]

A long series of experiments followed, at first making structures using mainly aluminium cans and cement such as the Thumb House in 1972. He also built with bottles and, finally, with tyres.

'In nature,' he wrote, 'there is no such thing as garbage. Garbage is simply a concept of the human dogma.

'If we don't know what to do with the by-product ... we shouldn't use the product.'[c]

He mentions in *The Coming of Wizards* that he is developing an earthship as 'a prototype for a design to be used by the homeless.'[d] In recent years too, Reynolds has taken teams to places that have been hit by natural disasters in order to build shelters for people who have become homeless – in Haiti, after the earthquake, and in Little Andaman in the Andaman Islands after the Indian Ocean tsunami on Boxing Day, 2004. The implicit message is that the people in disaster zones have to try to build with whatever is available to them – and often that means mostly rubbish – garbage.

The Little Andaman Island building is shown in the film *Garbage Warrior*[e]. Reynolds, of course, is the eponymous hero of the film and it follows him as he battles the New Mexico State authorities in a bid to establish a test site where he can experiment with building structures that may not comply with regulations.

Battling with authority and the law is a common theme: he has been stripped of his licence to practise architecture – and had it reinstated – in his controversial career. That's partly because he is extremely passionate and angry. He feels that not enough is being done to encourage building in a way that is less harmful to the planet and less stressful to people. This tends to bring him into conflict with bureaucracy.

'While other people and professionals may take this forward in different ways,' he says, 'we're right now planting the seeds, and, if humanity is to survive, they will have to do something like this. [...]Earthships can make it so more people can simply survive in an uncertain future, but if introduced in a large way soon enough, they can change that future.'[f]

References and notes

(a) Reynolds M. A coming of wizards: a manual of human potential, Taos, New Mexico, The High Mesa Foundation.

(b) Ibid, preface.

(c) Ibid, pp 122–124.

(d) Ibid, p 134.

(e) www.garbagewarrior.com.

(f) Email from Mike Reynolds to Kevin Telfer, January 2007.

Community Habitat (REACH was started in 1989, and is located on 22 ha of mountains above Valdez, near Taos[30]). All of the communities are either self-built or have been built by Earthship Biotecture, and house around 200 people with no centralised utilities[30]. In each new build the idea is to tailor the concept to suit the particular environmental conditions, and Reynolds sees the flexibility and constant evolution of the earthship systems, on an individual earthship-by-earthship basis, as being part of their intrinsic value, derived from homeowners taking responsibility for their own 'life support'.

The form of an earthship can be very varied, although after all the different elements are taken into consideration they tend to be fairly similar. There is the potential to create numerous different forms using the central principles embodied in the building; the approach is not prescriptive but pragmatic. However, there have been only a few variations built to date. These are the rectilinear 'packaged nest' earthship, which in the USA includes options for prefabrication, and modular earthships based on a combination of 'U-shapes' and (circular) 'huts'. The U-module means that there is mass on three sides, and multiple modules combined can create an entire dwelling. Earthship France is a nest 'packaged' earthship. Earthship Brighton is a hybrid earthship that is composed of a nest and a hut.

The design of earthships in Fife, Brighton and elsewhere in Europe reflects the ecology and lessons learned from the experiences of building and living in Taos. But the key question is whether the transition of the design idea has been successful – and that is one of the main topics of this book.

DEFINING PRINCIPLES

We have decided to explain what earthships are in two key ways – first by describing what we see as the five defining principles of earthships, and second by describing in brief their specific design features.

The defining principles are:
- comfort for people
- site harmony
- sustainable resource use
- autonomy and self-sufficiency
- aesthetic functionality.

Comfort for people

The primary purpose of earthships is as residential structures, designed specifically to provide comfortable shelter and homes for people. Most modern housing comprises thin-walled shells that would be completely uninhabitable were it not for centralised, grid-derived resources to drive the space heating, hot water, electrical input and fresh water that fuel them. Mike Reynolds described them as 'compartments that we pump life support into'[32]. By contrast, earthships provide the vital apparatus for human life embedded within the building.

Figure 9: Split-level earthship (Taos, New Mexico) © Kirsten Jacobsen

Figure 10: Earthship Fife visitor centre (Kinghorn, Scotland) © Kevin Telfer

The 'life support' for conventional housing consists of mains electricity, gas, water and sewerage that help to make homes comfortable to live in. These rely on centralised infrastructure that transports these services into people's homes. At the moment, in most developed nations that infrastructure is reasonably reliable in that, when people turn a tap, water will come out; when they flick a switch, a bulb will light up; and when they flush the toilet, waste goes away. Yet there are also significant elements of risk involved, and the provision of these services is generally completely out of people's individual control. Examples of risk include extreme weather and other natural events, such as heat waves leading to power outages due to too much demand or rivers being too hot for cooling power stations, or hurricanes and flooding damaging electricity pylons and substations. Most experts agree that there will be more and more extreme weather events due to the impact of climate change, and therefore more risk of infrastructure being damaged[33]. Another risk is cost, with the prices of domestic electricity and gas rising above inflation across Europe, meaning that more and more people are falling into fuel poverty. Currently one household in seven in Europe is in, or on the margins of, fuel poverty, and this figure is likely to increase, according to the European Fuel Poverty and Energy Efficiency group[34].

Most energy supplied through mains infrastructure is also very carbon intensive, because in most countries it is generated using large amounts of fossil fuels such as coal and gas. The easy availability of energy through the grid has meant that, for a long time, architecture has not considered the wider implications of energy-hungry buildings. Paul Hyett, a former RIBA president, has argued that there exists:

'an architecture that is increasingly incapable of serving its most primitive purpose: providing safe shelter. Our modern cities continue to be torn apart to accommodate ecologically destructive buildings that have insatiable energy demands for even the most basic functions of ventilation, lighting and cooling.' Paul Hyett[35]

There are major advantages to infrastructure as well, and some of the arguments around whether it is better to be off-grid or connected to centralised systems are discussed throughout this book, but especially in chapter 5 (on power systems) and chapter 6 (on water).

Earthships are not meant to be about privation in any sense; they aim to provide human comfort by supplying warmth, shelter, water, electricity and light. They also aim to provide security and a degree of economic freedom by placing all the essential systems for life directly within the control of the homeowner. It is not necessary to work to pay utility bills, because there are none, although there are increased upfront capital costs with the renewable energy systems. Earthships heat themselves in winter and cool themselves in summer, but sometimes require backup heating, depending on where they are located. They harvest water every time it rains or snows, and recycle that same water for multiple uses. Whenever the sun shines or the wind blows, electrical energy is generated and stored for use. However, Reynolds points out that occupants should not expect to be able to consume resources at the

same rate as they might in current, unsustainable housing: 'our usual amount of needs must be reduced,' he writes[36]. Electricity use is limited by the amount that can be generated from renewable power systems and stored in the batteries. Water is limited by the amount of precipitation and the storage capacity of the tanks. The systems are finite, but, if they are designed correctly, they should be adequate for human comfort.

This also means that the building produces a low level of carbon emissions during operation, and uses only renewable natural resources to sustain life. The only use of fossil fuel in most earthships is bottled gas for cooking. The concept is that the building works for its inhabitants, rather than the other way round.

It may sound like a tough dream to achieve, and the same hurdles are presented by the site selection, planning process, construction and capital finance requirements as are involved in any building. But people who have lived in earthships in the USA for the past 20 years – and now, more recently, in Europe – say that the dream can come true. Lisa and Oscar, who built their earthship in Spain, have said that they've found off-grid living to be 'miraculous'.

Figure 11: Oscar and Lisa pounding tyres in 2005 (Earthship Valencia) © Lisa-Jane Roberts and Oscar Briz

'The first time I had a shower in the earthship,' says Lisa, 'I had a real physical sensation of wow! I had this feeling of showering in water from the sky, powered by the sun.'[37]

And this is where the descriptive nature of the name earth 'ship' becomes apparent. The earthship has no connection to mains water, the national power grid, the gas main, or the sewage system – the utilities that most conventional buildings in Europe are tethered to. Therefore it could be said that the earthship is 'free floating', like a yacht or ship that uses only the natural resources of the wind, tide and currents to sail from place to place. Similarly, the earthship uses the sun, wind and rain to achieve its primary aim – providing comfortable accommodation for its inhabitants. The significant point is that the earthship provides comfort for the occupants from sustainable sources derived directly from the site itself.

Site harmony

The use of renewable natural resources harnessed on any site, such as sunlight, wind and rain, immediately draws comparison with 'systems' found in nature. In many ways, the earthship seeks to mimic some of these natural systems, which provide instruction in what might be called 'site harmony'. The deciduous tree is a good example. It is a solar-oriented structure that uses its leaves as solar collectors for harnessing energy. The branches of a tree grow in such a way as to promote the greatest possible exposure of its leaves to the sun so that it can collect as much energy as possible. The tree's root system obtains both water and nutrients from the soil, and helps in the process of recycling those nutrients as leaves drop off the tree and get absorbed into the soil once more. The wind spreads the seeds of the tree, and removes dead branches from its structure. The tree is able to – and in fact has to – obtain all that it needs from its immediate site and surroundings. It is a highly successful organism that is endemic across the world, despite pressures from human intervention. Trees also provide habitats for other forms of life – and live in synergy with their surroundings.

Like trees, the earthship seeks to establish a connection with nature that is not exploitative, but is balanced by using the resources that the site offers to the building's maximum advantage. Although the earthship concept is universal, each building needs to be tailored to the site where it is located, to take full advantage of the particular characteristics of the unique local environment. For example, in dry climates the angle of the front glass façade can be tailored to be perpendicular to the angle of the winter sun at its lowest point in the sky, to maximise solar gain in winter and minimise it in summer, or the roof can be designed to catch either snow melt or rain, depending on weather patterns. In temperate and cold climates of the northern hemisphere all earthships will face south, to receive the maximum amount of sunlight available in the colder months, although large amounts of glazing can lead to extensive heat loss, as discussed later in the book; the main demand onsite choice here is that the area must have a southern aspect. This can be flat or on a south-facing slope; the last characteristic means that the earthship is suitable for developments into steep, south-facing cliffs. The most extreme example of how this is possible is the REACH community in Taos, New Mexico, which is halfway up the side of a mountain. The systems for micro-generation will also be specifically tuned to the particular site, with photovoltaic (PV) arrays facing south for maximum solar capture; with wind turbines sited in the most advantageous location, if suitable, with minimal obstacles interfering; and with the possibility of employing other forms of site-specific generation, such as micro-hydro, if there is a stream or river on, or near, the site (as at Earthship Fife).

As the sun is the generator that fuels the planet and its weather systems, it is inevitable that the earthship should try to make best use of the sun's free energy. The solar orientation of the earthship is the single greatest factor in ensuring successful passive solar heating. By human standards the sun is a virtually inexhaustible power source that provides, according to author Godfrey Boyle, more than 10,000 times humanity's current rate of use of fossil and nuclear fuels combined, so it seems remarkable that more use is not made of the sun, in almost all senses[38]. The earthship attempts to provide an alternative vision to the current situation where elements – sun, wind and rain – constantly interact with our buildings, yet most of the built stock takes very little advantage of that interaction.

The earthship, though, gathers and uses all of its resources from immediately around it. The elements that interact with the earthship are either used directly – such as passive solar heating, for example – or converted into electrical energy, or stored for use as they are needed, including periods when the resource may be scarce – for example, storing rainwater to be used during dry periods or heat in the thermal mass during cold periods.

Sustainable resource use

The way in which earthships address the human exploitation of resources by relating use to the actual physical footprint of the building provides a solution to the problem of overuse of resources across the developed world. According to the Bioregional/WWF One Planet Living model, the average European consumes resources as though there were actually three planets, and the average American's resource use would require five planets[39]. This is a clearly unsustainable way of living that is also highly emissions-intensive, as well as creating other pollutant by-products and generating massive levels of waste.

The earthship, by contrast, seeks to use the resources around it to minimise its environmental impact on the wider world, restricting its resource implications to its own footprint. Using only renewable resources is one component of what has been called 'one planet living', although it may not always be appropriate to use only onsite renewables. This is discussed in more detail in chapter 5.

Figure 12: Bottle wall in the Groundhouse (Brittany) © Daren Howarth

Autonomy and self-sufficiency

The importance of site harmony, and systems that are able to run independently of networked structures, means that earthships are not just able to be autonomous and self-sufficient, but have been specifically designed and powered down (ie have a reduced energy demand) to allow human comfort in just such a situation. This was how they originally evolved in a location where no infrastructure existed. But that need for self-sufficiency created a building that cannot use and does not need more than it has immediately available to it. This sets up a model that is in opposition to the whole concept of large-scale infrastructure.

The social implications of autonomy and self-sufficiency are also central to the evolution of the earthship concept. The idea has evolved so that earthships are not just about having a low impact on the environment, but also about improving the quality of life for their inhabitants without negative consequences for the environment. This is in itself, of course, an attractive lifestyle proposition for many people. And the financial element is central to the whole concept of autonomy. With highly inefficient homes, homeowners are paying large utility bills for space heating, electricity and water. These houses can be thought of like credit cards with large balances on them that are accumulating debit interest. That 'interest' is the utility bills that need to be paid every month because the home is too inefficient and badly designed to be able to heat itself, or provide the electricity and water its inhabitants need. By contrast, the earthship can be considered as a savings account, with the positive interest being the free natural resources that enable the home to function effectively without any costs beyond the initial capital outlay and a little maintenance. However, at present, the capital outlay – particularly for electrical generation in the form of PV and wind turbines – is considerable, and payback times are long. Nonetheless, they protect the occupants from potentially devastating future energy price hikes.

Perhaps the most significant social aspect of earthships, though, is the personal empowerment they are designed to give their occupants – in the most literal sense. Homeowners of earthships have to take responsibility for generating their own electricity and regulating their own use of it, to ensure that they have enough water, and that all the systems in their building are operating satisfactorily. The full tools for life and survival are at the occupant's fingertips – a thrilling alternative, surely, to having an account number to quote down the phone to a call centre worker when something goes wrong. The earthship, in contrast to the status quo, offers an opportunity to form an unmediated connection with the natural resources that are essential for human life.

There are downsides to this too, though: the utility company provides support, and can send qualified engineers to fix problems, for example. It is also possible to sell generated electricity back to utility companies if the generation is connected to the network. This arguably enhances both financial self-sufficiency and provides a backup in case of a systems breakdown. But it may also encourage greater energy consumption, as the homeowner is no longer limited by being off-grid.

So, is an earthship that's connected to the grid still an earthship? One of the builds that is looked at in more detail in chapter 7 – Daren's Howarth's Groundhouse (Brittany) – is connected to the grid. That, along with a number of other design changes, accounts for why it is called a 'groundhouse', although in many other respects it fits the criteria for being considered an earthship.

Aesthetic functionality
The earthship concept is a universal approach for a building that provides all the functions that are needed to create a habitable space or shelter. Function is critical, and little emphasis so far has been placed on how the building actually looks.

Aesthetics are important to earthships, but performance has to come first. Performance in itself has aesthetic value, centred on the principles of harmony, equilibrium and site context that embody design elegance. By contrast, housing that relies on depleting unsustainable resources, and as a consequence pollutes the atmosphere and the world around it – housing that is fundamentally divorced from the natural world – is arguably ugly, or even disgusting. This debate is at the very heart of what aesthetics means in architecture, a human activity that is often looked upon as an art form, yet which also has profound implications for the physical environment. That tension is part of the

thrill of designing buildings, but it is a tension that in the main has been pulled away from major consideration of the implications for the natural world, either through an overemphasis on 'artistic statement' or, more commonly, through the 'bank statement' of profit margins.

James Wines, in his book *Green Architecture*, argues that:

'Nature is an instructive and inspirational influence that can expand the aesthetic horizons of the building arts and confirm the inalienable right of humanity to salvage a place on this planet before it's too late. The mission now in architecture, as in all human endeavour, is to recover those fragile threads of connectedness with nature that have been lost for most of [the twentieth] century. The key to a truly sustainable art of architecture for the new millennium will depend on the creation of bridges that unite conservation technology with an earth-centric philosophy and the capacity of designers to transform these integrated forces into a new visual language.' James Wines[40]

But the earthship also demands that there not be just a 'new visual language' but also an emphatic prioritisation of building performance above and beyond the idea of building services being non-sustainable, secondary to form, and supplied solely by external agencies. As Mike Reynolds bluntly puts it, 'housing should be a result of biology and physics, not a result of design prettiness. I am all for art and design, but if you make a boat really beautiful and it sinks, what the hell use is it?'[7]

Generally, function follows and is subservient to form, a form that in terms of numbers of units is actually dictated mainly by cost pressures, rather than by the need for artistic statement. Housing development is an industrial business, in which developers need to keep unit costs as low as possible to maintain their profit margins. But true profit is surely to be gained from genuinely sustainable, zero-carbon housing that does not damage or deplete the natural resources of the environment in which everyone collectively lives.

Human comfort in every sense is a key consideration with earthships; they are designed to be self-sustaining shelters for people to live happily in. The aesthetics of the living environment, then, is also important, and forms part of the 'performance' criteria of the building. Two key things that reflect this, and which have enormous qualitative impacts on the aesthetics of habitation, are the vast amount of sunlight that floods into earthships through the massive south-facing windows, and the fact that plants are an integrated part of the internal structure of the building. These are strong aesthetic and ergonomic statements within the earthship, which enhance the experience of the building's inhabitants.

Figure 13: Vine growing inside Earthship France
© Kevin Telfer

The earthship is commonly referred to as a pioneering building, but in truth it embodies and revives some of the most ancient ideas about human habitation. Wines explains that:

'On the most essential levels, troglodyte dwellings and structures made of sun-baked mud and other indigenous materials are ecologically friendly. Caves and underground habitats – including the subterranean villages of Shensi and Kansu in China, Cappadocia in Turkey, the Malmata area in Tunisia, and the Siwa region in Egypt – take advantage of virtually all that nature provides. They do not impose unreasonably on their environment, they do not negatively affect regional ecology, and they do not require high levels of energy consumption for heating or cooling since [they have] a consistently comfortable interior temperature.' James Wines[41]

The earthship in this sense is an echo from the past, a return to the pre-fossil-fuel age, although its application finds expression in post-industrial technologies and materials that allow the most pragmatic realisation of performance-related sustainable goals in the 21st century. Clearly, what human beings regard as being comfortable has also changed – and earthships are designed to try to cater for modern expectations rather than force people to have to adopt the toughness of cavemen.

Reynolds argues that 'a sustainable home must make use of indigenous materials, those occurring naturally in the local area. For thousands and thousands of years, housing was built from found materials such as rock, earth, reeds and logs. Today, there are mountains of by-products of our civilization that are already made and delivered to all areas. These are the natural resources of the twenty-first century[23].' Hence the reason why earthships are built from tyres, bottles and other low-embodied energy, salvaged materials rather than the hitherto more usual idea of ecological building materials such as timber, stone and straw bales.

DESIGN FEATURES

The following section introduces the main design features of earthships. They are:

- low-impact materials
- passive solar design
- renewable energy
- rainwater harvesting
- using plants to treat waste water
- food production.

All but the last of these are explored in more detail in other parts of the book. However, food production within earthships is not something that has been attempted in any significant way in Europe to date.

Low-impact materials

In the complete life-cycle analysis of a building, the embodied energy in the materials in con-struction is generally less than 6% of the total energy used[42], [43]. But once the building becomes low-to-zero carbon the figure increases, and becomes

Figure 14: Working on tyre walls in Almeria, Spain © Laura Davies and Dave Buchanan – earthship.es

a more significant percentage. So a primary aim is to reduce the embodied energy of the materials used in the construction of the earthship. According to *Building* magazine, 'Savings in embodied carbon emissions achieve significant "year one" reductions that will take many years to achieve through operational savings, for example, via onsite renewables or enhanced insulation'[44]. In earthships, the concept is realised through the use of a variety of 'waste' materials, from reclaimed timber and masonry to recycled glass bottles, tin cans and – most famously – used car tyres. Europe throws away over 3.2 million tonnes of car and van tyres a year, and the Landfill Directive, which came into full force in July 2006, has completely banned them from landfill[45]. When referring to used car tyres, Reynolds comments: 'The rubber (sometimes steel belted) automobile tire is indigenous all over the world as a "natural resource". Every city is a natural supplier of this item. It can be "harvested" with absolutely no technical devices or energy other than two human hands to pick it up and throw it into a pickup truck.'[46] A 130 m² earthship (such as that built in Zwolle) would typically use 1000 (or 10 tonnes) of used car tyres for the construction of its walls.

However, earthships have also been criticised for the amount of cement that is used in their construction; in most cases this could easily have been reduced, or replaced with a lower-impact alternative such as lime or Eco-Cement[47].

Passive solar design

The key to the earthship approach is to reduce demand, before trying to meet that demand through renewable or sustainable methods. Harnessing renewable energy, whether on- or offsite, to meet a demand that could have been designed out at the paper stage of a construction project is a waste of energy that could be put to better use elsewhere.

Earthships set out to be efficient buildings by reducing the conventional need for vast amounts of space heating. The earthship reduces its demand for external energy inputs because the structure is designed to harvest heat directly, which is the type of energy that most of the gas and electricity supplied to conventional buildings is converted to. The rammed-tyre walls of the earthship are earth sheltered, with over a metre of rammed earth used as backfill behind them. And behind the earth shelter is a 'thermal wrap' of rigid insulation, which embraces the building and makes the thermal mass of rammed tyres and earth act as a storage heater. Just like a stone wall on a hot day, the rammed-tyre walls retain heat, and then release it when the building cools. The thick walls, coupled with copious insulation, stabilise the earthship to maintain a comfortable temperature in any season, remaining warm in winter and cool in summer. This aspect of earthships is explored in more detail in chapter 8.

Renewable energy

Earthships are designed to fulfil many of their principal functions without the use of additional electricity generation; space heating and hot water are provided largely by solar energy, and the building is oriented and glazed so that it offers a large amount of natural light for its inhabitants. This makes it easier to generate the electricity needed for other activities from renewable sources. Earthships have no mains connections and therefore no fossil fuel is consumed for electricity generation or water heating. Instead, electricity is generated onsite from renewables and is stored in batteries before distribution in the building. This contrasts sharply with conventional buildings, in which centralised systems are vital for all functions and are essential to make the building fit for habitation. Earthship Brighton, for example, uses four renewable technologies for these ends: PV panels, a wind turbine, solar thermal panels, and a wood pellet stove as a backup space heater and boiler. Earthship Fife uses PV and a wind turbine, and also a micro-hydro turbine. A full list of the renewable power options used by European earthships is given in chapter 5.

Rainwater harvesting

Earthships have no connection to the water mains, but instead rely on rainwater harvesting and recycling to supply all their needs. Demand management and water conservation are used to make the harvested water go as far as possible. The roof collects water and channels it through a pre-filter before storing it in underground tanks. The storage capacity tends to be larger than that of most domestic rainwater-harvesting systems, as there is no mains backup for dry periods. Anecdotal evidence suggests that the rainwater-harvesting system, coupled with water appliances specifically designed

to reduce water use, and greywater recycling, has proved to be more than sufficient for residents' needs. The earthship approach is based on using the appropriate tool for the job. The water is purified in a two-stage filtration process, reflecting the fact that over 90% of water consumed in residential building is used for non-potable activities. With fairly high levels of rainfall in much of Europe, most buildings are well placed to collect and use rainwater onsite, and thus have a lower reliance on centralised mains water. These topics are explored fully in chapter 6.

Using plants to treat waste water

In an earthship, all waste water is treated onsite and grey and blackwater are dealt with separately. The greywater that is generated by the sinks and shower is treated with indoor planters or 'living machines', located next to the south-facing windows. The plants thrive in conditions of sunlight and nutrient-rich water and clean the water through natural processes such as transpiration, evaporation and oxygenation by their roots. All plants work well in the planters, but some hardier species with deeper root systems are good to start with, including bananas, avocados and geraniums. After cleaning, the recycled water is stored in a sump, and is then fed to the toilet cistern for flushing. The resulting blackwater leaves the earthship to settle in a septic tank before overflowing to a reed bed or other system for treatment.

Figure 15: Greywater planter in Earthship Fife
© Kevin Telfer

Food production

Reynolds has been exploring another element of earthship systems through the possibility of growing food all year round in the greywater planters – and even keeping fish in interior ponds for eating[48]. The only large-scale example of this so far is the Phoenix, built in New Mexico, which has a double greenhouse at the front: this allows a far larger area for food production, but also acts as an additional thermal buffer. In colder climates the earthship's thermal performance can be improved by adding a greenhouse, which acts both as a buffer and as an airlock, to reduce thermal loss when the occupants leave or enter the building. This can have the effect of making the indoor environment darker, so additional skylights may be needed.

Small amounts of food can be – and have been – grown in any earthship with planters. Crops that love sunny, warm conditions, such as tomatoes and courgettes, tend to thrive in an earthship environment. But lack of space means that the amount of food produced is negligible in terms of meaningful self-sufficiency. In temperate climates, such as those in France, the Netherlands and the UK, there is little need for indoor cultivation, as crops can be grown all year round, unlike New Mexico, where the harsh conditions make horticulture tough in winter.

CONCLUSION

The earthship is a building that combines several different strands of sustainable building in an integrated, holistic approach. It provides a powerful implicit critique of much current residential building design, which is predominantly inefficient, vulnerable to the elements, and dependent on centralised infrastructure. The earthship, by contrast, is a self-sufficient, off-grid structure that has all its functions embedded within its architecture and, in theory at least, interacts effectively with renewable natural resources to provide a comfortable, low-carbon home for its inhabitants. How effective has it has been in achieving this in Europe? This is what we look at in more detail in the rest of this book.

Greenhouse and planter in Earthship Brighton
© Kevin Telfer

INTRODUCTION

This chapter outlines the process of how to build an earthship. It starts with the selection of a suitable site and then describes the construction of the earthship from the ground up: foundations, ramming the used car tyres for the walls, timber framing, installing the power and water systems, and interior finishes. The stages are listed in order of works: for example, timber framing is described before earth plastering. The build process and techniques are for a generic earthship, but issues relating to earthships built in particular European climates are mentioned.

MODULAR APPROACH

Earthship design embodies a modular approach, based on simple geometric shapes – either U-shapes, known as 'nests', or round rooms called 'huts'. Smaller earthships tend to be a single module of either type – Earthship Fife, for example – is a single nest module whereas the larger earthships comprise a series of modules connected together and oriented towards the sun, such as the 'Hut House' in Taos that is two hut modules combined with a sunspace (conservatory). All modules are direct gain passive solar design, although sometimes indirect systems such as Trombe walls are used in the hut module as well[49]. The rule for combining modules is that they must be combined in a straight row on an east–west axis, or in a staggered row from east to west in proportion to the winter azimuth angle, or staggered up a slope, as demonstrated in the Gravel Pit Reclamation Project in the Greater World Community, Taos[23]. Crucially, all these combinations allow each separate module to maximise solar gain in winter.

Older earthship designs tended to be comprise a number of U-modules linked together, such

as the Earthship Biotecture offices in Taos, whereas later designs are more simplified, such as the packaged earthship, consist of a single, elongated U[50]. Earthships that combine any of the different basic module shapes nests or huts) are called hybrid earthships. The packaged earthship is a set of generic drawings extending the basic form in various standard floor layouts, designed to facilitate faster uptake of the concept and cheaper building projects[50]. In colder climates sunspaces are sometimes added to help thermal stability, with either vertical or sloped glass.

SITE SELECTION

In the northern hemisphere, where the aim is to maximise solar gain, earthships can be built on any land with an unobstructed south-facing aspect, whether flat or a hillside, except for the usual constraints – no boggy land or frost pockets, for example. In the southern hemisphere the building should be north-facing. Earthships require no special conditions, except that earth will be needed to build the walls and shelter the building, and so ideally will be available onsite. If earth is not available – on urban sites, for example – it could be obtained from other local building sites where it has been extracted for foundations; alternatively hardcore, rubble or other material could be used for filling the tyres.

Most earthships built to date have been single storey, although there are two-storey examples. This means that the footprint of a typical earthship, including the earth shelter around it, will require more land than a conventional two-storey house. All earthships up until now have been earth sheltered; this is not necessarily a prerequisite, though, but rather an aesthetic choice. Ideally the earthship should face due south, but it can be built within

20° east or west of this if site constraints so dictate; the crucial point is that, as with any passive solar design, the solar gain available to the building must be maximised[51].

GROUND PREPARATION AND EXCAVATION

If the earthship is to be constructed on a hillside, the site for it is excavated, cutting into the hill, and the spoil is piled in front of where the building will be. This pile of earth constitutes the material that will later be used both to fill the tyres and to create an earth shelter around the building. Reusing the earth in this way reduces transportation for disposing of it, and displaces the need for heavy masonry materials such as concrete block or brick for the walls. On a flat site the walls are rammed, and then a backfill

berm or earth shelter is moved to cover the walls on the outside of the building.

There are two excavation approaches. The choice between them depends on the climate and on the depth of the water table. In drier climates, such as New Mexico or the Mediterranean, it is possible to cut into a hillside, leave an earth cliff, and build the tyre walls directly off this. The cliff should extend 300 mm from the base of the rammed-tyre wall, and can be used only for walls taking a load from one side[52]. The advantage of the earth cliff technique is that tyre work is reduced. The technique is not suitable in wet climates, or in areas with a high water table, because of the resulting complexity of insulating and damp-proofing the tyre walls[50]. The approach has been used in some Spanish projects, but is inappropriate for temperate European climates.

Figure 16: Site excavation and preparation (Earthship Brighton) © Oli Hodge

Figure 17: Tyre wall built on earth cliff (Earthship Almeria) © Laura Davies and Dave Buchanan – earthship.es

Excavated soil that will be used for construction should be covered, kept dry, and have no organic matter in it. This material is for pounding the tyres, and for backfill to create the berm or extra thermal mass. The rammed tyres and walls have a depth of around 2 m, the tyres on average being 700 mm deep and the rest of the depth earth rammed behind the tyres. The use of onsite soil reduces transportation of heavy materials for the walls, as only the used tyres need to be brought to the site. The damp-proof membrane is installed under the base of the wall. The width of the wall, coupled with the earthship being built on undisturbed ground, means that generally no foundation is required, unless the build is in an area with a high water table, such as in places below sea level – Earthship Zwolle in Holland, for example.

THERMAL WRAP AND DAMP-PROOFING

The thermal wrap and damp-proof membrane are installed before the tyre work. Rigid insulation boards are placed behind the tyres and rammed earth, isolating the thermal mass of the walls from the earth shelter around the building. With 100 mm of insulation, a 2 m thick wall will have a U-value of around 0.18 W/m²K. In Earthship Brighton 100 mm Yelofoam X2i extruded polystyrene insulation was used and, at Earthship Fife, 50 mm Foamglas[53].

Figure 18: Installation of battery box thermal wrap (Earthship Brighton) © Taus Larsen

Figure 19: Backfill behind the tyre wall (the Groundhouse) © Daren Howarth

A tanking membrane runs behind the insulation from beneath the first course of tyres to the ring beam on the top course, completely encapsulating the earthship. It is usual to blind the site with sand before construction, to protect the membrane and provide a level surface to build off. In Earthship Brighton triple-layered Visqueen 1200 gauge heavy-duty plastic was used to damp-proof the nest module, and Rawell Environmental's RAWMAT was used to tank the round hut module. RAWMAT is sodium bentonite clay sandwiched between two geotextile layers[54]. This type of membrane is self-repairing, as the bentonite clay expands when it gets damp, and hence seals any punctures in the membrane. The Visqueen heavy-gauge plastic was triple layered and used in the nest module instead of the RAWMAT as it is a cheaper material. During

the design stage there was discussion of putting a French drain behind the thermal wrap and damp-proofing to improve drainage, but this detail was not constructed. At Earthship Fife, Voltex membrane was used[53].

In dryer climates, damp-proofing may not be required[50]. In wetter climates, in addition to damp-proofing, a French drain can be incorporated to reduce the risk of damp.

TYRE WALLS: A METHODOLOGY

In earthships, used car tyres rammed with earth are used to replace loadbearing masonry. Rammed tyres are laid, like bricks, in stretcher bond to form virtually indestructible steel-belted rubber walls, as some car tyres have steel embedded in them to strengthen them. The shape of tyres lends itself to the construction of graceful, free-flowing, undulating curves and other organic shapes, similar to other forms of earth building such as earth bag and cob. However, after pack-out and plastering, tyre walls can also be equally good as straight walls.

The tyres are rammed or pounded a course at a time, up to 10 or 14 courses high. When fully rammed, each course is 250 mm high, so a wall of 10 courses would be 2.5 m high. The first course of tyres is laid on ground that is levelled, and free of organic matter, including plants and tree roots, and over a damp-proof course as described above[52]. The tyres in the first course must be at least as large in diameter as any other tyre used in the wall, and no tyre in subsequent courses can be larger than this, to prevent instability[52].

The tyres are laid out in a row, with a string line, and levelled. To help protect the damp-proof membrane, the tyres of the first course can be partially filled with sand, up to 50 mm. Earth is shovelled into the tyre and then compacted, at first by hand and then in a circular motion using a sledgehammer to pound the whole tyre equally until it is fully 'inflated' as solid thermal mass, and levelled with itself and with the adjacent tyres. If the tyre is overfilled it can be pounded back down, or if under-filled can be pounded up to reach the desired level. Each tyre takes between 10 and 45 minutes to ram, depending on the experience, strength and fitness of the person working the tyre. Any type of earth can be used, from chalk to clay, as well as hardcore and other building rubble, and there is no need to grade or prepare the material first. This is an advantage over other forms of earth building. Each tyre takes two to three wheelbarrow loads – approximately 50 kg of earth. People usually work in pairs when building tyre walls; one person fills the tyre with earth and the other compacts it. It is a very labour-intensive process. Earthship Brighton used over 1000 tyres of different sizes, with 230 in the hut module and 670 in the nest. It took approximately 500 hours to ram manually, as described. Earthship Fife used approximately 320 tyres. Tyre pounding is an example of a low-skill, community-building activity that can employ lots of volunteers – and the tyres are free.

Figure 20: First course of tyres being laid on a damp-proof course (Earthship Brighton) © Taus Larsen

Figure 21: Filling first course of tyres with sand to protect the damp-proof course (Earthship Brighton) © Taus Larsen

Each course is backfilled to the level of each completed course of tyres throughout the wall construction: this beds the tyres in, and provides both stability and a working platform for the next course. Between the tyre wall, 700 mm deep and thermal wrap (insulation) up to 1.5 m of earth is compacted to create very wide thermal mass walls that earth-shelter the building. Once backfilling is complete, the tyre walls are very stable, as each filled tyre weighs over 50 kg. Because rammed tyres are so heavy, it is best to work on them in situ, rather than ram them first and then move them into position. When building the round hut module, the courses of tyres are laid vertically on top of each other and when building rectangular nest or U-modules, they are set back 25 mm to retain the earth behind them. Generally the walls are around 2 m thick; this amount of thermal mass is designed to keep the earthship's temperature stable all year round[23]. Tyre walls over 10 m long in a straight run may need a buttress.

After the first course the tyres are double-lined with corrugated cardboard to cover the hole in the middle and then filled with earth. Once the tyre is filled with earth and rammed, the cardboard base becomes 'shaped' to fit the area it was rammed in, providing further stability after the tyre has been pounded. If necessary, the tyres can be further reinforced by 'pinning' every two or three courses with metre-long stakes of 12 mm reinforcing bar at 1 or 2 m centres.

The method of tyre construction described above can also be used for a variety of other structural or non-structural applications, such as the footing for the front two glass faces at the front of the earthship, or in straw bale builds as a foundation[55]. Potentially, any wall could be replaced by a rammed-tyre wall, although the depth of the wall can restrict deployment of the technique. Some case studies where rammed tyres have been used are outlined in chapter 7.

Alternative tyre techniques

Even if care is taken with the choice of tyre sizes, the wall may still need additional techniques to fill any uneven gaps. The two main techniques are 'squeezies' and 'half-block' pours[23]. Squeezies are empty tyres forced into the void between two rammed tyres, which are then filled and rammed in the usual manner. Half-block pours involve creating formwork with a plasterer's lathe or wood around the hole that needs to be filled, and then using a small pour of concrete or mortar or other material to fill the gap. Half-block pours can also be used to create vertical wall ends instead of tapering the

Figure 22: Working on the seventh nest tyre wall (Earthship Brighton) © Taus Larsen

Figure 23: Half-block pour (Earthship Almeria) © Laura Davies and Dave Buchanan – earthship.es

tyre walls down to the ground. Rainwater-harvesting tanks are usually installed during the construction of the tyre walls, and are buried in the earth behind the earthship.

Tyre issues

There are some issues surrounding the suitability of using rammed tyres in construction: the risk of fire, long-term durability, and the possible generation of hazardous chemical components through off-gassing or leaching[56]. Toxicity of tyres is explored in more detail in chapter 4, but some of these issues are briefly discussed below.

Piles of discarded tyres present a high combustion risk, as oxygen can flow freely through the structure. For example, the Heyope tyre dump near Knighton, Powys, in Wales is home to over 10 million used tyres, and it smouldered slowly for over 10 years[57]. The use of tyres in earthships is completely different from this, as they are rammed full of earth and covered with up to 25 mm of render. Oxygen is therefore unable to circulate between the tyres, so the resulting risk of fire is minimal. There is a notable example in *Comfort in Any Climate* of rammed-tyre earthship walls in a US construction that survived a forest fire, whereas the timber-frame part of the building was destroyed[58].

The possibility of leaching of chemicals into the ground or groundwater from rammed tyres in construction is very low if the tyre wall is adequately damp-proofed. Tyres are inert unless exposed to ultraviolet light, water or high temperatures, and the risk of this can be minimised by tanking and rendering the tyres. Various US university studies have explored aspects of this subject. There have been no specific studies on the longevity or long-term durability of tyres if they are protected from the elements that can degrade them, but anecdotal evidence suggests that they would last a very long time. There are earthships in New Mexico that have been standing for over 30 years.

Tyre sizing

Used car and van tyres come in many different sizes, and their performance varies when rammed with earth. Each tyre has a code on the side that describes its characteristics; a typical code might be 195/60/R16 82 H. Table 1 summarises what the code means.

Table 1: Tyre-sizing codes

Component	Example
Tyre section width (mm)	195
Aspect ratio/profile*(%)	60
Cross-ply or radial construction (C or R)	R
Diameter of rim (inches)	16
Load index	82
Speed rating (letter)	H

* The aspect ratio is the height of the section expressed as a percentage of the tyre section width.

Although there can be other markings, tyre section width, aspect ratio/profile and rim diameter are the only important considerations. Load index and speed rating are irrelevant in terms of the construction of tyre walls. Low-profile tyres should be avoided because of their small rim depth. The only other stipulation is that the tyre must not have a hole in the tread, or be worn through. Potentially this means that 'old' tyres stockpiled in tyre dumps can be used, as well as those more recently disposed of, as long as they haven't degraded.

Generally, the most common tyre size in the UK is 195 mm in various diameters; a smaller tyre holds less earth, and is lighter and therefore more difficult to work with, as it moves around during the ramming process. It is possible to use a variety of tyre sizes in a tyre wall, but it is easier to use one uniform size throughout, as the tyres can be laid evenly, like bricks, with the middle of each tyre over the gap between the two tyres in the course below. If a variety of sizes are used then the larger tyres should be used at the bottom of the wall and the smaller ones towards the top. Even if care is taken, it is likely that the wall may need use of the alternative techniques described earlier to fill any uneven gaps.

TIMBER-FRAME CONSTRUCTION AND GLAZING

After the final course of tyres has been rammed and levelled, the next step is to create a ring beam or wall plate, secured to the walls with a reinforcing bar, to which the roof structure will be attached.

The ring beam can be poured with concrete, or can be a wooden wall plate. In Earthship Brighton, for example, the beam is a 300 mm × 50 mm pressure-treated timber wall plate; the insulation thermal wrap and damp-proof course are tucked under the beam, effectively sealing the berm or mass behind the earthship.

Once the ring beam is in place, the rest of the timber frame can be built. From this point all of the techniques are fairly standard, other than the occasional tyre-related detail, and follow the pattern of a conventional build. Once the front timber frames, roof trusses and structure go up and the windows are fitted, the basic weathertight shell is completed and interior fit-out can begin. It is advisable to reach this stage before autumn so that internal work is protected from the elements.

Figure 24: Ring beam and roof trusses (Earthship Almeria) © Laura Davies and Dave Buchanan – earthship.es

Figure 26: Conservatory timber frame under construction (Earthship Brighton) © Taus Larsen

Figure 25: Attaching the nest wall plate to rammed tyres (Earthship Brighton) © Taus Larsen

Figure 27: Vertical timber face construction (Earthship Brighton) © Taus Larsen

Figure 28: Timber framing (Earthship France)

Figure 29: Attaching timber roof structure to wall plate and rammed-tyre wall (Earthship Brighton)
© Taus Larsen

Figure 30: Roof structure (Earthship Brighton)
© Taus Larsen

ADOBE-TYRE PACK-OUT PREPARATION AND PLASTERING

After the tyre walls have been completed, the walls are ready to be packed out with adobe (clay plaster) to create a flat, easy-to-plaster surface. The material used for pack-out varies between internal and external tyres. Inside, the material can be cob or mud, but the exterior material must be waterproof, and so could be mortar based on cement, Eco-Cement, lime or an equivalent. The voids between the tyres are filled with one handful of material and then a small bottle or can. Bottles and cans are used to save on the volume of material used, although aluminium cans should be avoided, and recycled instead, because of their high levels of embodied energy. The voids can be 'porcupined' with nails before starting, to create a better surface for the pack-out material to adhere to. Pack-out is repeated until all the voids are filled, and then they are left to dry.

Figure 31: Rammed-tyre wall pack-out (Earthship Fife)
© Sustainable Communities Initiative

The process is then repeated, and the next layer involves another handful of material with two bottles. After this a thin layer of scratch coat plaster should be applied to create a level surface ready for the final finish coat. All service infrastructure (plumbing and wiring) should be installed at this stage, and then another thin layer of scratch coat render should be applied to create a level surface for the final finished coat. Adobe can be mixed from clay, sand, topsoil and chopped straw obtained locally; the option of buying pre-mixed adobe is very expensive. Claytec is one example of a pre-mixed product that is available in Europe[59].

Figure 32: Tyre wall pack-out (the Groundhouse)
© Daren Howarth

FLOOR AND FOUNDATIONS

The footing for the front loadbearing faces can be constructed from two courses of rammed tyres, or poured as a conventional footing and then capped with a timber plate, and then the front timber frame can be attached. Once footings are in place, the floor slab can be poured. The Earthship Brighton slab is a 100 mm Eco-Cement slab over Visqueen 1200 heavy-gauge plastic blinded with sand on top of undisturbed chalk. Earthship Fife's slab was poured with limecrete. In Earthship Brighton and Fife there is no underfloor insulation; this is a mistake in temperate climates, because it leads to the floor being uncomfortably cold. Although insulating under the slab flies in the face of earthship orthodoxy, with its 'connection to the earth'

principle, it is conventional in most of northern Europe to insulate all external elements. Detailing appropriate for different climates is discussed in chapter 9.

The Earthship Brighton project experimented extensively with Eco-Cement for rendering, pack-out and other non-structural applications (including the entire floor slab), which throughout were poured with this material. Eco-Cement is the invention of Tasmanian John Harrison; it uses reactive magnesia and a pozzolan to replace two-thirds of the ordinary Portland cement in a mix[47]. Reactive magnesia has a lower embodied energy than cement, but at present it is difficult to source. Pozzolans can be easily obtained from a variety of sources.

WATER SYSTEMS INSTALLATION

The rainwater storage tanks are installed as the tyre walls are rammed. This makes it possible for them to be buried while the area behind the walls is being backfilled, with service penetrations through the tyre walls where appropriate. There are various options for rainwater tanks, ranging from purpose-made plastic tanks and ferro-cement tanks to recycled orange juice containers. The vortex filter for pre-filtering rainwater can be installed at the same time as the tanks, but the bed of gravel is built after the framework and roof are finished. The water-organising module (WOM) can be fitted at the same time as the rest of the plumbing fixtures; once this is installed, the supply side of the water systems is complete. These systems are described in detail in chapter 6.

Once the front frames are in place and the floor slab has been poured, the greywater planters can be built. These can be a trough dug into the ground, a masonry wall built to retain the raised bed, or a combination of these. The trough is built to the required depth and prepared with sand to protect the damp-proof membrane. The trench is lined with an EPDM (ethylene propylene diene monomer) rubber membrane, which is attached to the sides, and then the edges are rendered over to them. An additional inner membrane of EPDM or equivalent can be placed inside as well, to protect the outer EPDM membrane from any sharp gravel or stones.

Next the plumbing fixtures are installed, and rock bulbs are created around all pipe fittings, to help fast draining into and between planters. Rock bulbs are piles of rock larger than the gravel that will be used to fill the planters. The large gaps between the rocks enable water to drain faster in and out of the system. Once all the bulbs are in place, the planter is filled with 20 mm gravel to the level the greywater will reach, up to 75 mm of sand, and 150 mm of topsoil as the final layer. A grease and particle filter can then be installed, as outlined in chapter 5, and the plants should be planted when all other building work is completed to avoid damage, dust and disruption. Once the plants are in place, it can take several months for the ecosystem that cleans the water to develop. The septic tank or other blackwater system can be installed towards the end of the project. Once this is in place, the rest of the water systems can be plumbed in and connected to the WOM. A water quality test is advisable after the system is complete, to ensure that the water is safe for human consumption, and that the quality complies with the relevant drinking water standard.

Figure 33: Preliminary greywater planter wall preparation (Earthship Brighton) © Taus Larsen

NATURAL CROSS-VENTILATION

The earthship ventilation system relies on convection created between low-set windows at ground level and skylights in the roof. To ventilate the building, the convection-fed skylights are opened to exhaust unwanted hot air, which rises out and draws in cool air through the low windows to replace it. Earthship France uses the earth berm at the rear of the building to cool the incoming air by drawing it through metal tubes that are buried in the berm. The advantage of the cross-ventilation system is that it enables the earthship to lose a lot of heat very rapidly during the day when it's hot in the summer months, or to change the air very quickly in winter. In winter this method of ventilation can lead to extensive heat loss and uncomfortable draughts, and the standard design is difficult to make airtight when shut. Increased airtightness with additional mechanical ventilation is discussed in chapter 9. Mechanical ventilation systems are a departure from earthship orthodoxy, although there was experimentation with a thermosiphon (moving warm air) system in Earthship Zwolle.

In Earthship Brighton there are two Monodraught Monovent sunpipes, which act as passive stack vents to change the air in the kitchen and bathroom. The sunpipe in the kitchen has the added bonus of dramatically increasing the level of natural daylight in an area of the building that is very dark, because of the 6 m plan depth, the layout of internal walls and the conservatory. The earthship ventilation system could be easily modified to draw cool air in from under a wooden deck or a pond in front of the building for more effective cooling in summer.

LOW-IMPACT AND NATURAL MATERIALS

Most earthship projects benefit from a large supply of voluntary labour, which has enabled them to prepare and use a range of salvaged and reclaimed materials. If the cost of these activities – for example, de-nailing and sanding reclaimed timber from skips – were factored in, the cost would probably be prohibitive. Earthship Brighton used 2 tonnes of cans and bottles; 1500 cardboard boxes; reclaimed timber, including elm, oak cladding, and 150 m of reclaimed floorboards; 90 salvaged granite blocks; 5 tonnes of granite offcuts;

and 35 reclaimed paving slabs. At present it is still cheaper to purchase new materials in volume, than to prepare second-hand materials and craft them into the build process. The use of low-impact materials is also discussed in chapter 4.

BOTTLE WALLS AND GLASS BRICK METHODOLOGY

The first step in building a bottle wall is to measure its size, in order to determine the length of the glass bricks needed, and help calculate the number needed to fill the space. For this calculation a gap of 25 mm should be allowed for between each course, and between each brick. Next the bottles can be collected, and grouped in terms of size and colour; two bottles of the same diameter are needed for one glass brick. Using a wet tile cutter, the bottles are cut to half the length of the glass brick, with the neck half being discarded. Glass dust is extremely hazardous, and adequate safety precautions should be taken at all times. The bottom halves are then cleaned and, when dry, two are taped together with gaffer tape to make a cylindrical glass brick. For a deep colour, two bottles of the same colour can be used, or for a lighter shade a clear bottle can be taped to a coloured bottle; when used, the clear end should be on the sunny side. The glass bricks are then laid in courses set in cement, leaving a minimum of 25 mm between bottles, with no more than six courses being laid a day. Once all the bricks have been laid, they are rendered over, and while the plaster is still wet it is thoroughly cleaned with wet sponges and clothes to reveal the glass bottles beneath. It is possible to build can walls in a similar fashion, but the cans are used intact.

Figure 34: Glass bottle brick wall (Earthship Brighton) © Kevin Telfer

Earthships show how materials such as tyres, which are usually considered to be waste, can be used as effective building materials © Jo D'Ambra

4   BUILDING WITH WASTE

INTRODUCTION

Arguably the most distinctive aspect of earthships – in the popular imagination at least – is the fact that they are built out of used tyres. To many people this may seem a strange choice of building material; after all, tyres were not created to be used as building blocks. Historically, environmentally-friendly construction has been associated with non-oil-based natural materials such as straw bales, rammed earth and wood. And, more recently, modern low-carbon buildings, such as the 2008 ZEDfactory-designed house at Grande-Synthe in France, have generally been built using conventional materials such as bricks, cement, glass and insulation in a considered way to achieve high building performance. But using tyres and other forms of waste material – what Mike Reynolds has called 'the natural resources of the twenty-first century'– is not a Mad Max-style gimmick[60]. Tyres perform valuable structural and thermal functions within the building. They also provide an implicit critique of attitudes to waste: if a material can still be useful, then shouldn't it be used?

Figure 35: The Hampole tyre dump, near Doncaster, in a disused quarry © Chemical Hazards and Poisons Division (London) Health Protection Agency, 2003

The disposal of waste tyres is a problem across the world. In Europe it has become a more visible problem as a result of the implementation in July 2006 of the 1999 EU Waste Landfill Directive, which banned the disposal of all waste tyres and their components to landfill[61]. This is a good thing, as it means that a use has to be found for a material that can still fulfil several functions. The legislation created the direct challenge of how to reuse and recycle the tyres rather than chucking them away. But there are a lot of tyres to deal with. Approximately 3.2 million tonnes of used tyres are generated every year in Europe according to the European Tyre and Rubber Manufacturers' Association (ETRMA), equating to around 300 million individual tyres, and including 479,000 tonnes in the UK and 571,000 tonnes in Germany in 2009[62]. Only 5% of these used tyres are now going into landfill across Europe, according to the ETRMA report for 2010. But whereas recycling rates, and the use of tyres for burning as a fuel, increased significantly between 1999 and 2009 across Europe, rates of direct reuse flatlined at around 10% during this period. In 2009, 37% of all used tyres were recycled across Europe, and 40% were incinerated to generate energy[45].

There have been two main problems with the use of tyres in buildings: legislative and regulatory difficulties, which stem from the legal classification of used tyres as waste; and concerns about the specific properties of the material itself, regarding leaching, durability, off-gassing and fire risks. Tyres are not the only type of waste used in building earthships – bottles, cans, salvaged masonry and timber are also often used as well – but they are our main focus here. This chapter takes a look at the concept of building with waste in general and scrutinises the regulatory basis and scientific concerns surrounding building with tyres in particular. Some pioneering European builds have tested the regulatory position in their respective countries. It is impossible to summarise the position of every local decision-making body across Europe, but this chapter notes the key points of contestation where they have occurred. The aim is to help clarify the questions 'Is building with tyres a good thing?' and 'Is it widely accepted by regulatory bodies?' Both questions have been mired in uncertainty in Europe for the last decade.

Figure 36: Rammed-tyre wall at Earthship Fife, with aluminium can infilling © Taus Larsen

WHY USE TYRES?

'We don't desperately need tyres, but they're growing as fast as trees, if not faster!'
Mike Reynolds[63]

One of the best reasons for using tyres as a material in earthship design is to find a use for a small fraction of the millions of tyres being thrown away globally every day. Tyres are lying around, waiting to be reused. They do not need to be manufactured specifically for the purpose of building. They are often free, and sometimes people are even paid to take them away. They require low levels of energy to bring onto the construction site and convert into building blocks. It is a perfect demonstration of how reusing materials is a more efficient use of resources than recycling them, as it uses less energy. The tyre, which Mike Reynolds describes as being 'indigenous all over the world as a "natural resource"', is ideal under these criteria, not least because it has such a generic design (no specialist sourcing required), and can be used for the purposes of building without any chemical or mechanical modification[64]. And, in fact, 'the very quality of tyres that makes them a problem to society (the fact they won't go away)

makes them an ideal durable building material for earthships'[65].

Tyres also allow another vital material in earthship construction to become more easily manageable – earth. One of the most important factors about earth is that it does not have to be transported onto site; it's already there. And unlike traditional rammed-earth buildings, rammed tyres do not need to be so fussy about the type of earth that is used. This is because, instead of ramming earth into formwork, section by section, in order to construct walls (as in traditional rammed-earth buildings), earthships are constructed by pounding earth into tyres with sledgehammers. The tyres are then stacked on top of one another in order to construct the walls of the earthship. Pounding tyres is a fairly low-skill technique that is easy to learn and transfer, whereas rammed-earth construction is a skilled and precise technique that requires some level of expertise. The correct soil composition is essential to the viability of a rammed-earth wall, as the wall is freestanding, and liable to structural weakness if the wrong type of earth is used. By ramming earth into tyres, individual building blocks with absolute structural integrity and great mass are created.

Figure 37: Oscar Briz levels rammed tyres at Earthship Valencia, 2005 © Lisa-Jane Roberts and Oscar Briz

Figure 38: Tyre walls going up at Earthship Valencia © Lisa-Jane Roberts and Oscar Briz

Pounding tyres is a low-tech process. It merely requires earth, a conventional car or van tyre, a piece of cardboard to prevent the earth from falling through the tyre, a sledgehammer, and a human being who is unafraid of a few blisters. The earth is packed in by hand to begin with and then compacted with the sledgehammer until it is firm. The process continues, ramming as much as 75 kg of earth into the tyre, until it is packed tightly and swollen by about 25% from its original depth, eg from 200 to 250 mm height. The tyre then needs to be levelled to ensure that it can form a stable building block that is flat and can form part of a wall. The stability also comes from this building block being so wide: at just under a metre in width, earthship tyre walls are three to four times thicker than conventional walls: this means that they do not require conventional foundations as they support their own load.

The low-tech approach and the direct reuse of waste without modification, mean that the carbon emissions from the production of this 'brick' are negligible. The main downside is the amount of time and labour it takes to produce each brick. But the resultant product has some fantastic qualities: in particular, it is highly durable, structurally stable and has excellent thermal mass. Indeed, Mike Reynolds has said: 'If I was paid $30 million to invent the best thermal mass brick I could, I would invent a tyre'[7]. Thermal mass is crucial to the design of earthships; coupled with the passive solar capacity of the building, thermal mass enables the structure to soak up energy from the sun. This energy is retained by the walls and 'radiated' back into the building during cooler periods. Space heating represents approximately 75% of the average European household's domestic energy use[66]. This requirement is enormously reduced in the earthship, due to its thermal mass and passive solar design. The passive solar aspect of earthships is discussed in more detail in chapter 8.

Shape is another consideration. It's an obvious point, but tyres are round: this makes them an excellent starting point for building free-flowing, undulating organic shapes. Brick and blocks tend to be square or oblong, which means they are ideal for building rectilinear forms, but they require more thought and skill as well as careful detailing to create curves and other shapes. The shape also helps to exaggerate one of the architectural influences behind the appearance of the earthship – the adobe pueblo buildings of the south-western USA, which are also characterised by rounded undulating surfaces.

Tyres are an excellent material for earthships, because they help to fulfil some primary aims of the structure: to build with reused materials, and use as little embodied energy as possible; to integrate large amounts of thermal mass into the structure, to reduce space-heating requirements; and to provide a stable, durable, low-maintenance structure to shelter the inhabitants from the elements. As noted by Sutherland Lyall in *The Architects' Journal* Specification focus on Earthship Brighton in August 2006, there is probably a marked degree of scepticism in the general architectural community about the use of tyres as a structural device[67]. 'Architects,' he wrote, 'may cavil at a used-tyre main structural element, especially when the tyres just sit on the local Brighton chalk, scraped back to an undisturbed layer'[67]. Indeed, some architects feel that tyres are simply not an appropriate material for a serious building. But the earthship refutes that sentiment and Lyall goes on to assuage the doubts of the anti-tyre brigade: 'We are too used to complicated and responsibility-proofed modern foundation systems,' he argues. 'It turns out that earth/chalk-filled used tyres spread relatively light domestic loads very efficiently – a proposition which building control was not disposed to fault. As the steep, internal side of the berm, they worked successfully as a retaining wall'[67].

Figure 39: Section of Earthship Brighton, showing rammed-tyre wall at rear and footing at front
© Taus Larsen

LEGISLATIVE AND REGULATORY POSITION

The moment a car tyre is removed from a vehicle because it is no longer considered suitable for its intended purpose, it becomes legally classified as waste. And building with what is classified as waste has become complicated from a legal and regulatory point of view in most European countries. In the UK this has largely been due to the Waste Management Licensing Regulations 1994, which require that all activities involving waste be either licensed or exempted[68]. This provides a framework for tracking waste and ensuring that it is being disposed of responsibly and under controlled conditions. The EU Landfill Directive 1999/31/EC has had an impact across Europe, as it ensures that other uses have to be found for waste tyres, because the legislation completely banned the dumping of all conventional tyres in landfill as from July 2006[61]. The negative aspect of the present legislative framework is that it has complicated permissions for building earthships in some places.

Of the projects we look at in detail in this book, the earthships built in France, Spain and Sweden have not had any regulatory difficulties with building with tyres. Builds in the UK and Belgium, though, have faced significant hurdles. The Belgian project, called Earthresidence, was denied permission to build with tyres. However, the builders (Earthship Belgium) negated the tyre issue by filling sandbags with earth instead of pounding tyres. In Sweden, on the other hand, there have been anecdotal reports of local municipalities going so far as to find tyres for earthship builders to build with.

The regulatory battles that we have the most detail on are those that have taken place in the UK. These were also written about in the first edition of this book, although there have been significant developments since then. The main point of interest in a more global sense is that the regulatory bodies involved in the decision making in the UK have been environmental agencies. And, regardless of the background waste management legislation, they seem to have mainly taken pragmatic decisions based on potential environmental impacts. In the case of the UK's Environment Agency, those impacts are:

- risk to water, air, soil, plants or animals; or
- causing nuisance through noise or odours; or
- adversely affecting the countryside or places of special interest[69].

If earthships can satisfy such criteria for environmental impact, this therefore goes a long way towards answering, with rigorous independent scrutiny, the question of whether building with tyres is indeed a benign technique – something that is looked at in more detail later in this chapter. Given the fact that it is almost 10 years since the Environment Agency was first consulted on this issue, though, it seems extraordinary that there is still no true clarity on it. Sorting through the history of what has happened in the past decade reveals a sorrowful tale of what the *Daily Mail* might call 'bureaucracy gone mad'. However, for anyone who has an interest in building with tyres, this history should be essential reading.

Regulatory history of UK builds

Earthship Fife was the first UK earthship to apply for an exemption from the Waste Licensing Regulations 1994 under schedule 3, paragraph 15, on the grounds of 'beneficial use of waste'[68]. It is under this exemption, for example, that tyres can be used as fenders on boats, or as swings in children's playgrounds. The alternative paragraph 19 exemption covers certain specific, named types of waste to be used for construction purposes: this includes, for example, the reuse of certain types of demolition waste as hardcore. However, the paragraph 19 exemption does not name used tyres – whether whole, shredded, crumbed or baled – so this exemption cannot apply.

An application from Fife was made to the Scottish Environmental Protection Agency (SEPA), and the exemption was granted in 2002 (exemption reference number WMX/E/0003204)[70]. When Earthship Brighton made a similar application on the same grounds to the Environment Agency in England in autumn 2002, it was rejected. This may seem surprising: although Scottish law is different from English law, the Waste Management Licensing Regulations are exactly the same in the two countries. But there are reasons for this inconsistency. The first is that the definition of waste had changed between SEPA's exemption and the Brighton application: it incorporated more items as 'waste' than previously, and those items remained classified as waste for a longer period of time. This made the regulators think harder about waste, and re-evaluate all associated issues. The paragraph 15 exemption (beneficial use of waste) that Earthship Brighton had applied for is pertinent only if the waste being used is not processed or changed in any way from its original form. Although the rubber in a tyre is not changed by being rammed with earth, the tyre itself becomes solid and its physical form is changed. The Environment Agency therefore deemed that a paragraph 15 exemption did not apply in this case.

The second conceivable reason for the inconsistency between SEPA's ruling and that of the Environment Agency is the possibility that SEPA's position was not strictly in accordance with legal precedent. Case law suggests that the Environment Agency's decision for Earthship Brighton is one that would have been upheld in court. So, if an exemption was not granted, how did Earthship Brighton end up being built? The Environment Agency, realising the groundbreaking nature and unusual circumstances of the Brighton build, decided to take the extraordinary position of allowing the project to continue without either an exemption or a licence. It is worth quoting from the letter sent by the Environment Agency to the directors of the company building the earthship – the Low Carbon Network Ltd (LCN) – in February 2003:

'As the legislation stands at the present time there is no exemption from the need to hold a Waste Management [Licence] for the activity you wish to carry out. As such a Waste Management Licence would be needed if you wish to continue with the project. However I am in sympathy with the trials you wish to carry out, and your desire to demonstrate and prove the concept, particularly with respect to Building Regulations issues. I have also noted that this is the first project of its type in the UK. Accordingly therefore I have taken the exceptional step of giving you authority to carry on with the demonstration project without the need for a Waste Management Licence. This letter can be taken as that authority. I must make it clear that, as a demonstration trial for the UK, this has to be a one-off situation and that it forms no precedent for any further requests from you, or other groups across the country.' Environment Agency[71]

This gave the go-ahead for Earthship Brighton to proceed with construction. It was an 'enforcement position' – a local decision, made by the regulators (the Environment Agency) on the basis that the earthship was a 'low risk' activity and that a Waste Management Licence was not appropriate. It recognised that, technically, LCN was acting unlawfully, but the regulatory powers would not be enforced in this case. This applied only to Earthship Brighton. At the time this did not set a precedent, and individual enforcement positions were still necessary for other builds.

A subsequent invitation from the Environment Agency for LCN to participate in what they called a 'stakeholder dialogue' created the opportunity for significant lobbying to ensure that future earthship builds would not have to labour under the same regulatory and legislative ambiguities. The result of this dialogue was a report issued in June 2004 on seeking solutions for waste tyres, entitled *Required Exemptions to Waste Management Licensing for Tyre Recovery*[72]. The needs of earthship builders were taken into account in this report, which was recommended to the Department for Environment, Food and Rural Affairs (Defra) by the Environment Agency. Among the recommendations was a key amendment to paragraph 19 of the 1994 legislation to allow whole tyres as a waste form used in construction. The Environment Agency has stated that, until these recommendations are enshrined in law, it will take the 'lightest regulatory stance' in relation to future earthship builds, provided that the local authority has granted planning permission[71].

When the first edition of this book was written, the Environment Agency seemed to recognise the low risk posed by earthship construction in terms of specific environmental risks, which we look at in detail below. The risk assessment system used at the Environment Agency when evaluating builds would make giving them the go-ahead a much easier decision to take than previously. Low-risk waste activities are brought to a national panel every six weeks by local environment officers, who assess the risk and make a decision whether to allow the activity to take place. This was not an exemption, or a waste management licence, but a pragmatic position that we hoped would allow for earthships to be built with relatively little bureaucracy until the 1994 legislation was amended.

More recent developments, though, suggest that there has been little change in the Environment Agency position, and that the use of whole tyres in construction is no longer considered low risk. The most relevant development was a discussion that came out of plans to build a tyre-wall structure at Schumacher College in Devon in summer 2010. Because there is no statutory authorisation for building with tyres, the college had to take the issue up with its local Environment Agency environment officer. The Environment Agency said that its concern was now not an environmental one, but was based on the fact that criminals had recently been exploiting the softened stance taken towards baled tyres, by illegally disposing of them in large dumps, resulting in a clean-up bill that could run into millions of pounds. It was worried that by providing permission for building with whole tyres, it might create a situation in which criminals would begin to dump them illegally in this manner as well[73].

This seems a strange position to take. Why not, for example, provide a permit to build with tyres only once planning and building control permission for a building has been obtained? This should make it straightforward to see the difference between legitimate and illegitimate uses of tyres. Linking the permission to use tyres into standard construction bureaucracy would seem to be the easiest way to enable the activity and enforce non-compliance. There seems to be a precedent for this too. A low risk position has been adopted by the Environment Agency in respect of tyre bales (used tyres compressed into bales) that are being used in a variety of civil engineering construction contexts such as slope failure repair, lightweight embankment fill and road foundations over soft ground[74].

The position became even more confused when, in July 2010, the Environment Agency issued a regulatory position statement relating to the Schumacher build which stated that 'we will allow the trial of the use of waste tyres in the Schumacher College "Earthship" project without an environmental permit'[71]. The Environment Agency justified this position on the grounds of it being a monitored trial:

'Storing or using waste tyres requires an environmental permit and this trial will inform our future decision making by helping us to understand the environmental risks around using waste tyres as a construction material.' Environment Agency[71]

In other words, the position is almost identical to that taken more than seven years previously for Earthship Brighton. The Environment Agency is slow to change, and its decision-making processes seem opaque and muddled. The environmental risk factors have long been available for monitoring, the objections to providing a permit for the Schumacher project were based around criminal activity, and yet the ultimate decision was to withhold a permit and treat the project as a test site.

An Environment Agency spokesperson told us that 'Tyres can be used for lots of things; I can't see why building with tyres can't be a potential future use of tyres. We have an industry growing of baling tyres and their use in construction is growing. The principle is there and we won't stand in the way of that. Construction is a potentially valid use of tyres.'[75]

However, he also added that 'The key for us is to make sure that we don't encourage activities that will abandon tyres – that has been a big problem in the industry. We are nervous about low risk positions, which is why we pulled back from that.'[75]

This situation suggests that there is no imminent likelihood of statutory permission being available to build with tyres in England and Wales, despite there being no significant adverse environmental findings. And although the Schumacher project has been treated as a test site, it seems unlikely that this will change the long-term position. The Environment Agency has clearly decided to restrict small scale tyre construction to being a peripheral activity while continuing to *sound* supportive about it. Meanwhile SEPA continues to be more practically supportive, with permits granted to projects in northern Scotland and at Greenhead Moss, near Glasgow. Across Europe, decision making varies in different territories, depending on interpretations of waste legislation. But, assuming local agencies are convinced by the environmental risk factors, they should be able to make pragmatic local decisions to allow building with tyres, as many – in France, Spain and Sweden – have already done.

RISK ASSESSMENT CONCERNS

In terms of the specific environmental risk assessment for tyres, the main concerns are issues regarding durability, off-gassing (fumes leaking into the living space), leachates (liquid run-off into surrounding soil) and fire risk.

Durability

Tyres are extremely durable, as the natural rubber is combined with synthetic rubber, and the resulting compound is treated with chemicals. This means that they can stand up to wear and tear from water, sunlight and acidity, the pressure exerted by the load of the vehicle they are carrying, and abrasion and friction with the road surface. Nonetheless, over three years on the road a tyre typically loses 1.5 kg or 20% of its weight[76]. By the time tyres arrive on an earthship site they have already been worn down to a degree where they're no longer considered roadworthy, yet they retain their basic structural integrity, which is what makes them a superb building block.

Once the tyres are integrated into the structure, they are buried behind a layer of damp-proofing, insulation and plastering, which means that they have no direct interface with either the interior of the building or the open air. They are therefore isolated from the principal forces that would cause them to degrade in a static environment: water and sunlight.

This suggests that concerns about durability may be misplaced: how can a substance placed in an essentially inert environment conceivably disintegrate enough to (a) create structural problems and (b) leach harmful chemicals into the outside environment or the building itself? Anecdotal evidence points to the fact that tyres are highly stable and durable as building blocks; the oldest earthships in New Mexico have so far been around for approximately 25 years without any structural problems.

However, in Fife, Scottish Building Control provided a five-year licence for the building, on the basis that the longevity of tyres was an essentially untested element[77].

The fundamentally durable properties of tyres, and the conditions in which they're placed in the building, suggest that there is a low risk of marked disintegration. The true test, though, is time itself:

unlike other building materials, tyres have only had a relatively short period in which to prove how durable they really are. In the meantime, the most critical aspect is the assessment of whether off-gassing or leaching pose significant environmental risks.

Off-gassing and leachates

Many of the chemicals that are added to tyres to make them more durable are also ones that can cause problems for human health and the natural environment: the aromatic hydrocarbons benzene, toluene, xylene and petroleum naphtha; synthetic rubber compounds, such as butadiene and styrene; polycyclic aromatic hydrocarbons, including phenols and benzo(a)pyrene; heavy metals, such as zinc, chromium, nickel, lead, copper and cadmium; and other chemicals, such as carbon black and sulphur[78]. Some of these are also volatile organic compounds (VOCs). The World Health Organization classes VOCs as the group of organic compounds occurring in air that have a boiling temperature of between 50 to 100°C and 240 to 260°C. VOCs are linked to a range of health issues, from irritation of the eyes, nose and throat to headaches, nausea, fatigue, dizziness, respiratory difficulties, and an increased risk of developing certain cancers[79].

Used tyres are a problem when they are stockpiled in an open environment, as they can leach chemicals into watercourses; this is one of the reasons why the EU classifies them as hazardous waste. However, as the tyres in an earthship are shielded from the ingress of water, the leachate problem seems extremely unlikely. An anecdotal report suggests that local regulators in Sweden were concerned when a damp-proof course was not placed beneath a tyre wall on one build, but insisted they would be happy if there was one there.

The greater concern is that tyres in earthships may be off-gassing VOCs into the building. VOCs are common in most existing household products, such as paints, insulation, vinyl tiles, carpets and other textiles. Smells such as those of new carpets, freshly painted walls, and clothes just back from the dry-cleaners are created largely by VOCs. But at least 50% of the chemicals off-gas from their source within the first year[80]. This is also relevant to tyres, as most tyres are at least three years old before they are used in earthship construction.

The Solid Waste Bureau of the New Mexico Environmental Department (in the US state where the earthship concept was pioneered) did some research into tyre off-gassing, based on the report *Use of Scrap Tires in Civil and Environmental Construction* by the University of Wisconsin-Madison. It concluded that:

'The production of such vapors will be proportional to the vapor pressure of the compounds producing the vapors. The NIOSH pocket guide lists the vapor pressure of carbon black as 0 mmHg (approx.). This is an extremely low vapor pressure. In other words, this chemical produces almost no vapor. What this means is that the potential for tires to affect indoor air quality will be severely limited by the extremely low vapor pressure of the source chemical.'[81]

Whereas the vapour pressure of carbon black as listed in the NIOSH pocket guide is 0 mmHg (approx.), it is only one of many chemicals and components[82]. By comparison, the solvents toluene, xylene and benzene (all commonly used in rubber processing) have vapour pressures of 21, 9 and 75 mmHg respectively, and *do* off-gas[83]. Therefore it could be stated that the New Mexico example is selective with its data, although by volume the amount of carbon black and other filler, at around 30%, is significantly higher than that of solvents (less than 1%)[84].

There are two ways in practice to measure tyre off-gassing: either in isolation in a laboratory, or in situ in a house. The first method involves an emission test chamber and monitoring over time to the international standard ISO 16000-9, varying the conditions of temperature, humidity, airflow and duration[85]. This would provide a detailed breakdown of pollutants, but it would not reflect an actual indoor environment, with the effects of infiltration and ventilation, as a test chamber is a sealed unit.

The second method would use sampling equipment such as a Perkin Elmer tube in an earthship, to measure the average concentration of pollutants. However, although this method would study the tyres in a wall, it would be very difficult to distinguish the gases relating to the tyre from the background of gases from other materials. This could be partially overcome by testing the other

materials in an emissions chamber and removing them from the results by a process of elimination.

To our knowledge neither of these methods has yet been used in a scientific study to monitor tyre off-gassing. Clearly, a study is required. Anecdotally, there have been no reports of any symptoms from people living in earthships that might be related to unhealthy levels of VOCs. Earthship Biotecture states on its website that 'There has never been one instance of illness or even awareness of any off-gassing of tyres in 30 years of research and development'[86].

The obvious retort to this is 'They would say that, wouldn't they?' And in contrast to the anecdotal reporting is the example of a factory worker in a Wolverhampton tyre plant, who was severely affected by solvents in a lubricant paint sprayed on the inside of tyres, and collapsed while working. Obviously the level of exposure was far higher than anyone would experience while working with used tyres, but it does emphasise that tyres contain some noxious and dangerous chemicals[87]. Only an independent, authoritative study will properly reveal the answer. As it is, though, the necessarily tentative conclusion at this stage is that there is no direct evidence to suggest that VOC concentrations are higher in earthships than they are in other dwellings.

VOC concentrations are generally mitigated by ventilation: studies have shown that indoor VOC levels are on average 10 times greater than those outdoors[88]. So by refreshing the indoor atmosphere with air from outside, dangerous build-ups are generally avoided. The difficulty is that for buildings to have high thermal performance they also need to attain high levels of airtightness. This includes earthships. At the moment, airtightness is not a major factor in earthship design, but we argue in this book that it should become more so, if earthships are to deliver the full extent of their performance potential. However, this also raises the dilemma that occupants may be exposed to higher concentrations of contaminants that might otherwise be dissipated by background infiltration. This also highlights the need in airtight buildings for a ventilation system that can supply an adequate level of indoor air quality and remove the build up of pollutants. This is discussed later on. An airtight house would correspond more with the results from an emissions test chamber. Further rigorous testing needs to be done in order to find out how low VOC levels can coexist with high airtightness.

Fire risk

'The fire was described on the front page of one of the tabloids as a "burning inferno" on the first day of the year, I suspect that the papers were short of news, but it made a dramatic headline none the less. However, it has become a forgotten fire. My objective is to give a balanced view and to come up with serious suggestions about how it can be tackled, while stressing the legitimate fears of my constituents for their community and for the precious environment in this lovely part of my native Wales.'[89]

This quote, a report made to the House of Commons on 26th July 1990 on the fire at the Heyope tyre dump by Mr Richard Livsey MP for Brecon and Radnor, is a dramatic demonstration of the fire risk of tyres. We wrote in the first edition of this book that the fire risk with tyre walls in earthships is practically non-existent. This was demonstrated when an earthship in the USA was burnt in a forest fire. The only parts left of the earthship were the tyre and glass bottle walls; the timber frame had been completely burnt away[58]. This demonstrated the resilience of tyre walls.

However, in March 2010 the Greenhead Moss earthship near Glasgow was burnt down by arsonists, and this potentially reopened the issue of whether tyres *do* pose a fire risk. From photographs of the structure after the fire, it looks as though the timber was badly burnt, and, although the tyres retained their structural integrity, the rubber was badly burnt where it was exposed to the air. The main risk seems to be at the pre-pounding stage, when the tyres are in storage, waiting to be used onsite. Once they have been filled with earth the risk becomes much lower, because they are stacked with non-flammable material. The risk becomes even less once they have been rendered over, so that the flammable element is completely hidden.

OTHER RULES ABOUT WASTE HANDLING

Any project that involves building with tyres will also have to comply with various different rules regarding their transport and storage. This relates to the classification of tyres as waste. Earthship builders are advised to check on the local regulations in their particular country.

Figure 40: Greenhead Moss Earthship after blaze © Wishaw Press

Figure 41: Aluminium can wall (Earthship Valencia) © Lisa-Jane Roberts and Oscar Briz

OTHER LOW-EMBODIED-ENERGY MATERIALS

Tyres are the 'headline' material of earthships, but they are not the only form of waste used in their construction. The idea is to try to reuse as many waste materials as possible. Instead of packing out the spaces between tyres solely with cement, for example, infilling with various types of waste, such as bottles is used in an attempt to reduce the amount of cement being used overall. Even so, earthships have been criticised for the amount of cement used in their construction.

Figure 42: Aluminium can wall (Earthship Fife)
© Sustainable Communities Initiative

Non-loadbearing walls, in particular, offer the opportunity to experiment with different types of 'brick' that might otherwise merely be discarded into landfill. These include aluminium cans and glass bottles. Reynolds states that 'the material we have found … is a little durable aluminium brick that appears "naturally" on this planet. It is indigenous to most parts of the planet that are heavily populated. It is also known as the aluminium beverage can'[27]. The aluminium can is often used in US earthships to create eye-catching features such as panel walls, domes and vaults. This technique evolved in the 1970s in the desert, where there was no recycling infrastructure. However, non-ferrous metals have the highest embodied energy of any material that is used in volume in any industry or sector in society, and it is better that they are recycled conventionally in order to reduce the need for raw material extraction. This is particularly the case when the aluminium can is not a functional element – that is, it provides no structural or thermal quality to the building.

This is true with glass bottles too. Glass bottle walls also form a visually impressive feature in many earthships. They can easily be shaped into 'bricks' by cutting the necks from two bottles with a generic

Figure 43: Glass bottle brick wall in construction (Earthship Brighton) © Mischa Hewitt

Figure 44: Close-up of glass bottle brick wall in construction (Earthship Brighton) © Mischa Hewitt

Figure 45: Finished glass bottle brick wall with render (Earthship Brighton) © Mischa Hewitt

cutting tool and sticking them together with some tape. The result is a uniform cylinder that is easy to work with in creating a non-loadbearing wall. This significantly reduces the embodied energy that would come in the form of a brick specified for the same job. And there is a genuine aesthetic beauty to glass bottle walls, which allow light to permeate through them, with a delicate interplay of shape and colour that creates a great dynamic against the solidity of the wall in which they are set. It is a real skill to achieve such an effect, which delivers a realisation of the amazing capacity for rubbish to be turned into something inspiring. Various bottle walls have now been built using clay or lime as the mortar instead of cement.

Reclaimed timber and salvaged masonry are also used in earthships wherever possible. Earthship Brighton benefited from using the Brighton & Hove Wood Recycling Project for all the doors and floorboards used in construction. The Wood Recycling Project states that 'every day a huge amount of waste timber is generated by industries working in construction, demolition and manufacture, wooden packaging waste and non-returnable pallets. Brighton & Hove Wood Recycling Project aims to rescue, reuse and recycle some of the tonnes of wood going to landfill locally by collecting waste wood from local businesses'[90]. It then sells the timber it collects to clients such as Earthship Brighton, who were happy to use a material that might have otherwise gone to landfill.

Figure 46: Exterior view of glass bottle brick bathroom wall at the Jacobsen earthship (Taos, New Mexico) © Kirsten Jacobsen

Stone is another material that is often discarded at various stages of its lifetime in construction, including when it is first extracted from the quarry. There is waste in the form of offcuts that don't quite make the quality control grade. The Earthship Brighton build benefited from a donation of end-of-vein offcuts of this type – in this case Portland stone from the company Albion Stone. This was used for the meeting room, kitchen and bathroom floors. Reclaimed granite offcuts from a local stonemason were used in a mosaic style for the hut and conservatory floors to make best use of the irregular shapes that had been sourced. Mosaic is a common style in earthship builds, because salvaged materials are often used in a best-fit sense. One of the most impressive uses of mosaic in earthships is seen in Earthship Zwolle in Holland. There is a genuine design and craft skill in incorporating these materials into a build in a way that enhances the basic structure and functions of the earthship itself, and creates a welcoming and comfortable environment for the inhabitants.

Figure 47: Mosaic and bottle wall detail in Earthship Zwolle © Harald Walker

JUNK AESTHETIC

The heterogeneity of material in earthships creates an unusual agglomeration of visual styles that could loosely be defined as a 'junk aesthetic'. Like a set design in a post-apocalyptic film, earthships can seem as though they are built from the scavenged remnants of industrial society. This may sound pejorative, but the earthship is a building that deliberately makes use of, and indeed often makes beautiful, manufactured materials that have been dumped and discarded, as well as organic materials that have already been harvested and have been judged to have reached the end of their usefulness. This means that the reuse that occurs is twofold. First, it makes use of the man-made materials that are so readily available, short-circuiting the manufacturing process and reducing the overall embodied energy. Second, it negates the need for direct harvesting of virgin natural materials such as timber, by using reclaimed materials instead. The final visual result of this combination of materials may look strange to some, and indeed people sometimes describe the overall look as 'post-apocalyptic'. But the underlying rationale behind the building is function and performance according to human habitation and environmental criteria. The earthship challenges conventional aesthetics and the sense of what is beautiful in buildings, mainly through its rootedness in performance and its direct connection with the natural elements. Building a self-sufficient, high-performance home for people using materials that have been rejected by the rest of society is arguably, in itself, an immensely artistic and beautiful thing to do – as long as it works.

CONCLUSION

Waste materials are not the only materials that are used in earthship construction. Inevitably, the greater part of the specification involves newly manufactured products that are needed to make the earthship the high-performance structure that it aspires to be. This means that some items have to be of extremely high-grade specification, such as the PV panels, the glass and the insulation. These are all absolutely crucial to the performance of the building and it is impossible to compromise on them without compromising the very nature of the earthship itself.

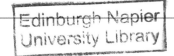

However, the waste products that are used are significant in terms of the overall resource outlook of the building and, indeed, as a provocation to the rest of the construction industry and to society as a whole. The provocation is the statement 'Look what can be done with what we throw away every day', and it is arguably a major part of what can be learned from earthships – that rubbish can be useful.

The most obviously useful waste material in earthship construction is the reused tyres. Thanks to the pioneer builds across Europe, regulatory case histories have begun to emerge that will support future builds, although there remain ambiguities in different territories, especially in England and Wales, and in Belgium. More work also needs to be done on monitoring issues crucial to the credibility of building with tyres.

Photovoltaic cells at the Hockerton Housing Project
© Hockerton Housing Project

5 RENEWABLE ENERGY AND POWER SYSTEMS

INTRODUCTION

'The operation of a sailing boat requires an understanding of the concepts and schematics of sailing and knowing the patterns and nature of the wind. There are many differences between the operation of a gasoline powered speed boat and a wind powered sail boat. The major difference is that in a sail boat you will never run out of gas. Other differences involve pollution, noise, wear and tear, and repair of moving parts. The differences between conventional electricity and solar electricity in a home are similar to the differences between a speed boat and a sailboat.' Mike Reynolds[27]

Similar to sailing ships, earthships directly employ the elements they encounter, so the analogy of a yacht or sailing ship using renewable natural resources – the wind, tide and currents – to travel effortlessly seems appropriate. This is especially the case when we consider the ship's freedom to travel using only these abundant, renewable and free natural resources without recourse to non-sustainable fuels. The earthship is similarly unconstrained as it is designed to be unconnected to the national grid or other utilities. The aim of the earthship is to provide comfortable shelter for its inhabitants through a set of sustainable means analogous to those of a sailing boat, although the 'wind in the sails' of the earthship is not for movement, but for providing space heating through thermal mass and the energy generation to power the systems required for human habitation. The planning of these systems also means thinking about those times when there is no wind in the sails – what sailors refer to as 'the doldrums': days when the earthship's natural resources such as sun and wind are not so plentiful.

There is a clear and pressing need to decarbonise our power. Earthships do this by reducing space-heating needs (traditionally supplied by fossil fuels) and relying instead on renewable sources to generate electricity, although there are many issues with this, such as the capital costs involved and the ongoing maintenance of such systems. This chapter explores the power systems of the European earthships, and the nature and limitations of off-grid power.

Figure 48: Earthship Brighton, showing a wind turbine, photovoltaic cells and solar thermal panels
© Mischa Hewitt

DESIGN OUT: ENERGY DEMAND MANAGEMENT IN EARTHSHIPS

'Photovoltaic electric systems can be very complicated and almost prohibitively expensive for conventional "energy hog" housing. Earthships are the result of energy-conscious design and, by their very nature, come a long way towards reducing the electrical requirements of living.' Mike Reynolds[27]

The earthship's energy strategy is twofold: first in terms of energy-efficient design that reduces the need for external energy inputs of any sort, even those of a sustainable kind; and second in terms

of the actual micro-renewable energy generation systems that provide electricity and hot water to the building. This can be looked at from a supply and demand perspective: the first step is to slash energy demand so that the second step (supply) can be easily met with renewable sources. A process of system sizing – evaluating an earthship's capacity requirements, and integrating the correct level of supply to meet those requirements – needs to occur in order to balance the books. The system-sizing spreadsheet for Earthship Brighton is included here as an example (Table 2). Note how the supply side is much greater than the demand side. This

Table 2: System-sizing spreadsheet for Earthship Brighton								
Outgoing energy								
Device	Voltage	Wattage	Current	Hours/day summer	Hours/day winter	Inverter efficiency	Total daily summer (Ah*)	Total daily winter (Ah)
DC loads								
Fridge	24.00	140.00	5.83	18.00	12.00	n/a	105.00	70.00
Pump	24.00	6.00	0.25	8.00	8.00	n/a	2.00	2.00
Pump	24.00	6.00	0.25	8.00	8.00	n/a	2.00	2.00
AC loads								
Laptop	24.00	30.00	1.25	8.00	8.00	0.90	11.11	11.11
Laptop	24.00	30.00	1.25	8.00	8.00	0.90	11.11	11.11
Laptop	24.00	30.00	1.25	8.00	8.00	0.90	11.11	11.11
Printer ink jet	24.00	50.00	2.08	4.00	4.00	0.90	9.26	9.26
Projector	24.00	800.00	33.33	1.00	1.00	0.90	37.04	37.04
Stereo	24.00	75.00	3.13	4.00	4.00	0.90	13.89	13.89
						Totals (Ah/day)	202.52	167.52
Incoming energy								
18 × 62 W Unisolar electric panels	24.00	1116.00	46.50	6.00	–	3.00	279.00	139.50
900 W Whisper H40 wind turbine	24.00	900.00	37.50	2.00	–	4.00	75.00	150.00
						Totals (Ah/day)	354.00	289.50
						Ah	151.48	121.98

* Available excess energy

overcapacity is essential, because the renewable technologies in use – wind and solar – are weather dependent, and may not produce the peak outputs they are capable of when needed ('the doldrums').

The design is energy-conscious, but it also relies on the occupants using energy frugally. They are in command of their energy production, but with that power comes responsibility. With off-grid buildings it really is a case of tailoring activities, and using any excess power at any given time, for example using a washing machine on sunny days, as storage capacity is expensive. The earthship concept suggests that profligate and wasteful consumption of energy is a thing of the past. This general idea seems to be gaining increasingly widespread acceptance: for example, the use of low-energy light bulbs is now widespread, and the increasing prices of fuel are forcing people to reassess their energy needs. But at the same time there is an increasing demand for energy-hungry air-conditioning units and a proliferation of electronic devices and gadgets, balancing out this energy-saving impulse and maintaining the overall upward trend of electricity consumption.

The significant point is that comfortable living – what we might call low-carbon living in luxury – is designed to be easy in earthships without resort to the high energy usage seen in most of the present European building stock, where demands even for basic services such as space heating and hot water represent a massive drain on the grid, mainly as a result of poor design. And this is before we assess the impact of the arsenal of modern appliances: TVs, computers, Wi-Fi, hairdryers, and other gadgets from iPads to hedge trimmers, games consoles to dishwashers.

The combined passive solar and thermal mass capacities of earthships are crucial factors in reducing the energy requirements of the building, although – as will be shown in chapter 8 – the earthship is not zero energy, and space heating does need to be provided in cold weather. Passive solar features such as large amounts of south-facing glazing mean that additional lighting is seldom necessary during daylight hours, even though the rear of the building is earth-sheltered (skylights and sunpipes compensate for the lack of north-facing windows). But the fact that earthships allow light to flood in to them is also emblematic of the primacy

of the sun in their overall design. Earthships are powered by the sun, and many design features, from the building's orientation to its thermal mass, and from its large glazed area to its water recycling, are all solar-oriented. The building is like a rechargeable battery that uses the sun to keep it charged and functioning, while collecting and using as much solar energy as possible through various means.

'You get up in the morning. It's cloudy. O.K., you're not going to do a wash today. You don't turn up the heat because your Earthship inherently provides it. You don't need any lights during the daylight hours for the same reason. As a matter of fact, you don't need any power today except for a few small things.' Mike Reynolds[27]

This sums up the essence of earthships: renewable natural resources are harvested not just for electricity generation but also for passive space heating and ventilation, lighting and water heating. By using these site-available resources to reduce demand, earthships are able to be off-grid and detached from some of the problems that are part and parcel of centralised infrastructure, such as consumption of fossil fuel, high levels of carbon emissions, inefficiencies in transmitting power, rising energy prices, and power cuts. Small-scale off-grid systems may be suitable for rural locations, but they may not be appropriate for denser urban locations, where community-scale power systems such as combined heat and power plants will be more efficient. The potential problem of a supply deficit is compensated for by storage batteries and an overcapacity of supply that is integrated during the formative stages of system sizing. There are negative implications of living with batteries, but they can be balanced against the benefits that earthships offer in general, and against the many negative aspects of centralised infrastructure. There is also the possibility of supply failure, despite techniques that are employed to prevent that happening. This is unlikely, though, and would also have less problematic consequences than a breakdown in a conventional infrastructure-dependent home, where fewer services are embedded within the building itself.

Earthships are pioneers of what can be achieved through micro-generation, and show that non-grid-based solutions are viable on a single-dwelling basis. However, there is a fine balance between economy and efficiency of scale. The earthship shows how basic, freely available resources can provide all the energy that is needed, when onsite renewable energy systems are integrated into a design, and as long as people are prepared to be flexible with their lifestyles.

ONSITE MICRO-RENEWABLES

This section introduces an overview of the systems used in the various European earthships, and the subsequent sections discuss the detail of the various technologies. Stand-alone systems are closed, so they require a method of storing energy. Also, as the amount of power generated is relatively small, they must be carefully balanced to match supply,

storage and demand. The tailor-made nature of such systems can make them inflexible. Table 3 summarises the differences between grid-linked and off-grid systems. All the European earthships are off grid, except for the Groundhouse in Brittany and Earthship Zwolle. Earthship Zwolle, which was built in 2009 by Earthship Biotecture, is not included in this book, because of a lack of detail on the project.

From Table 3, it can be seen that one of the main complexities of off-grid systems is the reliance on batteries. This is discussed in more detail below. The different European earthships have different power systems, enabling them to exploit the most accessible onsite renewable resources available to them. Most have either a solar array or a wind turbine, or both; Earthship Fife is unique in having a micro-hydro plant as well as both PV and wind systems. Some use solar thermal or wood for heating hot water. The European

Table 3: Comparison between grid-linked and stand-alone renewable energy systems	
Grid-linked systems	**Off-grid systems**
Grid connection to a regional electricity network	No grid connection to a regional electricity network
No onsite storage required	Onsite storage required – usually lead-acid batteries with charge controller
Less regular maintenance	More components require regular maintenance – eg topping up batteries
Less component replacement	Some components, eg batteries, have a relatively short lifespan and need to be replaced regularly
Any size of renewable energy system could in theory be installed, as they are not dependent on being balanced with other components in a closed system	Balancing of components to enable an efficient design will limit the size of renewable energy system, eg a photovoltaic array
Excess energy can be exported to the grid and sold	Excess energy cannot be exported, and so is usually dumped as heat. In some countries a feed-in tariff can still be claimed if power is not exported
Affected by regional power cuts	Unaffected by regional power cuts
Upfront capital cost for renewable energy systems and synchronous inverter only, but grid tie may be required as well where none is present. This may be expensive, depending on proximity of grid	High upfront capital cost for whole system, and ongoing costs to replace components that wear out

earthships' power systems are summarised in Table 4. The following sections divide the technologies into those that produce hot water and those that produce electricity. There is a general introduction to each technology in each section, and then a brief discussion and summary of how these are deployed in the European earthships.

HOT WATER

Solar thermal: domestic water heating

Solar thermal is a relatively simple technology that can be used to supply hot water for domestic applications such as dishwashing and showers. Bob Everett of the Open University says that 'domestic water heating is perhaps the best overall potential application for active solar heating in Europe.' According to Everett, a typical UK household uses approximately 15 kWh per day for domestic water heating, although much of this energy is lost as waste heat through uninsulated pipes and hot water tanks[91].

Solar thermal systems can provide hot water all year round in southern Europe and for most of the year in northern Europe. The main issue in northern Europe is the paucity of sunshine in winter, meaning that solar thermal alone cannot exclusively supply hot water all year round, and backup is required. It can supply enough hot water the rest of the time, though. The European earthships that have solar thermal systems are summarised in Table 5.

Table 4: European earthships' power systems

| Earthship | Hot water | | Electricity | | |
	Solar thermal	Biomass	Photovoltaics	Wind turbine	Micro-hydro
Almeria*	Yes	–	Yes	Yes	–
Brighton	Yes	Yes	Yes	Yes	–
Fife	–	–	Yes	Yes	Yes
France	Yes	–	Yes	Yes	–
The Groundhouse	Yes	Yes	Yes	–	–
Valencia	Yes	Yes	Yes	–	–

* The intention is to install solar electric and solar thermal panels in the near future.

Table 5: European earthships' solar thermal systems

Earthship	Manufacturer	No. of panels	Area (m²)	Anticipated annual yield (kWh)
Brighton	Filsol	2	4.0	1636
France	Ferroli	1	1.2	–
The Groundhouse	Solex	–	10.0	–
Valencia	Chromagen	2	2.0	–

Biomass

Biomass is energy derived from the sun that has been converted by plants into material such as wood and straw. As plants fix atmospheric CO_2, as long as forests are sustainably managed, then the fuel forests are sustainably managed then the fuel should be almost carbon neutral, although the environmental impact is a hotly debated topic[92]. The crucial aspect of the use of biomass, though, is that 'provided our consumption does not exceed the natural level of production, the combustion of biofuels should generate no more heat and create no more carbon dioxide than would have been formed in any case by natural processes'[93]. However, it is a complex dynamic issue, as the quantity of CO_2 released by combustion is not absorbed immediately, but over a longer period of time as the tree grows.

There is also the possibility of the sustainable production of biomass as purpose-grown energy crops, but this has issues as well, such as the amount of land required reducing arable land available for food production, transport and processing implications, and air pollution from combustion. Nonetheless, it is a promising form of renewable energy that can be used effectively on a small scale. Only three of the European earthships use biomass, and these are summarised in Table 6.

Table 6: Biomass systems for European earthships			
Earthship	**Manufacturer**	**Fuel source**	**Rated output (kW)**
Brighton	Extraflame	Wood pellet	15.00
The Groundhouse	Hwam Vivaldi	Wood	5.00
Valencia	Plate steel wood fire with an oven on top	Wood	–

ELECTRICITY

Wind power

On a large scale, wind is one of the most cost-effective sources of generating renewable electricity, but there can be issues with smaller-scale machines. There are three factors that determine the amount of energy in the wind that can be harvested from a site: the density of air, the swept area of the blades, and the wind speed. The first two are known entities, but the wind speed varies enormously, depending on the time of year. The most important consideration is turbulence, created by obstructions such as trees or buildings, which lowers the wind speed and removes energy from the wind. Hugh Piggott, in Windpower Workshop, provides some figures to illustrate this point (Table 7).

Table 7: Typical wind speeds provided by different site conditions[94]	
Site conditions	**Average wind speed (m/s)**
Trees and buildings	3.0
Open fields, with few hedges	4.5
Hilltops or coasts (open sites)	6.0

Figure 49: Extraflame wood pellet stove (Earthship Brighton) © Mischa Hewitt

The average wind speeds show that, unless you have an open site, the potential wind resource available may be quite small. This caveat covers most sites, and correlates with the Energy Saving Trust's recent report *Location, Location, Location*, which concluded:

'Local topography and site characteristics can have considerable impact on the available wind resource and turbine performance at a site. As such, fewer sites than previously predicted should be considered suitable to install the technology.' Energy Saving Trust[95]

Another report by the BRE states that:

'A life cycle cost analysis of the systems included in this study suggests that, even in the most favourable location considered in the study, there is no financial payback within the expected life of the systems, with the current system and electricity costs.' Phillips et al, BRE[96]

Nevertheless, four of the European earthships have small wind turbines installed, but unfortunately no monitored data is available for the amount of energy harvested to show whether the above statements are borne out by experience. Anecdotally, at Earthship Brighton, the energy generated by the 900 W wind turbine was never felt until all the solar panels were stolen in autumn 2006, after which the wind turbine was the only source of energy, trickle-charging

the batteries. When the solar array was replaced in summer 2007, compared with the output of the PV panels the effect of the wind turbine was negligible. The European earthships' wind turbines are summarised in Table 8.

Table 8: European earthships' wind turbines			
Earthship	Manufacturer	Model	Rated output (W)
Brighton	Whisper	H40	900
Fife	Proven	WT600	600
France	South West Wind	Air X	400

Photovoltaics

'The PV panels are as integral a part of the Earthship as the headlights on a car. Therefore, they should be treated as such.' Mike Reynolds[27]

Solar cells or PVs are increasingly becoming a promising renewable energy source as the technology develops and the price drops. Once manufactured and installed, the panels produce no pollution, require little maintenance, and – as the sun is a virtually infinite source of energy – can deliver a consistent amount of power. Indeed, as Godfrey Boyle has pointed out, the net solar power input to the earth is more than 10,000 times

Figure 50: Installing Whisper wind turbine (Earthship Brighton) © Daniel Holloway

humanity's current rate of use of fossil and nuclear fuels, although as it is a less dense power source than those, it is harder to collect[97].

PV cells convert sunlight into electricity. They use both types of light: diffuse light (no direct sunshine) and direct light (sunshine) for conversion into electricity. Direct sunlight produces the most energy, and therefore the orientation of the PV system is very important in achieving maximum output. The amount of diffuse light available can be high, though, and should be used for natural daylight and passive solar gain. In Europe, the various different climates mean that the proportion of direct-to-diffuse light varies considerably, as will be seen in the Nicol graphs in chapter 7.

All the European earthships have a solar array, and the details are listed in Table 9.

The only monitored data for these systems are for Earthship Brighton. Data has been collected over a three-year period from August 2008. The system harvests very little power between November and March; the majority is collected during spring and summer.

Figure 51: Photovoltaic panels at the Eden Project
© Mischa Hewitt

Table 9: European earthships' photovoltaic systems

Earthship	Manufacturer	No. of panels	Rated output per panel (W)	Peak output (kW)	Anticipated annual yield (kWh)*
Brighton	Unisolar	18	62	1.12	1050
Fife	BP	4	75	0.30	218
France	ET Solar	10	200	2.00	1848
The Groundhouse	Sharp	14	200	2.80	2860
Valencia	Prosolia	8	158	1.26	1584

* Earthship Brighton figure collected from monitored data. All other yields calculated using PV-GIS[99].

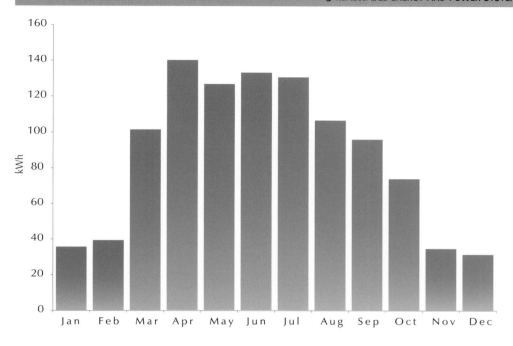

Figure 52: Earthship Brighton average monthly output

Micro-hydro

Hydroelectricity on a mass scale is already a successful and widely exploited form of renewable energy: it provides about a sixth of the world's annual electrical output, and over 90% of the electricity produced from renewables[98]. There are ecological and social impacts of large-scale hydro, though, not least the displacement of people in the area to be flooded. Also, it is a far less universal resource than sunlight and wind, and not every site will be able to harness it. The point, though, is about site harmony and opportunism – using the resources that are available to contribute to the overall demand. The main advantages of micro-hydro are that the water flows all the time, so it is a constant background source of available energy, and unlike wind turbines it is not dependent on weather. Generally there are higher water flows in winter. The only European earthship that uses a micro-hydro turbine is Earthship Fife, which has a 1 kW Turgo Runner Stream Engine.

Figure 53: Turgo Runner Stream Engine micro-hydro turbine © Sustainable Communities Initiative

DESIGN LIMITATIONS

Storage

'Learning to sail a boat takes practice. Likewise, living in a solar home takes practice. An experienced solar fanatic could take a small photovoltaic system and never have a problem or care. However, an inexperienced believer who has spent all of his or her life with an abundance of power could get into trouble quite often during the first year or so of solar living. Good advice to the novice is to have a backup source of power if possible' Mike Reynolds[27]

National grids are not storage mechanisms, but networks for delivering electricity, although some do contain limited storage capacity, such as the Dinorwig pumped storage plant in Wales. The fundamental principle of the grid, though, is that it fills real-time demand for electricity with real-time generation and supply. The main challenge for an off-grid building such as the earthship, therefore, is to achieve exactly what the grid does – to match its ability to generate and supply electricity to meet the demand at any given time, even though supply may be intermittent. But earthships have nowhere to import electricity from if there is a deficit. Instead,

they compensate for likely potential deficits by using deep-cycle lead-acid storage batteries. Therefore, surplus energy can be stored from peak periods of production, to be used at a later time. This is a controversial approach, though, because of the limited longevity of lead-acid batteries, global supplies of lead decreasing and the fact that lead is exceptionally poisonous, which means that this approach creates some toxic waste.

Batteries can be considered as a 'transitional technology', because more sophisticated technologies for energy storage are under development. If a cleaner alternative to lead-acid batteries could be found, then there would be very few downsides to the off-grid earthship model. In the meantime earthshippers must be prepared for regular maintenance and replacement of batteries. The battery systems for the European earthships are summarised in Table 10.

Table 10: European earthships' battery systems			
Earthship	**Manufacturer**	**Model**	**Number**
Brighton	Trojan	L-16P	40
Fife	–	–	12
France	Rolls	4 KS 25P	6
Valencia	Exide	Classic OpzS	12

Figure 54: Trojan batteries before installation (Earthship Brighton) © Mischa Hewitt

Figure 55: Power organising module: controller, inverter and fuse box (Earthship Brighton) © Mischa Hewitt

Off-grid construction and suitability of rural locations

'Small is beautiful, big is practical.'
David Olivier[100].

In developed countries in Europe there is little direct need for off-grid construction, thanks to the extensive infrastructure that meets most demand. It is only in rural settlements that there is a need for buildings to be off-grid, and therefore the demand for autonomous homes is not large. So why is the off-grid approach being adopted with earthships? There are various reasons, but the primary reason is that the philosophy of these buildings is about complete self-sufficiency; connection to outside utilities of any sort is essentially an admission of non-self-sufficiency. Within the wider green movement there is a drive towards 'small is beautiful' self-sufficiency, and the earthship echoes this sentiment.

An earthship uses only the resources that are immediately available to it, and thereby doesn't extend the footprint of the building beyond its means. This does have an impact on the amount of land required for systems that take a lot of space, though, such as reed beds. By contrast, homes that require utilities to be piped and wired into them in order to house people comfortably can be seen as fundamentally failing to deliver their most basic aim: to provide safe and comfortable shelter. In the event of any kind of breakdown of utilities this ability is severely compromised, and such homes are quickly rendered uninhabitable as demonstrated by the quote from Mike Reynolds below:

'Decentralized utilities can completely eliminate the expensive and invasive web of wires and pipes that currently deliver centralized utilities. Both the manufacture and delivery of centralized utilities put people in a powerless and vulnerable position with respect to security and evolution.' Mike Reynolds[101]

For all this to really make sense, it needs to be related to the wider picture of energy use in Europe. Electrical energy forms roughly a third of total energy use; heat energy also constitutes a third, and transport the final third. So the emphasis should not rest entirely on electricity generation, as it sometimes does. Various countries are increasingly relying on electricity for a wide variety of applications, and so decarbonisation of the grid is a priority. The question is: What is the best and most practicable route for a massive reduction in all building-related carbon emissions? Is it through enormous investment in grid-based renewable solutions, or through mass devolvement of generation appropriate in scale, from individual dwellings through to private wire grids? Is it desirable – or even realistic – to turn our houses into power stations, or is the solution to be found through a combination of all these means? All the solutions have to begin with demand reduction and energy efficiency before considering how the various supply options can provide clean, low-carbon energy to those homes.

Financial implications

There are significant cost implications of being off-grid. A single, up-front capital expense upon construction means that the building will run on a perpetual 'income' of natural resources that cuts out utility bills entirely – as long as the systems function. Mike Reynolds estimates that earthships require, on average, a 10% greater initial capital investment than a conventional home in order to realise this possibility[42]. In a time of massive instability in energy prices, which has seen large price rises for the provision of gas and electricity right across Europe, protection from exponentially rising fuel prices is an envious financial position for the off-grid householder to be in. It also adds a further tier to the concept of freedom that the earthship embodies; freedom from regular utility bills is something that everyone would like to achieve.

Figure 56: Filsol solar thermal panels and Unisolar photovoltaic panels (Earthship Brighton)

Reynolds also sees off-grid living as a way in which humans can rapidly evolve more appropriate systems to face numerous environmental and structural challenges, whereas centralised infrastructure remains sluggishly slow to evolve. 'Decentralized utilities can completely eliminate the expensive and invasive web of wires and pipes that currently deliver centralized utilities,' he says. 'Both the manufacture and delivery of centralized utilities put individual people in a powerless and vulnerable position with respect to security and evolution'[102].

For many, off-grid living is a lifestyle choice. There are examples of people living very cheaply off-grid, such as the 'No Money Man', in extreme privation, almost a Thoreau of our times, but for most people it is not much cheaper than mainstream on-grid living[103]. Hugh Piggott comments on the capital cost of batteries that:

> 'It has been calculated that just the cost of replacing the batteries can be roughly the same as the cost of buying the same amount of power as the system produces in this period, for the mains supply.' Hugh Piggott[94]

The technology that enables individuals to escape from the 'invasive web of wires' that Reynolds describes is micro-renewable power, mainly in the form of PV generation and occasionally of micro wind turbines, as described above. The earthship is a pragmatic building, dictated by function. It is therefore open to any renewable form of energy to meet its demands: Earthship Fife uses three different types of technology, for example, and Earthship Brighton uses four.

CONCLUSION

> 'We can't solve problems by using the same kind of thinking we used when we created them.' Albert Einstein

We live in an age where there are many large-scale problems. At first glance it would seem that the problems are caused mainly by people, and their resource-hungry lifestyles. In turn, these lifestyles are fuelled and powered by large-scale infrastructure, so it would seem that such systems are part of the problem, if indeed not the entire problem. Perhaps,

as Albert Einstein suggests, we can't solve problems by using the same thinking that created them, but the real issue is probably the continuing application of 'one size fits all' thinking, rather than the use of technology at an appropriate scale. This is the type of thinking that needs to change.

At one end of the scale, there is large-scale infrastructure. At the other end, there are earthships: built by pioneers, demonstrating what is possible at the cutting edge of small-scale self-sufficiency. It's not necessarily that one end of the scale is better or worse than the other; it's how they are deployed that matters. The point here is not to defend current polluting, large-scale, fossil-fuel-based infrastructure, but to emphasise that while 'small is beautiful', it is still small. For rural buildings, where it is difficult to connect to the grid, the level of autonomy that the earthship concept offers is desirable and appropriate, but for urban settings, where houses are closer together, other systems may be more effective. Is it better for a housing estate composed of entirely independent houses, to be connected to a community-scale combined heat and power plant, or to be linked to many other estates using large-scale low-carbon infrastructure? This is a complex question. Consideration of the unique context of each location is paramount in answering it successfully. It is most likely that the middle ground will become increasingly attractive, as people continue to develop micro grids and other ways of distributing renewable energy on a medium scale. Just as there is no such thing as a free lunch – in the sense that running an earthship is bill free, but it has high upfront capital costs – so there are no hard-and-fast rules either.

The Groundhouse has done something new and innovative in Europe. And by demonstrating a grid-connected earthship, it may set a trend. The earthship shows the importance of minimising energy use in a house, and the crucial importance at the design stage of analysing energy requirements thoroughly, and reducing them wherever possible. Design out, before designing in. At a small, medium or large scale, this approach is essential for powering a low-carbon future.

As this chapter has shown, there are many issues to consider in maintaining off-grid energy systems. The next chapter continues the discussion by exploring the complexity of off-grid water systems.

Rainwater-harvesting system in action at the Eden Project's 'Core' building © Mischa Hewitt

6 WATER

INTRODUCTION

'If there are energy shortages, individuals will have water problems.

If there is ecological damage, individuals will have water problems.

If there are economic crises, individuals will have water problems.

If there are computer glitches, individuals will have water problems.

If there is political turmoil, individuals will have water problems.

If there is war, individuals will have water problems.' Mike Reynolds[104]

Water is one of the most precious natural resources. Of all the water on earth, only 1% is fresh water and, of this, only 1% is suitable for human consumption; the rest is either locked up in ice caps or is inaccessible. Water stress is an ever-increasing problem in the 21st century. People lead increasingly water-intensive lives, and, around the globe, levels of abstraction from the natural environment are causing problems and political unrest. In parts of India, for example, production of cotton and other cash crops means that the water table is dropping by 6 m a year, and in the USA the mighty Rio Grande, which once surged through the south-west US states, no longer reaches the coast; instead it silts up before it reaches the sea[105]. This pattern is commonplace throughout many of the world's rivers and aquifers and many people face severe water shortages. The earthship, by harvesting and recycling rainwater, demonstrates a solution without the need to draw water from the ground or from rivers, so that freshwater reserves, and the environment they support, can be conserved.

This chapter is about earthship water systems and how they minimise their occupants' water footprint by collecting, purifying and distributing water onsite with no mains connection. This can work well for rural locations, but earthships are designed to use the same strategy wherever they are built. And sometimes connection to the water infrastructure might be a positive thing. The chapter starts by looking at large-scale water distribution and typical levels of domestic demand. After a brief discussion of alternative water sources, the earthship rainwater harvesting, grey and blackwater recycling systems are explored in detail, with reference to the techniques and technologies applied in the European earthship projects.

CONTEMPORARY SITUATION: LARGE-SCALE DISTRIBUTION

Most European housing uses centrally supplied potable water for all domestic purposes, rather than small-scale private water supplies harvested from rain. Yet there are issues with this system. In urban areas of many countries water is supplied directly to houses through large-scale centralised systems. These systems, and the availability of water, rely on a variety of factors, ranging from the level of rainfall, through the infrastructure in place to collect, treat and distribute it, and the standard and quality of treatment, to the number and location of consumers. Any imbalance in this complex dynamic can lead to interruptions in supply, water shortages, or water stress. Water is abstracted from rivers or aquifers to be stored in surface reservoirs; it is treated, and then distributed through a vast network of pipes. All water supplied through this system is treated to a drinking quality standard, but is used for all activities, from washing clothes, preparing food, irrigation, and bathing through to flushing the toilet.

In the last decade there have been several water shortages in Europe, for example in winter 2006 in the UK, in 2008 in Spain, and in 2011 in France[106], [107]. In the UK in 2006 Defra made the decision to allow permits for the increased abstraction of water from rivers and other watercourses – with dire consequences for many aquatic ecosystems. Elliot Morley, the environment minister at the time, concluded that 'In many parts of the country, water is a precious resource that we can no longer simply take for granted'[108]. The Environment Agency agreed, saying that 'In some cases existing [water abstraction] licences are already damaging the environment'[109]. This situation is not an isolated incident, but a pattern that is occurring with alarming regularity. With changing weather patterns, attributable to climate change, likely to increase, there is a pressing need to adopt more careful water management practices.

DOMESTIC WATER USAGE

The average volume of water consumed in Europe is between 200 and 300 l/day[110]. This water is used for a variety of activities, and compares with 575 l/day in the USA and less than 10 l/day in Mozambique[111]. The minimum required for drinking and personal hygiene, as stipulated for short-term survival by UNICEF and the World Health Organization, is 20 l/day[112]. In the UK the average amount of water used per person, at 150 l/day, is lower than the average in Europe[113]. All the water is treated to a drinking water standard, and is used for all activities in most houses, which includes many non-drinking activities such as toilet flushing or watering the lawn. As a demonstration of this, the two charts in Figures 57 and 58 look at the breakdown of average use. Figure 57 looks at all activities, and Figure 58 groups the activities into those that require potable water and those that can use non-potable water. Around 83% of the water used by a typical person does not need to be treated to a drinking quality standard. The fact that all water

is supplied at this quality contrasts starkly with the significantly increasing sales of bottled water.

RAINWATER HARVESTING

People have been harvesting and using rainwater for millennia, and there are many early examples of this technology being used by the Romans and others. In more recent times the idea has been mostly overlooked in urban areas, as large-scale, centralised collection and distribution of water are considered safer and more convenient. Now, with the increasing cost of water supply, rainwater harvesting is beginning to seem more financially viable, although it is likely that the cost or the embodied energy of such a system will not be recovered during its life cycle. Some studies suggest that negative environmental impact of small-scale rainwater-harvesting systems is greater than that of mains water[115]. This highlights the way design considerations for small-scale water systems depend on location, and their impact should be considered carefully before they are installed, if mains water is available. This may change in the future, though, with the increasing cost of mains water and the possible use of energy and carbon intensive desalination.

There are high levels of rainfall in all but the very driest areas of Europe, and so there is great potential for rainwater harvesting. This technology is already widely deployed throughout the rest of northern Europe. The environmental consultancy ech$_2$o calculates that it is possible to collect 1700 l of rain off a roof of 100 m² area for every 25 mm of rainfall per year[116]. So, for example, for a roof of that size in an area that receives a moderate rainfall, such as Berlin (588.70 mm) or Rome (792.90 mm), it would be possible to harvest around 40,000 and 54,000 l/year, respectively[117].

Rainwater-harvesting systems need large underground storage tanks, and this means that it can be difficult to fit them retrospectively to existing properties in towns and cities, and they are expensive. A popular small-scale exception to this is the rainwater collection butts used by many gardeners. The situation is different for new build, as the tanks can easily be installed during the groundwork phase. Most systems are designed to supply rainwater to flush toilets and other non-potable activities, such as clothes washing or irrigation, but with additional filters they can easily supply drinking water as well. Most systems are dual supply, as they are backed up by mains water for times of low rainfall when the tanks are empty.

The fundamental issue with the lack of water in certain parts of Europe, even with a widespread variation in climate, is not a lack of rainfall, but rather a lack of efficient collection and distribution. Most buildings do not store rainwater, even though it falls freely onto their roofs. Buildings do not have the capacity to take advantage of the precious rainwater that flows down their gutters into the drains and finally to the beleaguered sewers.

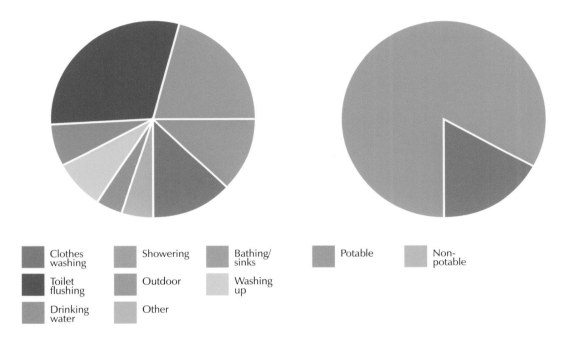

Figure 57: Average domestic daily water consumption (source: Waterwise[114])

Figure 58: Average domestic potable/non-potable consumption (source: Waterwise[114])

CURRENT GREYWATER AND BLACKWATER RECYCLING

In most conventional housing all waste water is mixed together, so that what is often relatively innocuous greywater, from activities such as dishwashing and showering, joins raw sewage (blackwater) and a cocktail of chemicals such as bleach and other detergents, and is then sent off to the sewage treatment plant. The waste water is then treated and, most often, pumped out to sea. In a situation where there are water shortages in the UK this seems an incredibly wasteful form of water management. And it takes energy to treat sewage, so it is desirable to reduce the volume. Mike Reynolds points out the fundamental craziness of this equation in his book *Water from the Sky* when he writes:

'…normally a person would use brand new fresh water from an aquifer to take a bath in. They throw that away down the drain into a sewage system and mix it with everybody else's shit and turn it into sewage. They then would use brand new fresh water again to water indoor plants. They would then use brand new fresh clean water to flush their toilet. Then they would use brand new fresh clean water again to water outside. And what we're doing with this system is using the same water four times to do these four tasks.' Mike Reynolds[118]

This is achieved by recycling the greywater in botanical (plant containing) cells, pumping the treated water to the toilet cistern for reuse, then sending sewage out to contained outdoor botanical cells. Water recycling is a statement of how important water is as a resource. It is also an implicit critique of the way in which water is currently treated in our profligate society. The fact that there are so few greywater recycling schemes illustrates how little is being done to conserve an important resource. One of the problems with the recycling of greywater is that it's a low grade of water, and so using lots of energy to clean it could be considered a waste. There are simple systems, such as waste diverter pipes or hand pumps, to move bath water out into the garden for irrigation, but most greywater systems use electrical or chemical energy to clean the water. Potentially this could have more impact than if fresh water were used in the first place, and this is also true for rainwater-harvesting systems.

One fairly low-impact system is Ecoplay[119] which treats only bathroom greywater in a small settling tank; kitchen greywater is more problematic, because of its higher grease content. Hair and other debris is separated as it floats to the top or sinks to the bottom of the tank and is

Figure 59: Blackwater treatment lake at the Hockerton Housing Project © Hockerton Housing Project

flushed away, leaving only water, which is then treated with a small amount of benzalkonium chloride, a common alkaline disinfectant. The system also has a timer on it so that greywater doesn't sit in the tank for more than a day, which means that it doesn't get a chance to fester. The main barrier to most people with this system is cost – it is priced at around £2000 a unit. Some building standards, such as the UK's Code for Sustainable Homes, require greywater to be recycled to achieve an 80 l/day water supply per person limit, to achieve higher levels of the Code for Sustainable Homes[1]. This has led to criticism of such requirements, on the grounds that they force designers to employ technologies to provide alternative supplies of water, although mains water may be less carbon intensive.

Sewage (blackwater) is not as easy to deal with as greywater, because it is potentially much more harmful, and contains a rich mixture of nutrients. In environmental terms, the key aim is to try to limit the impact that sewage has on the ecosystems in and around human habitation, so that the nutrients don't pollute rivers and streams, and result in algal blooms and fish death. Reed beds, such as that employed at the Hockerton Housing Project, are a popular alternative for processing sewage onsite in rural locations. The roots of reed mace (bulrush) and common reed supply oxygen to bacteria in the water, which consume the sewage. Pathogens present in the sewage have a limited lifespan once outside of the human body. Dealing with blackwater onsite is a complex design consideration, based on a variety of factors such as site availability, the cost and feasibility of connecting to the sewage main, and the users' willingness to maintain the system.

However, despite all the novel solutions to blackwater treatment, the most efficient method for dealing with this type of waste is to not create it all, by using composting toilets. Sewage is mostly water, and the sewage treatment process is designed to treat the small amounts of solids and nitrates contained within it. Culturally, the wet toilet has been widely installed in housing only in the last 150 years. The Groundhouse has only a composting toilet, which obviates the need for any blackwater treatment.

Figure 60: Diagram of Earthship Brighton harvesting rain © Daren Howarth

EARTHSHIP WATER SYSTEMS OUTLINE

'Water should be used many times before being put back into the earth. When we do put it back, it should be in a way that works with the existing nurturing forces and phenomena of the earth. Present day human life has static shelter that is dependent on "life support" systems running to and from individual units. For there to be a future of human life, we must develop housing units that are of the nature of the earth. These dwellings must dynamically "be" their systems.' Mike Reynolds[120]

The earthship typically has no connection to mains water, and so it relies purely on rain and snow melt for its supply. The earthship's water systems combine rainwater harvesting, greywater and blackwater treatment systems with other water conservation measures. They have evolved through 40 years of practical experience, design and construction of many systems in a variety of climates. The strategy is that the earthship can provide enough water to survive in any region in the world where annual precipitation is greater than 200 mm; other than desert, this is true for most of the world. It is not clear why this is the threshold, but using the ech$_2$o rule of thumb outlined above, a 100 m^2 roof could provide a yield of 13,600 l/year.

The concept is that water is harvested, filtered and then used, recovered and reused four times within the earthship water system. First, rainwater is captured and purified to a level that is safe to drink or wash with. Second, the waste water that flows

Figure 61: Roof materials (Earthship Brighton) © Taus Larsen

from all the sinks and showers – greywater – is used to water the plants in greywater planters, which clean the water. Third, this recycled water is used for flushing the toilet; and finally it is discharged as blackwater or sewage to a reed bed, where it is fed to reeds and plants to be treated back to harmless water and returned to nature.

The water here isn't literally used four times, but the point is that the earthship is designed to extensively reuse the nutrient-rich resource, wherever possible, in a closed-loop system. In the desert and other dry regions these water systems help to facilitate survival, but in temperate climates with more rainfall, although they demonstrate a low-impact model of water conservation and onsite treatment practice in new build, they may not be necessary.

Table 11 lists the various stages of the earthship's water systems, from the first drip to the last drop.

Collection and roof materials

Rainwater lands on the earthship roof, runs through the guttering and rainwater goods, and is then filtered before storage. From its evolution in the deserts of New Mexico, the earthship roof has been designed with a low pitch that is oriented towards the sun, so that snowfall on the roof can melt and flow into the tanks before it evaporates. Similar roofs are featured on earlier European projects, such as Earthship Brighton. Earthship Fife has a flat roof; in Earthship France and Earthship Zwolle the design was adapted, with the pitch away from the sun, as

Table 11: Earthship water systems summary		
Water type	**Stage**	
Rainwater	1	Collection and harvesting
	2	Pre-filtering
	3	Storage
	4	Potable and non-potable filtering
	5	Drinking, sinks and shower
Greywater	6	Removal of grease and other particles
	7	Indoor treatment by plants
	8	Recycled water pumped to toilet cistern
	9	Toilet flushing
Blackwater	10	Blackwater settles in septic tank
	11	Outdoor treatment by plants
	12	Clean water soakaway

most water harvested is rain, not snow melt, and the rate of evaporation off flat roofs is much higher than that off pitched roofs.

As some of the harvested rainwater will eventually be used for potable activities, the choice of roof materials is crucial. They must be both durable and inert, to remove the possibility of chemical leachate into the drinking water supply. The choice of roof materials can be much wider for rainwater systems that are designed only for non-potable activities. Earthship Brighton used a combination of Pro-panel steel profile metal roof and thermoplastic polyolefin (TPO) single-ply membrane. Pro-panel is a commonly used material for earthship roofs. If a metal roof is used this is important to make sure that any enamel coating is lead free. The roof shape channels the rain into wide, TPO-lined timber, guttering; where the gutter narrows, the metal roof has a splash guard. When Earthship Brighton was constructed in summer 2003, the Flagon TPO EP/PR membrane was the only single-ply membrane on the market in the UK that had WRAS (Water Regulation Advisory Scheme) certification. The final, baked-enamel finish on the surface of the Pro-panel roof minimises any leachate into the water. On Earthship Fife the roof material used was EPDM rubber membrane. This is a material that is widely used on earthships in New Mexico, and can also be used for lining the greywater planters. It is higher maintenance than other roofing solutions. Earthship France also has a Pro-panel roof, whereas the Groundhouse has a TPO and slate roof.

The choice of roofing materials on European earthships is summarised in Table 12.

Pre-filtering

Before storage, the water must be pre-filtered to remove leaves, twigs, sediment and other debris. There are various ways of doing this, ranging from a simple bed of gravel built into the roof structure to more expensive, but lower-maintenance, vortex filters. Vortex filters exploit the surface tension of flowing water to filter it through a fine mesh filter, with sediment being washed into the drain with the remaining water[121]. Around 90% of the water flows through the filter and the pipe to the storage tanks; the rest, which is mixed with detritus, falls through the centre to a waste water run-off and soakaway. Vortex filters are also self-cleaning. Some projects use either gravel or vortex filters; others, such as Earthship Brighton, use both types. At this stage there is also the option to add an extra tank on the overflow pipe from a vortex filter to collect the run-off water for irrigation. The gravel in the gravel bed filter has to be changed every six months as plants start to seed in the sediment that builds up. The pre-filters for the European earthships are summarised in Table 13.

Storage

After the particulate matter has been mechanically removed, the water flows to underground storage tanks. The advantage of storing water underground

Table 12: European earthships' roof materials

| | Earthship | | | | | |
	Almeria	Brighton	Fife	France	The Groundhouse	Valencia
Roof area (m²)	100.0	135.0	31.5	170.0	140.0	215.0
Main roof pitch	22°	4°	Flat	8°	4°	8°
Roof material/ surface	Bitumen/acrylic paint coating	Pro-panel/TPO	EPDM rubber membrane	Pro-panel	Slate/TPO	Pro-panel

Table 13: European earthships' pre-filters

| | Earthship | | | | | |
	Almeria	Brighton	Fife	France	The Groundhouse	Valencia
Pre-filter	Gravel	Gravel/0.28 mm WISY vortex	Gravel	Gravel	0.28 mm WISY Vortex	Flyscreen mesh

is that it maintains a cool temperature, which reduces the risk of bacterial growth. In earthships, storage capacity is generally larger than that of most domestic rainwater-harvesting systems, which are typically designed to store 4000 to 5000 l, with mains water backup, if needed, that can recharge the tank when the volume of the water in it drops below 5%.

The annual rainfall yields for various European earthships are summarised in Table 14, using the following equation[122]:

Annual rainfall yield = Roof area × Average annual rainfall × Run-off coefficient × Filter efficiency

Note: Run-off coefficient is the percentage of precipitation that appears as run-off after the rest has evaporated. Filter efficiency is the percentage of rainwater that flows through the filter after filtration.

Table 14 shows that Earthship Brighton, for example, can harvest up to 48,000 l of water a year. Since rainwater harvesting began there in August 2003, the tanks have always been at least half full, even though tens of thousands of litres of water have been used for local agricultural irrigation. The tanks have a large capacity, but they are designed to overflow several times a year after heavy rainstorms; this is important for clearing any matter floating on top of the water. Based on this rainfall yield, and assuming the typical daily consumption of 150 l, the water system would provide 320 days of water

per person, or 80 days' worth for a family of four. In practice the actual consumption figure would be lower than this, as there are other technologies in place in the earthship to reduce demand. For example, one of the features of the water system is that different types of nutrient-rich waste water are treated separately with plants at each stage, maximising reuse at every opportunity, and minimising the amount of fresh water needed; this is discussed in more detail below. Using a reduced figure of 94.4 l/day per person, which reflects these systems, the supply from rain harvesting is extended to 127 days for a family of four[123]. This is not enough water, unless people are prepared to use only 33 l/day per person, which is only 13 l more than the UNICEF/WHO minimum threshold outlined above. This calculation correlates with the conclusion of a recent academic paper about earthship water systems by Kruis and Heun, which states:

'In most climates there is not enough precipitation to supply the entire water demand of a family of four, even with intensive water conservation efforts. The catch water and gray water systems of an earthship can still be used in conjunction with a backup connection to local aquifer supplies. Such a design effectively conserves water while ensuring a consistent potable supply.' N Kruis and M Heun[124]

At Earthship Brighton the rainwater is stored in four Eco-Vat tanks; each has a volume of 5000 l, and they are linked in series to create a total storage

Figure 62: Rain storage tanks before backfill (Earthship Brighton) © Taus Larsen

Figure 63: Rain storage tanks after backfill (Earthship Brighton) © Taus Larsen

Table 14: Annual rainfall yields for European earthships

Earthship	Roof area (m²)	Average annual rainfall (mm)	Run-off or drainage coefficient	Filter efficiency	Annual yield (l)
Almeria	100.0	204.0	0.5	0.9	9180
Brighton	135.0	789.7	0.5	0.9	47,794
Fife	31.5	676.2	0.5	0.9	9600
France	170.0	687.0	0.5	0.9	42,556
The Groundhouse	140.0	726.0	0.5	0.9	45,738
Valencia	215.0	464.0	0.5	0.9	44,892

Table 15: European earthships' storage tanks

	Earthship					
	Almeria	Brighton	Fife	France	The Groundhouse	Valencia
Type of tank	See note*	Eco-Vat tanks	Reused water tank	Unknown	WISY	Unknown
Number of tanks	1	4	1	2	2	4
Storage capacity (l)	2000 (7000) †	20,000	4546	10,000	10,000	34,000

* Future plans are to build a tyre/cement water cistern[52]. † Current capacity is 2000.

capacity of 20,000 l. This, coupled with other water conservation measures, is enough for two to three months' supply, based on average annual rainfall patterns for the Sussex area. The tanks are buried in the hill and below the roof level, but above the level to supply the earthship, so the whole system is gravity fed until it reaches the filtration panel inside the building. Underground tanks also offer a dark, cool environment that tends to discourage bacterial growth.

The storage tanks for the European earthships are summarised in Table 15.

Potable and non-potable filtering

Rainwater is gravity-fed from the underground water tanks to the WOM, described by Earthship Biotecture as 'a self-contained filtration unit designed for catch water home'[125]. A standard WOM treats water to two standards: potable and non-potable.

The supply of private water is governed in many countries; the relevant law in the UK is the Private Water Supply Act 2009 (PWSA). In addition, The Water Supply (Water Quality) Regulations 2000 classify rainwater as raw sewage, because of the potential contamination from bird faeces, so thorough filtration to remove pathogens and other harmful elements is critical for what can legally be classified as a 'wholesome' supply[126]. The standard WOM as supplied by Earthship Biotecture will be described in this section, a WOM redesigned to ensure that water quality complies with the PWSA is outlined in the next section as an illustrative example. Although this legislation is not legally binding across Europe, it is a good indication of the level that water needs to be purified to before it is considered fit for human consumption.

When the water first enters the WOM it passes through a 500 μm mesh filter to remove sediment; this filter serves to protect the 12 V direct current (DC) pump, which with the aid of a pressure tank pressurises the system to 50 psi (approx. 350 kPa), or conventional household pressure. The pump is adequate to push the water through a second, finer-grade (5 μm) mesh filter, and after this the water is ready for all non-potable uses, including showering, bathing, washing clothes and cleaning dishes. Both these filters are removable, and can be easily cleaned. This is the main house supply.

To treat the water to a drinking water standard it is filtered using charcoal and then a carbon block. After the WOM the water system is a typical domestic system. Many of the earthship projects in Europe have the standard WOM, as described, fitted as pre-constructed units from Earthship Biotecture and shipped from the USA. Some also have ultraviolet (UV) light sterilisation units installed. The standard WOM components are outlined in Table 16.

Some WOMs are adapted with additional features such as water meters after stages 5 and 7, to measure the volume of water passing through the system; this helps with filter changing, as some components need to be replaced regularly. A UV sterilisation unit can be fitted instead of a carbon block filter, or additionally after stage 7. Finally, a valve can be fitted after stage 7 but before a sterilisation unit, to prevent untreated water passing through the system in the event of a power cut.

Table 16: Standard WOM components

Stage	Water quality	Component	Function
1	Non-potable	500 mm mesh filter	Protects pump from sediment
2	Non-potable	12 V DC pump	Pressurises system to 50 psi (350 kPa)
3	Non-potable	Pressurisation tank	Increases flow rate
4	Non-potable	5 mm mesh filter	Removes finer particulates
5	Non-potable	Pressurisation tank	Reduces need for pump
6	Potable	Charcoal filter	Protects drinking water filter
7	Potable	Carbon block filter	Removes pathogens, trace organics and inorganics such as chlorine and lead

The WOMs for the European earthships are summarised in Table 17 and shown in Figure 64.

The Groundhouse is connected to mains water, which simplifies things considerably, as off-grid systems require ongoing maintenance, monitoring of water quality, and regular replacement of filters.

Table 17: European earthships' water-organising modules

| | Earthship | | | | | |
	Almeria	Brighton	Fife	France	The Groundhouse	Valencia
Standard WOM	No	Yes	Yes	Yes	No	No
Bespoke system	Pump and reverse osmosis GEC filter	N/A	N/A	N/A	String/carbon filter	Pump, pressure tank and osmosis filter
UV sterilisation	No	Yes	Yes	Yes	No	No
Water tested	No	Yes	Yes	Yes	No	No

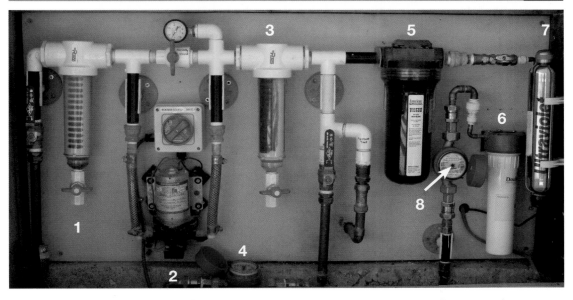

Figure 64: Water-organising module (Earthship Brighton) (see Table 18 for reference to numbers) © Mischa Hewitt

DRINKING WATER QUALITY LEGISLATION

The World Health Organization publishes guidelines on drinking water quality[127]. In the European Union the guidelines are the basis for the Drinking Water Directive (98/83/EC2), and set the standards for microbiological, chemical and organoleptic (sensory) parameters for drinking water in member states[128]. Although European countries may interpret the guidelines, the water quality and monitoring regime must comply with the minimum standards laid out in the Directive.

Collecting and purifying rainwater to drink is common in many parts of the world, but in Europe it is less common except in rural locations. As discussed above, in the UK any supply of water that is not mains, such as boreholes, wells, springs, lakes, streams and rainwater-harvesting systems from fields to roofs, is considered a private water supply, and is covered under the Private Water Supplies Regulations 2009. Wholesome water:

'does not contain any micro-organism, parasite or substance, alone or in conjunction with any other substance, at a concentration or value that would constitute a potential danger to human health; … it complies with the concentrations or values [of chemicals or compounds] …; and nitrate and nitrite levels are less than 1 mg/l'.[129]

Private water supplies may deliver less than 1 m³ per day to a single house, or much more to larger developments. Small systems for houses are exempt, but public buildings such as Earthship Brighton and Earthship Fife must comply with the standard of water quality.

REDESIGN OF WATER ORGANISING MODULE

Currently, the standard WOM is designed to supply water to two standards; potable and non-potable. Various European earthships have had their water tested, with varying results. In Earthship Brighton in 2010 the water was tested by Brighton & Hove City Council's environmental health department. To recap, non-potable water is supplied to the kitchen sink, bathroom sink and shower, with the potable water being supplied to a drinking water tap by the kitchen sink. While the results of the test indicated that the drinking water was fine, the non-drinking water had coliform colonies greater than 201 per 100 ml of water.

This level of non-harmful bacteria is not dangerous in itself, but is higher than is specified in the definition of wholesome water in the Private Water Supplies Regulations 2009. In addition this level of bacteria is a risk to children, old people, and those with a compromised immune system. The drinking water filters mean that the quality of potable water is of a wholesome standard, but the flow rate is low at 5 l/min. The Private Water Supplies Regulations 2009 doesn't set a minimum flow rate.

After consultation with the Brighton & Hove City Council environmental health department, a new design for the WOM was agreed that would deliver drinking-quality water throughout. This simplifies both the system and the future monitoring regime. The new WOM will have four pre-filters and then a UV sterilisation unit. Although water supplied to all fixtures will be potable, there will be a carbon block filter to improve the taste on a dedicated drinking water tap in the kitchen. This is simply to improve taste. The redesigned WOM components are summarised in Table 18.

Table 18: Redesigned water-organising module components

Stage	Component	Purpose
1	500 mm mesh filter	Protects pump from sediment; filter is washable
2	12 V DC pump	Pressurises system to 50 psi (350 kPa)
3	Pressurisation tank	Reduces need for pump
4	80 mm mesh filter	Pre-filter for UV sterilisation unit; filter is washable
5	25 mm mesh filter	Pre-filter for UV sterilisation unit; needs replacement filters every six months
6	5 mm filter	Pre-filter for UV sterilisation unit, needs replacement filters every six months
7	Back-flow prevention valve	Restricts water flow in the event of a power cut
8	UV sterilisation unit	Supplies 37.5 l of treated water per minute; needs replacement bulbs every six months
9	Water meter	Measures volume of potable water treated, for regular filter cartridge change or cleaning
10	Carbon block filter (optional)	Improves odour and taste for a dedicated drinking water tap in the kitchen

There are increased energy implications with the new system, but these outweigh the risk to the public. The use of UV sterilisation in off-grid buildings has implications for the capacity of the power systems.

LOW-INTENSITY, CHEMICAL-FREE GREYWATER RECYCLING

The first use of water in the earthship is in the sinks and shower. All sinks have a hot, a cold and a drinking water tap. The waste water, or greywater, that is generated flows through the grease and particle filter into a greywater planter or botanical treatment cell lined with EPDM or equivalent rubber. This lining creates a closed area, which becomes its own ecosystem that adapts to the treatment of waste water. There are various designs for grease and particle filters, but the simplest is merely a nylon stocking clamped over the end of the pipe with a Jubilee clip. The filter will need changing every 3 to 6 months. Stainless steel Jubilee clips are used for all fittings in the planters, for durability.

The grease and particle filter is placed inside a box with holes drilled in the bottom of it. This box is positioned over a pile of large (75 mm) stones, known as 'rock bulbs', which enable the outflow from showers, and other large volumes of water, to percolate into the system quickly. These bulbs are placed at all plumbing junctions to facilitate fast draining between sections, through the increased voids between the rocks.

The planters are designed to recycle greywater through a variety of natural processes, such as transpiration, evaporation and oxygenation, and through the rhizosphere – treatment by the bacteria that live around plants' root systems[130]. These processes deal with the various constituent parts of greywater, by consuming the suspended solids and reducing the bacteria level (the grease and fat have already been removed by the filter described above). A rule of thumb is that 25 ft² or 2.33 m² of planter area is needed for each plumbing fixture[104]. For example, Earthship Brighton has a kitchen sink, a bathroom sink and a shower; this means that the minimum planter area required would be 7 m². The two greywater planters, located in the conservatory

Figure 65: Rock bulb installation during greywater planter construction (Earthship Brighton)
© Mischa Hewitt

Figure 66: Plan view of greywater sump and rock bulbs during construction (Earthship Brighton)
© Mischa Hewitt

and the meeting room, and linked in series, have a combined area of 12.75 m², which means that 10% of the usable floor space is lost to greywater treatment. It is possible to link as many greywater planters as are required to treat the greywater; the only stipulation is that the greywater level must be the same throughout.

The greywater planter systems for the European earthships are summarised in Table 19. All systems are internal, except in the Groundhouse. A typical earthship greywater planter is made up of layers of up to 450 mm of 20 mm pea shingle (gravel), 75 mm of sand, and 150 mm of topsoil. This structure is a growing medium and stabilising environment for the plants, and maximises the opportunity for them to 'encounter' the greywater. The level of the greywater comes up to the height of the pea shingle, effectively forming a greywater table, with the sand keeping the soil from clogging up the gravel. The greywater planters are located next to the south-facing windows, creating a beneficial environment for the plants, which thrive in the nutrient-rich greywater and sunlight. In summer, as the plants grow, they offer increased shading from the intensity of the sun, and in winter

they can be cut back to increase the solar gain into the earthship.

At this stage the water has not been mixed with human waste; all blackwater is dealt with later in the process. The greywater planters have a three-way divert valve, which can be used so that the greywater bypasses the planter system and is discharged directly to the septic tank. The whole earthship water system deals with the water one step at a time, which makes it easier to treat it in a low-intensity fashion, with plants in low volumes. This approach differs greatly from the centralised municipal system, which has to deal with all greywater, blackwater, chemicals, organic waste and other contaminants as a sewage 'soup': therefore it has to be very large scale to deal with the waste *en masse.* The greywater system in earthships is designed so that there is no human contact with the greywater, and no opportunity for backwash; this is important, to avoid the risk of infection or contamination.

The choice of household cleaners that can be poured down the sink in an earthship is limited to those that will not upset the balance of the plants, bacteria and greywater ecosystem. This is

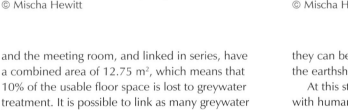

Table 19: European earthships' greywater planter systems

	Earthship					
	Almeria	**Brighton**	**Fife**	**France**	**The Groundhouse**	**Valencia**
Fittings	Shower, bathroom sink, kitchen sink	Kitchen sink, bathroom sink, shower, toilet	Two sinks, toilet	Shower, bath, basin, kitchen sink, washing machine and toilet	Two sinks, bath, shower	Kitchen sink, washing machine drain, bathroom sink, shower, toilet
Number of planters	1	2*	1	1	1	1
Length (m)	7.50	15.00	5.00	15.00	†	10.00
Width (m)	1.00	0.85	1.40	1.00	–	1.00
Minimum depth (m)	0.80	0.60	0.60	1.00	1.00	0.80
Maximum depth (m)	1.20	1.20	1.40	1.50	1.00	1.20
Area (m²)	7.50	12.75	7.00	15.00	10.50	10.00
Volume (m³)	7.50	10.20	7.00	18.75	10.50	10.00
Planter area as % of total floor space	7.5	10	22	9	Outside	5

* For the purposes of calculation the two planters are treated as one entity

† Two primary beds 1.5 m round and 1 m deep, alternated every two weeks, then two more beds in series at 2 m × 1 m, and then a 2 m × 1.5 m pond with an overflow soakaway.

equally important with the choice of chemicals used to clean the toilet, so that they don't impair the anaerobic bacteria that live in the septic tank and reed bed. It is important to note that in this method of water treatments, the plants and the ecosystem around them are the system. As the system is composed of natural components, it takes time for the plants to settle in and the greywater colony to evolve. In the first year the treated water may be discoloured until the plants have established themselves as a treatment system. To date, the quality of treated greywater supplied by the standard earthship planter has not been analysed.

Choice of plants in greywater planters

Virtually any plant can be planted in the greywater planter. Some of the most popular edible varieties are bananas, lemon and lime trees, grapes and avocados. The larger plants take up and treat larger volumes of greywater than those that

Figure 67: Greywater planter (Earthship Fife)
© Kevin Telfer

Figure 68: Filling greywater planter with gravel (Earthship Brighton) © Mischa Hewitt

Figure 70: Sand raked flat in greywater planter (Earthship Brighton) © Mischa Hewitt

Figure 69: Raking gravel flat in greywater planter (Earthship Brighton) © Mischa Hewitt

Figure 71: Greywater feed pipe for toilet and pump panel (Earthship Brighton) © Mischa Hewitt

have shallow root systems. In the arid desert of New Mexico the planters are used to grow food, and this aspect is now being explored with the extension of the planter systems, sometimes with a second greenhouse on the front of the building to incorporate large areas for food production. The Phoenix Earthship is the most recent example, which also boasts the possibility of raising fish as well[48]. In a more temperate climate, interior food production is not crucial, although it can usefully extend the growing season through the year, and demonstrates the innovative onsite reuse of waste water and the possibilities of utilising an undervalued resource. If greywater planters *are* used for growing food, only fruiting plants (eg tomatoes or grapes) should be used; root crops such as carrots and parsnips should be avoided, to eliminate any possible contamination by the greywater.

BLACKWATER SETTLES IN SEPTIC TANK

After treatment, the greywater gathers in a well at the end of the planter, until the toilet is flushed, which draws water through to fill the toilet cistern. Some earthships have an additional faucet so that the toilet can be flushed with rainwater. This means that advantage can be taken of periods of heavy rainfall. If there is more than one planter, then there is a recirculation pipe between them, powered by a dedicated solar panel and 12 V DC pump. This keeps the greywater moving continually through the treatment process until it is needed for toilet flushing, and ensures a higher quality of greywater by avoiding stagnation. The separate power supply does not use power from the main house supply, but works only when it is sunny.

The earthship has no connection to the municipal sewage system; in towns and cities this may not be practical for earthship developments, because of the lack of space. Blackwater is defined as water that has been mixed with human waste, and the autonomous sewage system contains and treats all blackwater onsite. Some earthships have a septic settling tank, as in Earthship Brighton for example, but others don't. The septic tanks for the European earthships are summarised in Table 20.

Onsite treatment by plants

There are many different designs for the treatment of blackwater in earthships. In Earthship Brighton, blackwater is discharged to settle in a 2800 l Klargester Alpha septic tank, located 20 m from the earthship, which then overflows into a 60 m^2 horizontal-flow reed bed, lined with EPDM rubber, and then finally to a soakaway. The Environment Agency granted permission for a facility to deal with waste water in this manner in 2004, and after the initial teething problems dealing with waste tyres as outlined in chapter 5, are generally very supportive of the project.

Earthship Fife uses an alternative system, very similar in design to the greywater planters. The blackwater flows down a soil pipe to settle in an infiltrator before overflowing into two planters, lined with 25 mm thick Voltex, in a greenhouse; the same natural processes as outlined above break the sewage down, and the plants feed on

Figure 72: Greywater planter (Earthship France)
© Gillian and Kevan Trott

Figure 73: Greywater planter (Earthship Valencia)
© Lisa-Jane Roberts and Oscar Briz

Figure 74: Blackwater treatment system (Earthship Fife) © Kevin Telfer

Table 20: European earthships' septic tanks

	Earthship					
	Almeria	**Brighton**	**Fife**	**France**	**The Groundhouse**	**Valencia**
Capacity (l)	3000	2800	N/A	1000	N/A	N/A

Table 21: European earthships' blackwater treatment systems

Earthship	System
Almeria	Septic tank drains to outdoor blackwater planter
Brighton	72 m² 300 mm deep horizontal flow reed bed to French drain
Fife	Two blackwater cells 24 m² in area and 24 m³ in volume to land drainage (4 m × 3 m × 2 m) contained in a greenhouse
France	Blackwater cell 20 m² in area and 32.5 m³ in volume to land drainage
The Groundhouse	N/A – compost toilet
Valencia	Blackwater cell

the waste. Voltex is a waterproofing membrane that comprises two geotextile layers with sodium bentonite clay sandwiched in between. The infiltrator stores the solid waste, which slowly breaks down through the continual process of drying out and then being washed by liquid waste every time the toilet is flushed. The two planters measure 3 m by 4 m, and 1 m deep, and are linked in series, side by side. The contents of the planters are very similar to the greywater planter outlined above: 500 mm of 20 mm pea shingle, 100 mm of sand, and 400 mm of topsoil. The heights of the various layers vary; the shingle is deepest next to the infiltrator, and slopes away to a shallower depth at the other end.

Blackwater treatment systems for the European earthships are summarised in Table 21.

The greenhouse is an important addition in some climates, such as for Earthship Fife, as it stops flooding of the system by rainwater, increases the temperature for the plants, and provides an opportunity for blackwater treatment all year round. Although Earthship Fife is a visitor centre, the capacity of the system is designed to deal with the sewage of a family of four, approximately 0.5 tonnes of sewage per year. In domestic situations the system would be sized according to the number of occupants. This sewage system has been approved by the local building control authority and SEPA[53].

CONCLUSION
The systems installed in the earthships in Europe are experimental and need to be monitored closely. It would be useful to study the water systems in depth, to gain accurate data on rainfall yield, water quality, and the adequacy of the rain-harvesting systems

Figure 75: Contained blackwater treatment in greenhouse (Earthship Fife) © Kevin Telfer

and the grey and blackwater recycling for end-use consumption. Consistent monitoring of the water systems over the next couple of years would allow for more thorough designs for the next generation of European earthships.

The 'living' systems are designed for domestic purposes, and yet they have been installed in public buildings, which have different needs. To compensate for this in Earthship Fife, members of staff in the building simulate a domestic situation of running the tap for five minutes and flushing the toilet a few times a week to feed the grey and blackwater planters. As a demonstration model this is fine, but clearly it is not an example of best water conservation practice.

The systems may also need further tweaking to work more effectively in a European climate: for example, the evaporation rate may possibly be less than at certain times in New Mexico, so future earthship builds may need a greater surface area of planter. Also, the level of water supplied by the earthship may not be sufficient and so a mains backup or other source may be required. (One of the authors of this book stayed in an earthship in Taos a few years ago where the water ran out, which meant that a tanker was required to deliver more.) The systems are also bespoke, and require monitoring, regular filter replacement and maintenance. Like most off-grid systems, they become part of a lifestyle.

Finally, the most important factor with any system is context. In a rural setting the earthship water systems make perfect sense, and are a variation on the many other systems that are already available for the same task. In an urban setting it is probably preferable to connect to mains water and sewage, in terms of overall environmental impact, the provision of wholesome water, and reduced maintenance.

7 EUROPEAN BUILDS

INTRODUCTION

One of the main reasons for publishing this second edition is to evaluate the earthships that have been built across Europe over the past 10 years. The pioneers who built these earthships have been testing – consciously or otherwise – a variety of things: the regulatory framework (which varies from place to place); the design effectiveness of earthships in different climates; and the actual experience of what it is like to build them and live in them. What has been the experience of the people building them? What obstacles have they faced? Was it worth it? Are there any lessons that can be learned for other earthship builders?

This chapter looks in detail at six builds: two in Spain, two in France, and two in the UK. The information about these builds has been gleaned from a combination of replies to a questionnaire, telephone interviews, site visits (all unreferenced), and other referenced source material. We have

Figure 76: Earthships in Europe: a map of projects in different stages of completion

listed some data for each project, to put them in context. This includes a climate description, using the internationally recognised Köppen climate classification. Each project also features rainfall statistics and a Nicol graph.

The Nicol graph was devised by Fergus Nicol to express how, in a free-running building (ie one with no human inputs), the thermal comfort requirement varies with the outdoor temperature[131]. Figure 78 outlines basic weather data for the location: minimum and maximum air temperature, and insolation (a measure of solar radiation energy received on a given surface area in a given time). It is a basic, rough-and-ready tool for assessing how much heating and cooling may potentially be required to make a free running building thermally comfortable[132]. It also has a line indicating the temperature that a person indigenous to the region might find comfortable. Nicol graphs are included for each project so that the climatic differences between locations can easily be seen. The solar radiation is included on the graph to give an indication of the contribution that the sun's energy could usefully make to passive solar heating. It is divided up into fractions of direct and diffuse radiations.

The builds are listed chronologically in order of completion.

This section also briefly summarises other builds – both finished and unfinished – in Sweden, Belgium, Estonia and Holland, and others in the UK.

EARTHSHIP FIFE

Project name: Earthship Fife

Project location: Craigencalt Farm, Kinghorn Loch, Fife, Scotland

Latitude: 56.079

Longitude: -3.192

Altitude: Just above sea level

Köppen climate classification: Cfc – marine west coast, mild with no dry season, cool summer

Average annual rainfall: 676 mm

Ongoing/completed: Completed 2004

Building function: Visitor centre, providing education and information on sustainable building; non-residential

Floor area: 31.5 m²

Project cost: £26,034 (materials only)

Renewables used: 1 kW micro-hydro turbine, 600 W wind turbine, 4 × 75 W PV panels

Website/blog: www.sci-scotland.org.uk/earthship_centre.shtml

Earthship Fife was built as a non-residential, community group project by a group called Sustainable Communities Initiatives (SCI) in collaboration with Earthships Moray and South Ayrshire Council. They set out to build a visitor centre on a site shared with the Craigencalt Ecology Centre at Kinghorn Loch in Fife in 2002. But Paula Cowie, the project manager for SCI, also saw it as an opportunity to test the viability of earthships as a potential solution for sustainable housing in Scotland.

She writes in SCI's publication *The Earthship Toolkit* that they wanted to build an earthship in the Scottish climate 'in open negotiation with our planning and building control system, and before the eyes of the Scottish people. Would it work? Would it pass the system? Would people like it? What would it cost?'[133].

This was the first earthship to be built in Europe, and as such it was a fantastic pioneering experiment, as SCI clearly realised. The plan was to build a very small building, consisting essentially of just a main room with a narrow greenhouse buffer at the front, a kitchen and a toilet: a total of 31.5 m². One of the main modifications of the earthship design to adapt it to the Scottish climate

Figure 77: Earthship Fife visitor centre © Kevin Telfer

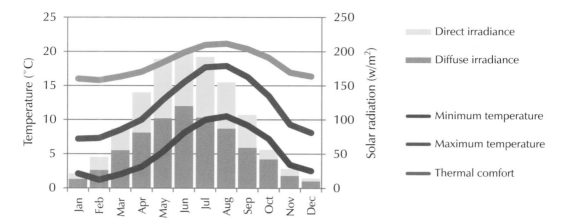

Figure 78: Nicol graph for Earthship Fife

was to make the front face of vertical rather than sloping glass, so that the low winter sun would reach the back of the building without reflection loss. The building was also oriented more to the east than usual, in order to make the most of the morning sun. In addition, SCI decided to build a separate greenhouse for the blackwater (sewage) treatment, as they were concerned that without it the temperature would be insufficient to break the waste down. They also decided to use a hydro turbine to generate electricity from a nearby millstream, in addition to the more conventional techniques (wind turbine and solar PV).

SCI paid to use Mike Reynolds and his team to get the build started in the summer of 2002. According to *The Earthship Toolkit*: 'We employed a team of 10 experienced earthship builders from Solar Survival Architects in New Mexico to transfer skills to 10 people from Scotland and England in the building methods'[134].

This meant that there were 20 people working on the building for the first eight days. The objective during this time was to transfer skills and complete the main shell. This comprised:

- constructing the tyre wall (pounding 616 tyres and placing them in courses)
- backfilling, and installing thermal and waterproof wrap
- berming the building with soil
- putting on the roof, with rigid insulation and rubber membrane
- starting pack-out of the tyre walls
- installing the front window frames.

After this intensive initial period of work, it took another two years before the project was completed. This was largely because approximately 225 volunteers, most of them completely unskilled, helped with the construction.

'With a large pool of unskilled volunteers, time was inevitably spent learning how to use basic tools, and experimenting with the building tasks and methods presented to them. On several occasions tasks had to be redone due to unacceptable standards or failure to achieve desired results.' P Cowie and S Kemp[135]

One of the other reasons for the length of the build is that the systems within an earthship are relatively complex: this is a building that is expressly not a mere shell, but a self-functioning, autonomous habitation. SCI estimate that, in total, 4000 person-hours were used to complete the building, with the caveat that none of these person-hours were input by construction professionals, and so the number is unrepresentative of the time a skilled workforce would take to construct an earthship.

'Good sense tells us that until an earthship is built by competent or skilled workers in a "commercial" way, we won't be able to work out the true costings for a UK earthship.' P Cowie and S Kemp[135]

Earthship Fife was completed in August 2004, and has since served as a visitor centre, providing information and education about sustainable building.

SCI calculated the total materials cost for the building at £26,034. For a building of 31.5 m² this returns a cost of £846/m² just for materials. No labour costs have been included in the Fife calculations, largely because most of the labour was provided by a voluntary workforce. SCI explained that:

'We don't feel it necessary to convert this investment of time into a monetary figure as the ethos of the Earthship concept is a lot about people being empowered to do it themselves, no matter how long it takes. For people not wanting to build their own earthship the potential labour cost, using Earthship Fife as an example, could be around £20,000–24,000.' P Cowie and S Kemp[135]

This would mean a total project cost per m² of between £1460 and £1587.

Earthship Fife was the first earthship to be built in Europe, and the approach to testing the regulatory framework and sharing their findings has no doubt inspired others to do the same. Indeed, the purpose of building Earthship Fife seemed to be as much the testing of planning and building control bureaucracy as it was the building itself. SCI concluded that 'planning permission is not going to be more of a problem for an earthship than a conventional house' and that 'issues raised by [building control] are all surmountable'[136]. A more detailed account of their conclusions can be found in *The Earthship Toolkit*, available to buy from their website (www.sci-scotland.org.uk).

Figure 79: Blackwater greenhouse (Earthship Fife) © Kevin Telfer

EARTHSHIP BRIGHTON

Project name: Earthship Brighton

Project location: Stanmer Park, Brighton

Latitude: 50.87

Longitude: -0.11

Altitude: 100 m

Köppen climate classification: Cfc – marine west coast, mild with no dry season, cool summer

Average annual rainfall: 789 mm

Ongoing/completed: Completed 2006

Building function: Education and community centre (non-residential)

Floor area: 123.6 m²

Project cost: £320,000

Renewables used: 18 × 62 W PV panels plus 900 W wind turbine; total capacity approximately 2 kW

Website: www.lowcarbon.co.uk/earthship-brighton

Daren Howarth (the Groundhouse) was heavily involved with the earthship built in Brighton between 2003 and 2007. However, the Brighton project, like Fife, was a community group project rather than a residential scheme by private individuals.

Daren's interest in earthships dates back to about 1994. In 2000 he invited Mike Reynolds over to the UK to give a talk at the Brighthelm Centre in Brighton. Reynolds' presentation was seen by 150 people, and it helped create the impetus to set up the Low Carbon Network (LCN) in July of that year. The organisation aimed to build an earthship community centre to provide education about the environment, and to be a meeting place for environmental groups. They quickly found a suitable site at Stanmer Organics – a cooperative based on land set aside for organic horticulture in Stanmer Park, on the edge of Brighton. The site is well served by public transport, with buses and trains connecting it to central Brighton and other areas (although a walk of a mile or so is also required). This is in marked contrast to many other earthship sites, which have very little access available through public transport.

Figure 80: Earthship Brighton © Mischa Hewitt

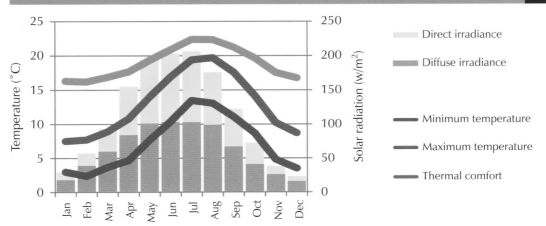

Legend:
- Direct irradiance
- Diffuse irradiance
- Minimum temperature
- Maximum temperature
- Thermal comfort

Figure 81: Nicol graph for Earthship Brighton

The design was completed in early 2001 and draft planning permission was granted by September that same year. As a new organisation, LCN had no funds of its own, so raising money for the project was the next significant piece of work to be completed. By July 2002 they had received enough funding from two main sources – the BOC Foundation for the Environment and a landfill tax credits grant (Biffaward) of £180,000 – to cover the entire project. Full planning permission was also granted that summer, and in late 2002 more detailed design work was undertaken to adapt the US model to the UK climate.

Only one significant bureaucratic hurdle remained for the LCN; they had to get clearance to build with tyres. This is discussed in more detail in chapter 4, but in essence both UK and EU legislation make it difficult to build with any material that has been designated as waste. In order to do so, either a licence or an exemption from holding a licence needed to be granted. LCN communicated closely with the Environment Agency about the issue – and the Environment Agency ended up taking an unprecedented local decision to allow the earthship to be built without either a licence or a special exemption from requiring a licence. However, they stressed that this was a decision based on Earthship Brighton being a one-off demonstration project; they were determined that this would not set a precedent.

Figure 82: Fastening the roof membrane at Earthship Brighton © Kevin Telfer

Figure 83: The roof of Earthship Brighton, looking south-west © Kevin Telfer

This go-ahead came through in February 2003, and in May of that year Mike Reynolds and his crew arrived onsite to start work on the project. They were onsite for a week, building the hut and transferring skills, and returned near the end of the project to help complete it.

The original construction plan was scheduled to take one year, but the experimental nature of the project, and inadequate budgeting, meant that it took longer, and additional funding was required for interior decoration, and for the renewable energy and water treatment systems. In all it took more than three years to complete, with the work occurring in a series of short bursts

as funding became available. There were no substantial technical difficulties with the build itself. The final tranche of funding required to complete construction was provided by British Gas in July 2006, and by the end of that year the building was completed.

Earthship Brighton consists of a hut module, which is used as an office, and a 'nest', comprising a large (10 m × 6 m) meeting room, kitchen, bathroom and greenhouse/conservatory. Power is generated by solar PV and a wind turbine, with additional warmth generated by a 15 kW wood pellet stove when required.

The earthship has been extensively monitored from 2004 onwards, and the results of an in-depth study are discussed in detail in chapter 8. There have been issues with thermal performance and ventilation.

Security has also been a problem at Earthship Brighton, perhaps largely because it is a non-residential property. The theft of PV panels meant that the replacement panels had to be installed with locks, to ensure they could not be ripped off by thieves.

The total cost of the building was £320,000.

Mischa Hewitt, one of the authors of this book, was heavily involved with Earthship Brighton in a project management role, and so it is difficult to be objective about the building's legacy. However, the monitoring of the building's performance should provide the opportunity to make significant improvements to earthship design in temperate climates. These are discussed in detail in chapter 9.

EARTHSHIP FRANCE

Project name: Earthship France 'Perrine'

Project location: Ger, Manche, Normandy, France

Latitude: 48.6829

Longitude: -0.7882

Altitude: 307 m

Köppen climate classification: Cfc – Marine west coast, mild with no dry season, cool summer

Average annual rainfall: 687 mm

Ongoing/completed: Completed June 2008

Building function: Residential – rental property and home

Floor area: 130 m²

Project cost: €188,000 (inclusive of labour)

Renewables used: 10 × 200 W PV panels, 1 solar thermal, 1 wind turbine 400 W

Website/blog: www.earthship-france.com

Kevan and Gillian Trott's earthship was the first full earthship to be completed on the European mainland, in June 2008 (although a hut module had already been completed on a Spanish build near Valencia by 2004 described later on in this chapter), and the first residential earthship to be completed anywhere in Europe. Its construction was slick and relatively speedy; it took just over a year from start to finish, with just 26 weeks onsite, and Gillian describes it as being 'really smooth running'. They were happy with the building too; there are some modifications they would like to make if they had the opportunity, but overall they feel that it is a 'fantastic design and a brilliant building'. Yet for a number of different reasons they have decided to try to sell it, and the building is on the market as this book goes to press.

Gillian Trott says that 'People think that earthships are very easy to build – but they're not. And they're not cheap, either: we paid a lot of money for the expertise that we received.'

The consultancy company she has been running with Kevan quotes a rough total cost estimate of €1000 to €1500/m² for earthship builds, which falls within the higher end of a survey of self-build

Figure 84: Earthship France in the village of Ger, Normandy © Kevan and Gillian Trott

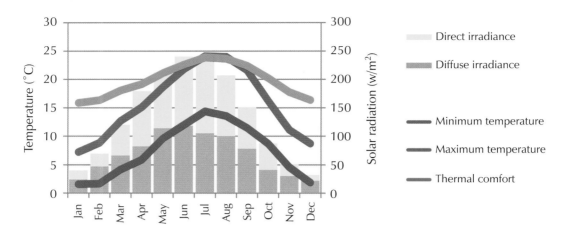

Figure 85: Nicol graph for Earthship France

Figure 86: Front face under construction at Earthship France © Kevan and Gillian Trott

costs compiled by *Homebuilding & Renovating* magazine[137]. (The Trotts' €188,000 project cost for a 130 m^2 earthship returns a figure of €1446/m^2, approximately the same as Earthship Brighton.)

If the earthship had been constructed solely as a self-build project (ie with very little or no additional expertise brought in to help), costs would certainly be much lower – perhaps as little as £500/m^2. But Gillian says that expertise is vital in earthship construction, rather than a DIY, make-it-up-as-you-go-along approach. And, in the main, expertise costs money.

Gillian praises their earthship for how cheap it is to run, both in terms of utilities (heating, water and electricity) and in terms of maintenance. In her eyes, the building is a functionally brilliant design that provides its inhabitants with a fantastic living space. However, the Trotts' experience suggests that high initial construction costs may tend to cancel out many of the financial gains of living in a virtually self-sufficient building.

Gillian and Kevan first got interested in earthships when they saw Mike Reynolds give a presentation in Brighton, where they were living. 'It was a lightbulb moment for both of us,' Gillian says. 'We both thought: this man's a genius, and everything he says makes sense.'

They were looking to start a business venture. They thought that with their backgrounds – Kevan was working as a council-employed chartered surveyor; Gillian has a background in education and a passion for environmentally-friendly living – there might be an opportunity for them to base a business on earthships. So they set up their own business, called Earthbuilds Limited, planning to bring the earthship concept to Europe in a big way. 'We wanted to get earthships in Europe into the mainstream,' says Gillian, 'out of the hippy fringe and into the mainstream – and generate an income for ourselves while we did it.'

Kevan started doing some work with Mike Reynolds on a possible 16-unit earthship development in Brighton Marina (which, although it got planning permission in 2007, has never been built). At the same time Gillian and Kevan found an inexpensive plot of land in the rural village of Ger in Normandy, northern France, and decided to buy it. This was where they were going to build their own earthship. They hoped to rent out the property as

Figure 87: Kevan and Gillian Trott with Mike Reynolds onsite at Earthship France © Kevan and Gillian Trott

Figure 88: A bedroom at Earthship France © Kevan and Gillian Trott

a holiday home in the short to medium term, and possibly move there permanently once their two children were older.

Gillian says that the planning process was straightforward: they submitted drawings done by Mike Reynolds and got full permission within a year. A French bank lent them 75% of the projected building cost and in April 2007 they began the build. They were helped by Mike Reynolds' own 'Commando Crew' – a gang of veteran New Mexico earthship builders who flew over from the USA to kick-start the construction process with a combination of muscle and expertise for the first six weeks. But they didn't come cheap – especially as Kevan and Gillian had to pay their expenses as well as a wage. They also had to contend with the tricky situation of getting the Americans out of jail after they arrived in France without work permits, and got locked up for the night as a consequence!

But they also had a large voluntary workforce for much of the build, formed of people who came from all over Europe to learn skills and find out more about earthships. 'The volunteers were fantastic,' says Gillian, 'and we couldn't have done it without them.'

'It was a really smooth construction – such a good build – incredibly well organised – workers at no time were waiting for materials. There were some minor problems, but they really were very slight. For instance, I remember planning to do some adobe in January – how stupid was that? My advice would be to pay for some expertise at the start – unless, that is, you have already done a lot of volunteering on earthship projects. What concerns me is that people are setting up in Europe without having enough expertise. We feel that our own skills contributed to the project being successful. But you have to have an exceptional demeanour to take this on yourself. So many have failed.'

The Trotts' earthship has three bedrooms, a bathroom, and an open-plan living room and kitchen. It is on the edge of the village, with views out over fields with apple trees and horses.

'The plot itself is great,' says Gillian, 'and the relationship with the village is excellent – you can walk to the butchers, patisserie, good restaurants etc. And also we've developed relationships with neighbours – rather than living in the wilderness and being car dependent.'

However, the village does not have any public transport connections, which means that getting to and from major centres (and travelling to and from the UK) requires extensive car use.

For various personal reasons Gillian and her family have not lived for more than a couple of weeks at a time in the earthship, and she says

this is a major caveat in terms of assessing the building's overall performance. They have had some problems with damp, for example, which she suggests might well not have arisen if the building had been constantly occupied. The building has not quite met expectations in terms of its thermal performance either.

Thermal performance is at the root of modifications Gillian suggests they would make if they had the chance to build their earthship again. These are:

- a double porch at both ends to provide greater warmth
- a separate greenhouse along the entire front face, for the same reason as above
- to move the chimney for the wood-burning stove to the lounge area corner
- a larger utility room
- a larger bathroom
- a wheelchair-friendly bathroom (other than this, it's an ideal environment for someone with a mobility problem)
- ventilation tubes in a different place (to address the humidity problem).

'In terms of the design, I still think [earthships] are fantastic. There's obviously an incredible amount of resilience in the design. In the main the technology has worked, and we have only paid phone bills in the house over the past four years and very little else.'

Numerous people have stayed in the earthship as a rental property, including the co-author of this book, Kevin Telfer, who wrote an article about his experience for the *Guardian*[138]. There are numerous glowing reviews of the earthship, such as these, which were written in the visitors' book:

'Had a really brilliant stay and enjoyed living off-grid.'

'We found the earthship inspirational.'

'We'd love to live in a house like this.'

For Gillian, the positive reaction to the earthship from its many visitors is what makes the fact that they are now selling it all the more poignant: 'People loved this building, and that's what's so tragic about it.'

EARTHSHIP VALENCIA

Project name: Earthship Valencia

Project location: L'Alcúdia, Valencia, Spain

Latitude: 39.2226

Longitude: -0.5053

Altitude: 50 m

Köppen climate classification: BSk – Mid-latitude steppe, mid-latitude dry

Average annual rainfall: 464 mm

Ongoing/completed: Completed 2009

Building function: Residential – home

Climate: Very hot dry summers (in the mid to high 30s most days), short but cold winters (minimum -6°C)

Floor area: 170 m² (main earthship), 18 m² (hut)

Project cost: €63,000

Renewables used: PV: Eight 156 W panels. All-AC system. No backup.

Website/blog: www.oscarlisabuild.blogspot.com

It took Australian Lisa-Jane Roberts and her Spanish partner, Oscar Briz, seven years to build their earthship, starting in 2002 and ending in 2009. When they began building it, completely on their own, they relied on a video as their main guide, which they watched '80 or 90 times'. This is a proper self-build story.

They admit that the environmental dimension of earthships has always been secondary to them. Their main interest at the outset was in self-sufficiency, self-empowerment and low running costs, and it remains so.

'The main reasons that we chose to build an earthship were what you would call social reasons,' says Roberts, who is small and spritely, and seems to have limitless energy, 'but self-sufficiency is also green.'

'We liked the philosophy of the earthship,' says the tall and laconic Briz. 'We found it inspirational and challenging. We like challenges. And also, the economic side of it. The possibility of building our own house by ourselves … trying to get away from mortgages … it's a question of freedom. We liked the idea of control with the whole thing – building it ourselves, modifying the building to suit our needs.'

Figure 89: Earthship Valencia © Lisa-Jane Roberts and Oscar Briz

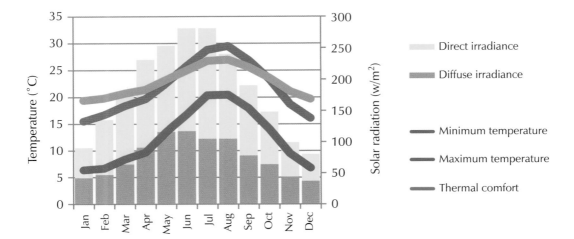

Figure 90: Nicol graph for Earthship Valencia

Figure 91: Lisa laying tiles © Lisa-Jane Roberts and Oscar Briz

They had the land – a plot opposite Briz's parents' summer home, nestled among orange groves near the town of L'Alcúdia south of Valencia – before they knew what they were going to do with it. But they decided that they wanted to escape from a culture in which people are meant to be in debt for most of their lives. They started doing internet research on alternative living. They stumbled upon earthships on the internet in 2001 and got interested enough to get directly in touch with Mike Reynolds. He suggested that they take a look at his books, and a video about building a hut.

They became what they call 'believers'. 'We wanted to believe we could build this house by ourselves,' says Briz. 'From watching the video it looked possible. I had helped other people building before, but had very little experience. 'Our idea was to build the hut first, and then be able to live in the hut while we built the rest of the earthship. This was a good idea.'

Using the video they built the hut, on their own, from scratch, in the summers of 2002 and 2003, and moved into it with their daughter in August 2003.

'And then in April 2004,' says Roberts, 'the [Mike Reynolds-led team] came over, we bought the plans, and we started the main building. 'I think they were surprised by how good the hut was. I remember

Figure 92: Earthship Valencia with retrofitted awnings to provide additional shading © Lisa-Jane Roberts and Oscar Briz

saying to someone that we'd done it from the video alone, and they were very surprised!'

The fact that they had selected a site prior to deciding to build meant that it was not ideal for an earthship, and they had to orientate the building facing further east than a conventional design would specify. 'But that is okay, because of the heat in the summer,' says Roberts. 'If it had faced due south it would have been far too hot.'

The mid-Spanish climate is fairly similar to that of Taos County, New Mexico, where the earthship concept was invented, although the winters are rather shorter and milder in Spain. But it is a similarly dry climate, with hot summers.

Despite the orientation, they say that it is still 'a little hotter than we would like in summer. But in winter it's very comfortable. We have recorded a

Figure 93: Oscar and Lisa with their daughter Carla and dog Luka (Earthship Valencia) © Lisa-Jane Roberts and Oscar Briz

temperature of -6°C outside, and yet the house has been 16°C inside without heating. However, we do also have a fireplace in the main living area, which we use when it is exceptionally cold.'

The main earthship took five years to complete, with the help of an enormous amount of voluntary labour made up of enthusiasts from all over Europe, who would come and work on the building in the summer in exchange for a bed and food.

The project ground to a halt at one point while they tried to raise enough cash to afford to build the rest of the earthship. 'For me the main thing when we built the earthship ourselves,' says Briz, 'was to have determination – go on, go on, go on – because you can really get stuck'. But by September 2009 it was finished and ready to move into, which was a relief, as the three of them had by then been living in the 18 m² hut for six years.

They estimate the cost at €60,000 for the main earthship, which has an enormous 170 m² of living space, and just €3000 to build the hut – less than €350/m².

They are impressed with what they have ended up with, and feel that the hard work has been worth it. There have been a few problems with the building, though. They say that the roof is too low at the front – a deliberate design decision, taken to prevent excessive sunlight coming into the building. This has also been a failure from a thermal point of view, as the building was still overheating in the summer. However, they have now fitted awnings that they use during the hottest months to decrease solar glare, and this has been effective.

There have also been some minor leaks and associated damp. The planter was smelly to begin with, although they have since modified it so that only water from the bathroom (shower and basin) goes into the planter, not water from the kitchen. This has improved the situation.

They're entirely off-grid and describe it as being 'miraculous'. 'We ran out of electricity this year,' says Roberts, 'but it was our own fault ... other years there had been such an excess ... I wasn't really checking the consumption. It won't happen again. The first time I had a shower in the earthship I had a real physical sensation of wow! I had this feeling of showering in water from the sky, powered by the sun.'

THE GROUNDHOUSE, BRITTANY

Project name: The Groundhouse

Project location: Central Brittany, France

Latitude: 48.4146

Longitude: -3.3178

Altitude: 50 m

Köppen climate classification: Cfc – Marine west coast, mild with no dry season, cool summer

Average annual rainfall: 687 mm

Ongoing/completed: Completed April 2010

Building function: Residential – rental property/home

Floor area: 140 m²

Project cost: Unknown

Renewables used: 14 PV panels with combined capacity of 2.3 kW

Website: www.groundhouse.com

Question: When is an earthship not an earthship?
Answer: When it's a groundhouse.

There are many interesting features about this building, but perhaps the most obvious is the fact that it isn't called an earthship, despite the fact that it seems to conform to many – but not all – accepted notions of what an earthship is, as discussed in chapter 2. The other thing that most obviously sets this building apart from others featured in this book is that it was covered on the prime-time British reality TV show *Grand Designs*. This provides high-quality documentary footage of some of the building process.

It's clear that Daren Howarth's Groundhouse, in a rural location in Brittany, France, has been influenced more by earthship design than by anything else: it is, after all, a passive solar building built with tyre walls. And Howarth's personal history is also relevant: he was one of the main figures involved in the Earthship Brighton project. But Howarth decided to call his building a 'groundhouse' because he felt there are also enough features to make it clearly distinct from an earthship.

Figure 94: The Groundhouse timber frame under construction – Daren is at the front and Adrianne on the right
© Daren Howarth

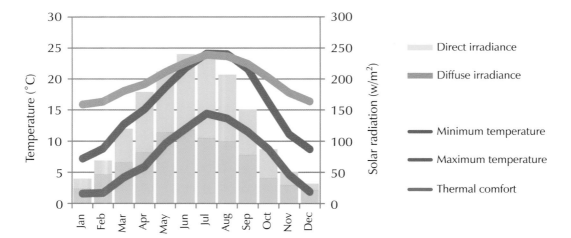

Figure 95: Nicol graph for the Groundhouse

Howarth says that he first found out about earthships in 1994, when he read a number of Mike Reynolds' books. They inspired him, not so much from an ecological point of view to begin with, but because of the self-empowerment, affordability and quality of life he felt the earthship offered. 'I had a dream,' he says. 'My dream was that I wanted to build an earthship of my own. But I soon found out it wasn't that easy.'

He started to investigate planning law and explore alternative living in the UK, after realising with dismay that 'it's even illegal to camp on a piece of your own land if you have not applied for permission to do so.' He spoke to residents of Somerset community Tinker's Bubble, and became involved with setting up The Land is Ours – a campaign to change the legal relationship between land and people. His initial interest with earthships was not an environmental one, but as he found out more about housing and the land he became more environmentally aware, and set up his own company – C-Level – as an environmental consultancy that focused on the impacts of climate change.

As part of his work with C-Level, he invited Mike Reynolds over from the USA to speak at a conference in Brighton. The positive reaction from Reynolds' talk was the beginning of the Earthship Brighton project.

Howarth had bought a plot of land in Brittany in the late 1990s. The original piece of land on the market was in woodland, but he also bought a field with a south-facing orientation that would be perfect for building an earthship. It wasn't until 2008, though, that Howarth managed to start building his own earthship, with his partner, Adrianne, and their children, and by then he felt he'd had enough experience to make some substantive changes to the standard design.

Figure 96: Laying roof insulation at the Groundhouse
© Daren Howarth

Howarth has identified seven major differences between his groundhouse and a Reynolds-designed earthship.

* connection to electrical infrastructure
* connection to mains water
* no greenhouse
* insulated underfloor space heating
* no indoor planters
* lime plaster instead of adobe
* operable front face (ie it opens and closes) rather than static.

Let's look at these individually.

Connection to electrical infrastructure

Probably the most eye-catching of these differences is the fact that the Groundhouse is connected to the grid, and to mains water supplies. 'We decided to be connected to the grid,' says Howarth, 'because we were unsure whether the PV would meet all of our energy needs, and also to have a backup in case of any system failure.'

He also points out that France's energy infrastructure produces significantly fewer CO_2 emissions than UK mains electricity: 'Most power is supplied by a combination of wind and nuclear in Brittany.'

It also means that he exports surplus electricity to the grid, purchased by his energy supplier EDF, instead of having batteries to store it in. He was unable to supply precise figures for how much this might be worth in a year (he suggested up to €1000), but it clearly seems to create a financial opportunity.

Connection to mains water

The Groundhouse also uses what Howarth describes as a 'dual system' for water. By this he means that there is both a self-sufficient system and a mains infrastructure backup. 'As with the electricity, we decided to have a backup,' says Howarth. 'This was essential when our 10,000 litre tank ran dry. However, we use extensive harvesting, and use significantly less mains water (which is metered) than we otherwise would. We use a basic filter that cost about a hundred pounds to filter our own harvested water. Overall consumption is less; bills are less.'

No greenhouse

Howarth comments that: 'We ditched the greenhouse. It would have been warmer if we had one, as the greenhouse acts as a thermal buffer, but there were a number of considerations that meant we did not choose to have one. Partly it was a choice about budget. We wanted to spend our money on operable front doors instead of on a greenhouse. Also, I've found that earthships with greenhouses tend to be darker at the back. The Groundhouse is really light. So much, in fact, that I don't feel as though we really need the skylights. These and the operable front doors mean that there is a little bit of a draught in the building, and it certainly wouldn't achieve Passivhaus standards of airtightness, but the proof of the pudding is that it is an extremely easy building to keep warm.

'I question whether you really need a greenhouse in a temperate climate.'

Insulated underfloor space heating

Howarth felt that heat loss through the floor was a major problem with Earthship Brighton, and wanted to do something to avoid this in the Groundhouse. He decided to use underfloor heating loops set in an insulated concrete bed to create constant background warmth in the cooler months. Hot water is pumped through the loops, powered by solar hot water panels heating a 1000 l accumulator tank with a 6 kW immersion coil backup. Howarth claims that the solar hot water panels are able to heat the water to 35°C in winter sunshine.

He also has a wood burner, but comments that the coldest days in winter are often the clearest, and so the solar thermal input is most significant when it is most needed. Howarth describes the underfloor heating as 'a great adaptation'.

No indoor planters

'We decided not to have planters for pragmatic reasons. Firstly we didn't want to lose the space that the planters take up. We wanted to have more space and less clutter. We decided to use a dry toilet and recycle our greywater. We were also wary about the fact that Brittany is a fairly damp place and so we did not want to add to the humidity inside the building by having the planter in there.' Instead, they have moved the planters outside and use them to help irrigate their kitchen garden.

Lime plaster instead of adobe

Howarth decided to use lime plaster because of the damp climatic conditions in Brittany relative to those found in New Mexico. Lime plaster is very breathable, and will allow moisture to evaporate from the walls, preventing build-up of damp.

Operable front face

The operable front face means that in summer the entire front of the building can be open to the elements, creating a seamless transition from inside to out. However, this was expensive, and has implications for airtightness, as mentioned above.

Howarth says it was important for them to build something that blended in both with the immediate surroundings and with the local built environment. This was something that they worked closely with the local planners to achieve. Local stone and wood are prominent. The 'turret' above the hut is a common local architectural feature in northern France. Howarth says that 'local people get it'.

The Groundhouse took two years to build, with extensive help from a voluntary workforce. Howarth said that the TV filming schedule meant they completed it in a lot shorter time than they would otherwise have done (the original plan was five years). And it also meant that they spent significantly more money than they originally intended as they wanted to make it look good for the cameras. Although coy about the exact figures, Howarth reveals that they had to sell their house in Brighton in order to help finance the project. Yet, at the time of writing, he and his family were back living in Brighton, as the experiment of living in Brittany had ultimately not worked out, because of what he describes as a combination of 'work, social life and the kids'.

He writes in the book that he and his partner Adi wrote about the build – *Groundhouse: Build + Cook* – that the building has been highly effective: 'The Brittany Groundhouse maintained an average inside temperature of 20.4°C during our first year in the new home. We are harvesting water, generating power, getting lashings of hot water, and growing food'[139].

And in spite of all the adaptations that went into creating the Groundhouse, Howarth is keen to make more changes and develop what he calls a hybrid building that will be more affordable to build. He imagines that this would have a couple of courses of tyre walls in the loadbearing back wall, with a straw bale wall built on top of these foundations, making it quick to erect but still highly insulated.

EARTHSHIP ALMERIA

Project name: Cuevos de Sol

Project location: Sorbas, Almeria, Spain

Latitude: 36.8507

Longitude: -2.46917

Altitude: 470 m

Köppen climate classification: BWk – Mid-latitude desert

Average annual rainfall: 204 mm

Ongoing/completed: Ongoing (began April 2007)

Building function: Residential home

Floor area: 81 m² (phase 1)

Project cost: Estimated at €17,000 for phase 1 (not inclusive of labour)

Renewables used: Wind turbine (planned)

Website/blog: www.earthship.es

At the time of writing, Dave Buchanan and Laura Davies, both Britons living in Spain, were in the process of building their first of two planned earthships in Almeria province, southern Spain, and aiming to complete it by the end of 2011 on a budget of just €17,000.

This review of their earthship is therefore a look at how they have got to where they are, something that is also extensively documented on their own blog (listed above). But, because it is unfinished, it does not, and cannot assess, how successful their building has been in meeting their expectations.

Dave and Laura, sensing a link between earthships and the cave homes that are found in some parts of Spain, have written on their blog that they hope their earthship 'will demonstrate how tradition and modern knowledge/technology can work together.'

As with the other Spanish earthship featured in this book, their first step to finding out about earthships – back in 2006 – was an internet search: 'I was looking on the internet for eco-friendly

Figure 97: Dave Buchanan and Laura Davies, intrepid builders of Earthship Almeria © Laura Davies and Dave Buchanan – earthship.es

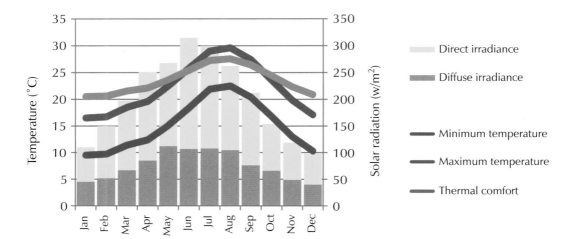

Figure 98: Nicol graph for Earthship Almeria

housing,' says Laura, 'and came across the Mike Reynolds site – and fell in love with the look of [earthships]. I liked the fact that they seemed so accessible. You don't need to have much building experience.'

They had previously spent five years renovating an old Spanish farmhouse, had gained plenty of knowledge and practical skills in doing it, and wanted a new challenge. They bought an elevated plot of land (about 470 m above sea level) in an area of almond plantations in the very dry province of Almeria, which has just over 200 mm of rainfall a year.

Then, after seeing the website, they bought a couple of the earthship books direct from Reynolds, and then, when they liked what they saw, bought some more. At this point, as they began to seriously consider the idea that they might build their own earthship, they decided to take a trip to Valencia to visit Oscar Briz and Lisa-Jane Roberts, who were already a few years into their own project. They were inspired by what they saw.

Laura, who is a graphic designer and artist, started drawing up some plans. 'I knew how we wanted to lay it out; the books were clear on what to do; it was fairly straightforward.'

However, they still had to contend with the Spanish planning system. On their blog, they note that: 'In his books Michael Reynolds suggests a

staged process of application for planning so as not to freak out planning departments who haven't come across earthships before'[140].

Closely following this advice, they decided to stagger their own planning application into three stages. The first stage was to put in an application for a small agricultural building called a *navé* – which would essentially be a 'test run' earthship. Stage two is an application to put up a wind turbine, and the final, third stage is an application to build a large earthship with a 350 m² footprint. They used local architects to formalise the drawings and advise them on conforming to regulations.

They got their permission to build a 35 m² U-module with an attached greenhouse in April 2007, and work began later that month with the excavation of the site. The permission was later extended to also include a circular hut, and so increase the footprint of the first test earthship to a total of 80 m².

They have spent the last four years working on the test earthship, which raises the question of how long it will take to complete their whole project. But Laura and Dave do not seem to be concerned. 'We only have our own deadlines,' says Laura. 'We're lucky because we already have somewhere substantial to live, whereas many people doing building projects do not.'

Figure 99: Painting the roof with acrylic paint (Earthship Almeria) © Laura Davies and Dave Buchanan – earthship.es

It has been a proper self-build project, with most of the work divided between Laura and Dave, family, friends and volunteers.

'Building walls in tyres is fairly straightforward – hard work but satisfying,' says Laura. 'The carpentry side has been a little more complex. But Dave has lots of practical skills that he has developed while we renovated our farmhouse. We've realised that you need to have a lot of patience when you're building an earthship.'

Dave gave an example of someone who had come to the earthship as a volunteer, who said that: 'This morning, when I first arrived, I was completely daunted, but now I understand that you need to do it little by little.'

They feel that taking their time over it has also meant that they've been able to adapt the design in different ways. They decided to use cork insulation, for example, and have had a chance to consider their options in terms of renewables. Dave's current idea is to use a wind turbine with backup PV for electricity as well as solar hot water. 'My thinking is that as we are fairly high up, a 1 kW wind turbine will give us on average about 300 W/hr – 7.2 kWh a day; and at the moment we're using about 6 kWh a day.' He is hoping to test the effectiveness of a wind turbine by using one borrowed from nearby permaculture NGO Sunseed, whose mission statement is to 'find and spread methods that will improve the living conditions and environment in desertified areas'[141].

Many of the volunteers on the earthship have also come from Sunseed. In such an arid area, access to water is of critical importance, especially as they do not even have the option of being connected to mains water. 'Water is a lot more highly prized here than in the UK,' says Laura. 'Water rights are held on to very tightly. You can buy a licence to drill a well, but the water table is falling all the time – so we didn't want to do this.'

They have decided to harvest rainwater, but their initial tank for the small earthship has only a 2000 l capacity. They ultimately want to create 50,000 l of capacity, although this is scheduled to be available only at the end of the final phase of the project.

In the hot, semi-arid summer climate, it seems possible that their earthship may suffer from overheating, but they do not seem overly concerned by this. 'We're not too worried about keeping cool in the summer; in the winter we want to get as much sun as possible.' Their main solution to prevent overheating seems to be to have a vine-covered overhang – a *brise soleil* – that will provide shade from the high sun in the middle of the day in summer, but will not interrupt sunlight in the spring, autumn and winter months.

Dave and Laura's earthship adventure is a fascinating story for anyone contemplating a self-build project of their own. And their blog is particularly interesting, full of decisions, sticking points, blood, sweat and tears – as well as the spirit of curiosity, energy and enterprise that they both seem to have plenty of.

PROJECT ROUND-UP: OTHER EARTHSHIPS AND RELATED PROJECTS

There are several other interesting European projects that are either in their early stages, or have been aborted, or about which we have been unable to collect sufficient information to feature them fully in this book. There are also projects that have been heavily influenced by earthships, but have been built with hybrid designs. This is a brief round-up of all these projects.

Earthship Zwolle, The Netherlands

A non-residential tea shop/cafe was built in a park in the town of Zwolle, about 130 km north-east of Amsterdam in 2008/2009. It was completed in spring 2009. It has been difficult to get an authoritative story about the building, but anecdotal reports indicate that it has not performed well, with issues relating to damp and poor thermal performance.

Mike Reynolds and Kevan Trott (Earthship France) were both involved with the building, but both of them have declined to comment on it. The earthship was designed by Reynolds, and is based on the packaged earthship layout of a single nest module with the addition of an extra entrance on the north side through the earth shelter (a unique feature in earthships, to our knowledge). Pictures show that there was a very high standard of interior finish, with mosaic floors and coloured glass windows.

Rehemetsa, Estonia

A small tyre-wall building was constructed in the village of Rehemetsa in Estonia, just south of the capital Talinn, as part of a project funded by the European Community Youth Programme[142]. It cannot be called an earthship, as it is just an uninsulated tyre wall with some glazing that was built as a rain shelter for walkers, rather than a fully functional building. The project, called 'Life Goes Around', was devoted to the idea that resources should be reused as much as possible. The aim of the project was as much about skills transfer to the young volunteers as it was about the actual construction of the building. Kevan Trott (Earthship France) was involved with this project.

Earthships in Sweden

Several earthships have begun construction in Sweden, including the Växhuset Sunship at Mobodarne, the Midgård Blackship near Skövde, and a further project at Skattyngbun, much further north in Sweden. Of these, the Växhuset project has stopped halfway through construction because of funding problems and a lack of momentum, and financial and planning problems have also meant that work on the Midgård Blackship has stalled. The Skattyngbun build is still in very early stages, after the project team decided to abandon their first design and start again with a design that they think is better adapted to their far northern situation. There is a small but active community of people interested in earthships in the country, and the possibility of future builds seems high.

Greenhead Moss, Scotland

Greenhead Moss is a community nature park between Hamilton and Motherwell, on the outskirts of Glasgow. At the beginning of 2008 work began on building an earthship that was to be a visitor, volunteer and community centre for the park. By the beginning of 2010 work had been going well, and the shell of the building had been completed. Systems were beginning to be installed. However, on 25 March 2010 the building was burnt down by arsonists, and the project failed to recover from the blow. Construction has stopped, and there is no intention of reviving it[143].

Skerray Hybrid Earthship, Scotland

Skerray Earthship is a two-floor, hybrid tyre/straw bale wall building in the north of Scotland. As this book goes to press it seems to be close to completion, and looks like a professional and impressive project. It is the first residential earthship (albeit a hybrid) in the UK. Photos of the project are posted on the Skerray Earthship Facebook page.

Rik Lander Bristol Studio, England

Rik Lander is a writer, director and producer based in Bristol. He decided to build a small blue-screen studio in central Bristol for production, rehearsal and events, using a hybrid tyre wall/straw bale/rock gabion design. More detail is given at http://bristolgreenhouse.co.uk/. The Low Carbon

Figure 100: Livingstone bat in flight © Dominic Wormell

Trust, which initially set up the Earthship Brighton project, was involved in a consultancy and construction role.

Rik notes that 'UK conditions are very different to the desert conditions experienced [in New Mexico] so designs for the UK have to be modified. I think we made some good innovations, but also some mistakes'[144]. In particular, he feels that better insulation detailing could deliver improved thermal performance: the lowest tyre course was resting directly on the foundation, and acted as a thermal sink. He has also experienced some difficulties with damp in some of the corners of the building, where the waterproof membrane detailing was inadequate. He suggests that this may also be a hangover from the New Mexico design, which was built in arid conditions; he suggests that in temperate climates more attention needs to be paid to the potential ingress of water.

Jersey Bat House, Channel Islands

Durrell Zoo on Jersey has a large collection of Livingstone and Rodrigues bats, which are native to tropical Indian Ocean islands. The bats had been housed inside in a large greenhouse, but they are at risk of suffering damage to the membranes of their wings whenever the air temperature drops below 10°C. With no thermal mass integrated into the greenhouse, at night the temperature dropped

dramatically, and some bats were in danger. The zoo chose to build a thermal mass polytunnel, with a rammed-tyre wall on two sides and straw bale insulation so that the structure would retain warmth and more closely resemble the bats' natural habitat.

You can see how the bats are getting on at the Durrell Zoo bat webcam: www.durrell.org/Home/Webcams/Livingstones-fruit-bat-webcam.

Belgian projects

Earthship Belgium is a non-profit organisation that has been at the centre of attempts to form a pan-European earthship movement in the form of EEBU – European Earthship Builders United. But it is also working on its own projects in Belgium. Its chairman, Willy Raets, says that it is planning a 22-unit earthship eco-village, although this is in the early planning stages. However, it has already started work on a project called Earthresidence – a living/working space for an artist. It failed to gain permission to build with tyres for this project, so instead is using earthbags. Willy Raets wrote on the Earthship Belgium blog in March 2011 that: 'It is now known that no permission will be granted for the use of tires. The project will take place anyway. The tires will be replaced by a wall of sandbags. This allows the concept of heat storage to be maintained. Other concepts will also be maintained'[145].

8 PASSIVE SOLAR DESIGN AND MONITORED THERMAL PERFORMANCE

INTRODUCTION

'Earthship is the name we have given to a home that is absolutely independent. It harvests its own power, harvests its own water, contains and treats its own sewage, heats and cools itself. It's built from by-products of our society, rather than largely trees like most housing is, and produces a certain amount of food and thus the name earthship is kind of like a ship that will sail on the earth and has everything that it needs to do so.' Mike Reynolds[26]

This chapter is about the passive solar design strategies used in earthships. The claim is that earthships use the sun to heat themselves, almost entirely negating the need for other forms of space heating. But does the claim stand up? Very little independent detailed monitoring has ever been carried out on earthships. However, an extensive study of monitoring has been carried out at Earthship Brighton, and the analysis of the data is at the heart of this chapter. The fundamental question is 'Do earthships work?' Of course, it's impossible to be quite that straightforward: data from one project is necessarily constrained by local factors. However, the intention is to provide a significant insight into earthship thermal performance, especially in a temperate climate.

In order to place this analysis in its fullest possible context we trace the history of modern low-energy building through the evolution of the passive solar and super-insulation movements in the USA in the 1970s, and the transfer of the approach to Europe. There is an outline of how passive solar strategies are used in earthships, with the thermal comfort reported by earthship residents, and a brief look at the academic papers that have been written about the thermal performance of earthships.

The chapter then focuses on the monitoring of the thermal performance of Earthship Brighton. This provides important lessons on how the performance can be improved in future earthships built in Europe. In the immediate context it opens the performance of the earthship to independent scrutiny, and demonstrates that without a consistent, inexpensive, independent monitoring scheme in place for all buildings, there is the danger of falling into the gap between design aspirations and what actually gets built. Mind the gap!

None of the strategies discussed in this chapter is new, and their deployment in earthships is not unique. There are plenty of other examples of buildings adopting a similar approach in Europe. Notable examples include: Port Sunlight, Liverpool (1899); the Hockerton Housing Project, Hockerton (1998); BedZED, Sutton (2002); the Sun Ship, Frieburg (2006); and One Brighton, Brighton (2010). These all demonstrate that they are viable techniques that are easily designed and incorporated into new builds.

BRIEF HISTORY OF MODERN PASSIVE SOLAR DESIGN

This section traces the modern passive solar movement from the 1970s onwards in the USA, and looks at the transfer of the passive solar approach to Europe. This is vital to understanding the design background to earthships.

Designing with the sun in mind is not new, and many indigenous American peoples built houses using passive solar principles. The Anasazi Indians, in what is now New Mexico and Arizona, built many south-facing dwellings and community

Figure 101: Taos Pueblo illustration from 1893
© Western History/Genealogy Department, Denver
Public Library

Figure 102: MIT Solar One House (1939)

buildings such as Mesa Verde, Pueblo Bonito and the Acoma Pueblo[146]. These villages and towns demonstrate sophisticated master planning of layout and orientation, which enabled all residents to have equal access to the sun[147]. The buildings were designed with the principles of solar architecture in mind, and were made from earth and built into the ground, providing passive cooling as well, through the temperature stabilisation of the earth's temperature and thermal mass.

In the earlier part of the 20th century, many passive solar houses were built: for example, George F. Keck's 'House of Tomorrow' at the 1933 Chicago World Fair, the various MIT Solar Houses in Massachusetts, built between 1939 and 1958, and the Howard Sloan House in Glenview, Illinois, in 1940. In addition, many others were built during the 1940s and 1950s, particularly to provide housing after the Second World War[147]. In more recent times the genesis of the earthship was the 'oil shocks' or global energy crisis of the mid-1970s. In 1973 an OPEC oil embargo in response to US supply of oil to Israel during the Yom Kippur war caused the price of oil to quadruple in price over a few months, from $3 to $12 a barrel[148]. Exacerbating this was the fact that US oil production had peaked in 1970, and the USA became steadily more reliant on imported oil[149]. The 'energy crunch' highlighted the vulnerability of large-scale centralised energy systems and dependence on foreign fossil fuel, and there was a renewed interest in energy efficiency, passive solar techniques and renewable energy sources.

As part of the drive towards energy efficiency in the 1970s, many passive solar experiments were built in California, Arizona and New Mexico, and a distinct style emerged[147]. The buildings were oriented towards the sun, had large amounts of glazing to collect as much sunlight as possible, and lots of thermal mass to soak up the heat to stabilise the internal temperature throughout the year. Passive solar buildings in New Mexico from this time include the Karen Terry House, the Fitzgerald House, and many others documented in the New Mexico Passive Solar Home Temperature Survey[49], [150]. As part of this wave, Reynolds states that, with the earthship, he was 'basically responding to the news'[7]. The approach evolved, with all of the typical passive solar features, as a practical response to the energy crisis, demonstrating the 'theory of how buildings can be made comfortable without centralised utilities or use of fuel'[151].

After the development of passive solar housing in the south-west, the approach was transferred to other parts of the USA, including New England and other eastern states. Whereas it had worked well in the south-western dry, hot climate, the challenge of adapting the design to a more temperate climate meant it didn't perform as well. The problem of transferring the approach for different climates is summed up in an article by Steve Bliss, former editor of Solar Age magazine:

'I interviewed two college professors living in a solar house in the Boston suburbs. When I got there, they were sitting in the house freezing – they were wearing down booties and down vests. They were suing their architect, who had used solar glazing formulas developed for houses in the Southwest ... It's certainly possible to heat a home with the sun. But these solar houses are unnecessarily complicated, and many have comfort problems. They often overheat on sunny days and get too cold at night. If you build a super-insulated house without any solar features, your heating bills will be lower, your construction budget will be smaller, and you're likely to be more comfortable'[152].

This highlights the gap between the design and the actual performance of passive solar buildings, and demonstrates the crucial need to optimise them for the climate they are built in. This theme will be explored later in this book.

SUPER-INSULATION

Other low-energy houses built during the 1970s had a different design ethos, minimising the need for heating rather than maximising the collection of solar heat – a subtle but crucial difference. These houses became known as 'super-insulated', and emerged as a distinct approach, separate from passive solar, although there is some crossover. Super-insulated houses still use solar and internal gains, but eschew classic passive solar features, favouring very thick levels of insulation of all external elements, high-performance glazing, good levels of airtightness, and some form of mechanical ventilation. Famous examples from the period include: the Lo-Cal House at Urbana, Illinois (1976); the Saskatchewan Conservation House at Regina, Saskatchewan, in Canada (1978); and the Leger House at East Pepperell, Massachusetts (1979). The Leger project is notable for having no 'classic' passive solar features at all, while the owner stated that the annual heating cost was $38.50[153]. In some ways it can be seen that the low-energy housing debate was starkly polarised between the two positions, but, as with all simplistic divisions, the reality was that lots of houses incorporated some features from each, while others were purist. While there was lots of development of superinsulated housing in the 1970s, unfortunately, by the mid-

Figure 103: Saskatchewan Conservation House

1980s, after oil peaked at $35 a barrel, the price dropped to below $10. This led one commentator to say:

'In North America ... the lessons of the Saskatchewan and Leger houses hardly spread beyond a small band of dedicated custom-home-builders. In the intervening 30 years, mainstream American builders completed tens of millions of leaky new homes, most with 2 × 4 walls haphazardly filled with fiberglass batts.' M Holladay[154]

Low-energy housing was the preserve of the few – a peripheral activity that was not adopted by the mainstream.

PASSIVE SOLAR DESIGN IN EUROPE

Passive solar design has a long and distinguished history in Europe, with examples dating from ancient times, such as the orientation of Greek housing to take advantage of the sun in winter and avoid overheating in summer[147]. As in the USA, there were many experiments with low-energy houses in the Europe during the 1970s, including the Kopenhagen Zero Energy House (1973), Maison à Ginestas at Aude (1979), and Maison de Velieux at Herault (1981). The last two examples were part of the wave of passive solar projects transferring the US approach, and were documented in the First European Passive Solar Competition in 1980[155].

Around the same time as these projects, several European countries such as Sweden and Denmark tightened their Building Regulations significantly, so that low-energy building became a legally required standard for new buildings, adopting high levels of insulation and airtightness. The experience in these countries, coupled with the earlier US examples of super-insulation, led directly to the first Passivhaus in Darmstadt-Kranichstein, Germany, in 1991. The Passivhaus approach will be touched on in chapter 9.

PASSIVE SOLAR DESIGN IN EARTHSHIPS

Exponents of passive solar design often state that the sun is so powerful that there is no need for any other energy source to heat homes. According to Bob Everett of the Open University, even a 'perfectly ordinary' badly insulated 1970s UK house is already 14% heated by passive solar, in terms of the sun's contribution to the gross annual heating demand of the building[156]. However, on average the remaining 86% net space heating demand will need to be supplied from fossil fuel sources – either gas or electricity from the grid – between mid-September and mid-May. The earthship, on the other hand, tries to achieve a 100% contribution to gross heating demand from passive solar input throughout the year, and to require zero, or negligible, additional heating.

The factors that influence the amount of energy a building can usefully harvest from the sun are orientation, shading, and the amount of glazing and thermal mass. The earthship has all the 'classic' passive solar features: southern orientation, floor-to-ceiling glazing facing the sun, and little or no glazing on the other elevations. Although solar energy can be collected from almost any direction, in the northern hemisphere, facing the equator, the solar gain is strongest from the south, and weaker from the east and west. From the north, the thermal loss

Figure 104: A Passivhaus in Austria. The house incorporates some passive solar features such as south-facing glazing and external shading devices

Figure 105: Solar gain section (Earthship Brighton) © Taus Larsen

Figure 107: Release of heat from thermal mass (Earthship Brighton) © Taus Larsen

Figure 106: Limiting solar gain in summer (Earthship Brighton) © Taus Larsen

Figure 108: Natural ventilation and convection (Earthship Brighton) © Taus Larsen

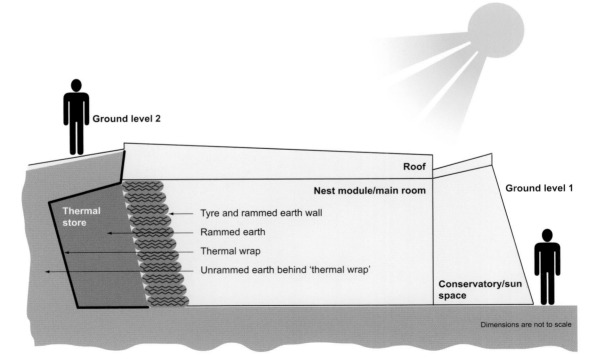

Figure 109: Exposure of thermal store at ground level (Earthship Brighton)

by far outweighs the thermal gain. In the southern hemisphere the opposite is the case.

In the temperate northern climate this means that the earthship must be oriented to the south to maximise the opportunity to exploit solar gain, although the building can face slightly to the east or west with only marginal loss.

With all the glazing on one side, the further away one is from the windows, the darker it gets. To optimise daylighting inside the earthship, the plan depth is calculated from the angle of penetration of the sun during winter, so that ideally the sun at the winter solstice should hit the base of the back wall. The depth is usually 6 m. The design of the interior layout needs to reflect this to avoid creating dark areas that may require extra lighting or skylights during the day. Also, the layout of an earthship puts the rooms next to the amenities that use them: for example, the kitchen is next to the greywater planter at the front of the building, to minimise pipe runs.

As part of the natural ventilation system the earthship has operable skylights at the highest point of the roof, which are normally towards the back of the structure. The daylight they provide may be insufficient, and so may need supplementing with sunpipes to increase the natural light level. The large amounts of south-facing glazing suggest that earthships may overheat in summer. However, the high levels of thermal mass, together with the natural ventilation, help to stabilise the temperature. The natural ventilation system was outlined in detail in chapter 3.

The real advantage of passive solar design is that the building structure or fabric is designed to harness and retain heat. If the sun's energy can be used directly, there is less conversion loss from other energy sources trying to meet demand, and therefore efficiency is very high, compared with heating using electricity or gas, and there are no moving parts that require maintenance. Earthships have two ways of collecting solar energy: a large expanse of south-facing glass in the nest module, and a Trombe wall in the hut module. In passive solar terms, nests are direct-gain buildings and huts are indirect-gain buildings. The Trombe wall works by the sun heating the air and tyre wall directly behind the glass. The hot air rises through the holes at the top, and cooler air is drawn through the holes at the base of the wall. This process of convection heats the space, and the holes can be plugged for control at night, on overcast days, or during summer. With both methods of harvesting heat, the warmth is stored in the wide thermal mass walls.

Figure 110: Earthship passive solar features (Earthship France) © Kevan and Gillian Trott

THERMAL MASS AND THERMAL WRAP IN EARTHSHIPS

'At even the outermost layers of the earth this heat can be felt. Just four feet below the surface, the ground temperature remains remarkably constant, especially compared to climatic conditions above the ground. At a four foot depth, the temperature is usually between 55° and 60°F (12.8° and 15.6°C), which is much more comfortable than weather conditions of both summer and winter. By tapping into this natural thermal constant, the Earthship can remain consistently comfortable, because this is only 10° away from the US comfort zone of 70° in winter via heat from the sun. In summer, this massive constant tends to drag the 100° air temperature down to 70°.' Mike Reynolds[157]

Earthships are a very heavyweight construction, either cut into a south-facing slope, as in the case of Earthship Brighton and Earthship Fife, or sheltered with earth on a flat piece of land, as Earthship France and the Groundhouse are. In either instance the walls – rammed tyres and rammed earth – are about 2 m thick, and offer a very large thermal store or 'battery' for winter. The tyre wall mass is a loadbearing structure as well, serving a dual purpose. Behind the backfill berm is a 100 mm thermal wrap of rigid insulation, which surrounds the building and isolates the thermal mass of rammed tyres and earth, making it act as a storage heater. Just like a stone wall on a hot day, the rammed-tyre walls absorb heat, and then slowly release it as the building cools. The earthship exploits it on a building-sized scale, capturing heat, storing it, and balancing it out to find thermal equilibrium.

Given that 9 of the 10 hottest years on record have been in the last decade, the need for a stable indoor temperature and the avoidance of energy-hungry air conditioning can only become more important[158]. Mass of this size, with its large repository of heat, provides temperature stability through diurnal fluctuations, but is a lot slower to react than lighter weight buildings. Table 22 summarises the amount of thermal mass in the European earthships. The mass to volume ratio is an expression of the amount of thermal mass in the walls in relation to the volume of air in the earthship module. The trend would appear to be that the ratio is higher for smaller earthships, such as the various huts and Earthship Fife, and lower for the larger, nest modules.

Thick walls, coupled with insulation, in theory enable the earthship to maintain a comfortable temperature in any season; the building's temperature is stabilised to remain hot in winter and cool in summer. However, although anecdotally this phenomenon is effective, there has been very little study into how effective it actually is. The reactions of residents to the thermal comfort of earthships are reported here.

Table 22: Volume of approximate thermal mass in walls of European earthships

Earthship	Module	Floor area (m²)	Mass in walls (m³)	Internal volume (m³)	Mass/volume ratio
Almeria	Nest	35.00	71.40	73.50	0.97
	Hut	19.63	66.00	41.22	1.60
Brighton	Nest	80.00	135.00	200.00	0.67
	Hut	12.50	58.00	31.25	1.88
Fife	U	31.50	101.25	78.75	1.30
France	Nest	130.00	123.55	229.00	0.54
The Groundhouse	Nest	109.00	89.82	241.20	0.38
	Hut	33.00	52.68	79.64	0.66
Valencia	Nest	150.00	163.20	382.50	0.42

Assumptions are: the thermal mass is 2 m in depth (rammed tyre 700 mm and 1300 mm of rammed earth/chalk). Internal ceiling heights are 2.4 m. The internal volume is for rooms connected to the thermal mass, and does not include greenhouses.

'Many underground houses have been built through the years. It has been customary to insulate these buildings away from the earth. An earthship must not be insulated away from the earth. It must interface with it, taking advantage of this tremendous thermal constant.' Mike Reynolds[157]

Most of the earthships built in Europe so far do not have underfloor insulation. This is a deliberate design decision by Reynolds to tap into the earth's core ground temperature, as expressed in the above quote. Earthships are dug into the ground, below the frost line, to access the natural temperature of the earth. This varies from place to place, but the principle is that it is much easier to raise the ambient air temperature from 10 to 12°C to a comfortable temperature, than for a similar structure built above ground. The variation of ground temperature at Earthship Brighton is actually much wider than this, and is outlined below. The principle does not take into account that the mean radiant surface temperature has an impact on thermal comfort as well, and a large area such as a floor can make people feel cooler by radiating lower temperatures.

Another factor with the lack of underfloor insulation is that there is an opportunity for a large amount of conductive thermal loss through the floor. If the stable temperature of the earth is lower than the temperature of the thermal mass in the walls, or the air temperature, then the floor becomes a thermal sink, although this factor will vary considerably, depending on the soil and moisture content that the earthship is built into. Once the sun's heat is inside the earthship, and has been stored in the mass, its movement needs to be carefully controlled, and heat loss needs to be restricted when heating is the priority.

THERMAL COMFORT REPORTED BY EARTHSHIP RESIDENTS

There is very little information on the recorded thermal performance of earthships, so some anecdotal reports of how residents feel about their homes are presented here. Reynolds describes the performance of the earthship approach for a cold climate by stating that:

'Once they [earthships] get stabilised and all the energy is trapped with insulation, there is so much mass that it stabilises the air space. And they'll hang, in a worst case scenario, they'll hang between 65°F and 75°F (18°C and 24°C) with no fuel being needed whatsoever.' Mike Reynolds[26]

This corresponds with the experience reported by the owner of the Touch the Earth Ranch Earthship, Colorado, who comments that:

'On the coldest of winter days the temperature inside never goes below 63°F, even when it's been very cold (-27°F [-32.8°C] our coldest night) and with no additional heat in the house, it was still 60°F. On the hottest of summer days (95°F outside [35°C]) inside temperatures don't go over 80°F (26.5°C) in the shade. It's always quite warm under the solar array windows, when the sun is shining.' NASA GISS[158]

In a temperate climate, with a higher proportion of cloudy days, the last point is crucial: how to store the sun's energy from the sunny days for overcast days to provide useful warmth in the winter period. The Touch the Earth Ranch Earthship was completed in 1994, and the owner reports that they do use a small wood stove to provide 'a flash of heat on snowy evenings or on "Arctic front" days'.

Another Colorado earthship owner comments on the internal temperature in winter by saying that:

'Friends in town have been running their furnaces for a month now while we have only had one evening in the last month when we lit up the wood-burning stove. In the last month it has usually been right around 70°F (21°C) in the house when we retire for the night around 10 pm.' P Cowie[53]

In Scotland, the SCI report that, after manually monitoring the internal and external air temperature over a period of three days each week during winter, Earthship Fife 'averaged 14.5°C over the winter months, without any extra heating'[53]. Temperature sensors have been installed in the sunspace at the front, in the main wall body of Earthship Fife, and at 33 cm, 66 cm and 99 cm depths in the back wall, and are monitoring the thermal performance on an ongoing basis. There is some data available, but unfortunately it is sporadic, and so has not been included in this book.

In Earthship France, built in Normandy, Kevan and Gillian Trott report that on 28 December 2008 the internal temperature in the bedrooms was 17°C, while the external air temperature was -14°C. The internal air temperature remained a fairly constant 16 to 17°C during this winter period[160]. Meanwhile, at the Groundhouse in Brittany, Daren Howarth and Adi Nortje report that the average spring temperature is 19.9°C, and that the average inside temperature was 20.4°C during the first year[161].

In Spain, the owners of Earthship Valencia have posted on their blog:

'We were at minus 2°C this morning and it hasn't got much above 7°C all day. The house is holding up pretty well. We have a gas heater, which we use at night in the living area. Without the heater the house is still warm. On cloudy days it stays around 16°C but if the sun comes out it gets up into the 20s.'[162]

To summarise these anecdotal findings, it seems the lowest internal air temperature that earthships drop to in a dry arid climate is 17.21°C, with the highest ranging up to 26.66°C, while in the maritime temperate climate of Scotland the lowest recorded indoor air temperature was 14.5°C and in Normandy, France, 16°C. All the temperatures given by owners are ambient air temperatures, which do not take into consideration the mean radiant temperature, convection (draughts) or relative humidity: therefore thermal comfort conditions are difficult to report. In most cases it seems that the people are happy with the thermal comfort their earthships are providing for them, even though they are operating below the threshold of what is usually considered thermally comfortable (18°C to 23°C) and in some cases below the World Health Organization guidelines for the minimum temperature for a healthy environment (15°C)[163]. This fits in with the findings that people are more forgiving of green buildings and the environment they provide. It would be useful to conduct a survey of people who live in earthships around the world to make the sample wider and more representative[164].

LITERATURE REVIEW: PUBLISHED ACADEMIC PAPERS ON THE THERMAL PERFORMANCE OF EARTHSHIPS

This section briefly reviews some of the academic papers that have been written on the thermal performance of earthships. To date there has not been much analysis of whether the earthships perform adequately or not.

The thermal behaviours of an earthship

This paper by Grindley and Hutchinson[165], written in 1996, was about the thermal performance of the Earthship Biotecture office in Taos, New Mexico. The offices are five connected U modules: the dimensions are 13.7 m by 6.9 m, with a gross floor area of 95 m². The earthship is earth sheltered, and has double glazing on the south façade. A pyranometer and thermocouples were used to take hourly readings of the internal ambient air and mean radiant temperatures, and externally readings were collected for insolation and ambient air temperature.

Data was collected over a three-day period during June 1995, and the internal temperatures recorded were between 24°C and 29°C, while the external ambient air temperature ranged from 4°C to 35°C. The readings were used to calibrate a thermal model using TAS software, based on weather and soil temperature data for nearby Los Alamos. The model covered the thermal performance of the building over the course of a year, which was then transposed to the south-east of England for comparison with a temperate climate. The results indicated that the earthship would overheat during summer in both the USA and UK, and that some form of solar shading would be required to reduce this. Also, they identified that additional heating would be required between October and March in the UK model, where the dry resultant temperature was below 18°C for most of the period.

The paper suggests that the heating load over winter in the UK model would be 325 kWh, which if correct is a fraction of the delivered energy used by the average existing building stock. However, divided over the usable floor area this equates to 3.5 kWh/m², and although the figure quoted isn't for the whole year, most of the heating load would be in winter, as identified above; this is very low, even for a low-energy building. The Taos TAS model was more thermally comfortable, ie between 18°C and 26°C for longer than the UK model. In summary, although the paper's findings are interesting, the sample of data used to calibrate the thermal model was very small. Also, the building studied was not residential, and the behaviour of the thermal mass in the walls was not considered.

The Brighton Earthship: evaluating the thermal performance

This report[166] was published by the University of Brighton's School of the Built Environment in 2005 as part of the Durabuild Project, and focuses on the initial findings from the monitored data from Earthship Brighton. Temperature sensors were installed throughout the earthship, and the data forms the basis of this report and the following two papers. For more details of the sensors and data collection see the section on the predicted and observed thermal performance of Earthship Brighton below. Findings were that the internal temperature was 'consistently higher than outside, responding to incident solar radiation'.

There are several limitations to the report; the building was unoccupied, and the sample of data, although very detailed, did not cover a complete year. For example, it would have been useful to see how the building dealt with summer overheating. However, the report does give an insight into the free-running state of the building, and analyses the performance of Earthship Brighton in terms of the levels of thermal comfort prescribed by the Chartered Institution of Building Services Engineers (CIBSE)[167]. The report concludes that Earthship Brighton is 'moderating the extremes of external temperatures, although these are generally still below thermal comfort conditions for the majority of the time within the main module, the Nest.' In line with the Grindley and Hutchinson paper, the report also finds that the earthship tends to overheat in summer.

The predicted and observed thermal performance of Earthship Brighton

The University of Brighton presented a paper[168] at the 2005 World Sustainable Building Conference in Tokyo. The paper's focus was on the performance of the thermal mass within the earthship, looking at the internal and external conditions, and

using Integrated Environmental Solutions' Virtual Environment (IES-VE) simulation software to model the thermal behaviour of Earthship Brighton for comparison.

The actual performance of Earthship Brighton was 'consistently higher than that predicted by the model', even though the air leakage rate assumed in the model was much lower than was actually the case. The actual rate of air change was unknown at this time, as a pressure test wasn't conducted until later. Three ventilation rates of 0.5 ach (air changes per hour), 3 ach and 5 ach were tested over a baseline infiltration rate of 0.4 ach. Also, the paper focused on Earthship Brighton's nest module, and did not include the hut module.

Analysis of the performance of earthship housing in various global climates

This paper by Kruis and Heun[124], presented at the Energy Sustainability 2007 conference in California, analyses earthships in four different locations and climates in the USA. Earthships are compared with a family of four living in grid-connected timber-frame houses in terms of thermal comfort, electricity and water supply, and financial payback over 45 years. The locations and climates are a broad range: Anchorage, Alaska – continental sub-arctic; Grand Rapids, Michigan – humid continental; Albuquerque, New Mexico – dry/arid; and Honolulu, Hawaii – tropical wet/dry.

The authors built a thermal model using the Energy Plus energy simulation program, and the results indicate that in all four climates earthships do not always provide a comfortable living environment: 'The inside environment created by earthships may be tolerable from a survivalist point of view, but before earthships can be marketable to the average family they must include centralised mechanical systems to moderate daily temperature fluctuations.'

The study uses high temperatures for its thermal comfort parameters: 21°C to 28°C instead of the lower 18°C to 23°C typically used in Europe. Also, other than the roof, the various elements in the models are not insulated to a high standard: walls are 0.23 W/m²K, floor 0.38 W/m²K (uninsulated in the Honolulu and Albuquerque models), and the glazing 0.31 W/m²K. In colder climates the amount of glazing is reduced from 25% to 13%.

The high levels of thermal mass may help to reduce heating costs in some situations, but in the tropical wet or dry climates houses do not need a robust thermal envelope, and ways of building with fewer materials will be cheaper.

The authors modelled stand-alone electricity systems at each location using PV-DesignPro-S to supply 8 kWh/day. This level of demand is high for an off-grid system, and other than for remote rural locations, onsite PV generation is not competitive when compared with grid-supplied electricity. For water supply, in three locations there is not enough rain to supply the amount of water needed, and between 44 and 86 additional l/day of mains water is required to top up. The assumption is based on the family of four using 370 l/day, with flushing toilets supplied by recycled greywater, and no water used for landscaping.

The conclusion of the paper is that earthships do not meet typical housing needs when compared with grid-connected timber-frame houses, and that they 'cannot provide: (a) a consistently comfortable environment solely through passive solar heating, (b) a consistent supply of water solely through catch water and gray water system, or (c) an adequate supply of electricity through a PV power generator at a reasonable price.'

Financially, when compared with mainstream timber housing, earthships are most viable in colder climates with higher heating requirements. The paper suggests that further research is required, including the evaluation of consumer acceptance and marketability of this type of housing.

Thermal storage: an evaluation of the thermal performance of the Brighton Earthship

This paper[169], from the School of Environment and Technology at the University of Brighton, looked at the thermal storage in the earth-rammed-tyre walls: average temperature, vertical and horizontal temperature gradients, and the thermal store over the first 77 weeks of operation. The paper covered the findings of the 2005 paper, and, in addition, considered the amount of energy stored in the walls.

THERMAL PERFORMANCE OF EARTHSHIP BRIGHTON

This section deals with the thermal monitoring of Earthship Brighton, from the setting up of the sensor system to the methods used to treat the data. The results are presented, with some analysis. The detail in this section is given in full for transparency, and the reader should feel free to skip this section and proceed to the results. The research presented here is original to this edition of the book.

Monitoring equipment and regime

As part of Durabuild, an EU-funded project to monitor low-energy buildings in the south-east of England, the University of Brighton's School of the Built Environment installed air and earth temperature sensors in Earthship Brighton in autumn 2004[166]. Thirty-two sensors were buried in different parts of the building (walls and floor), some placed on shelves to measure internal environmental conditions and other places to measure heat flow in the rammed-tyre walls. An onsite weather station was also installed to record specific conditions. The sensors took readings at different time intervals, ranging from every five minutes to once an hour.

Figure 111 shows the location of the sensors. Figure 112 shows a plan of Earthship Brighton. The raw data was collected and recorded on a centralised data-logging system, and were manually downloaded every month and archived (see the Appendix for a list of the sensors). This was not an automated process, and so there are some gaps in the record. Also, a change of personnel at the university meant that data was not collected systematically after March 2007. The weather station was vandalised in September 2006, and so readings for solar radiation and external air temperature are unavailable after that date.

The sensors were placed to measure environmental conditions – ambient air temperature, mean radiant temperature, surface temperature, relative humidity and temperature of the thermal mass – at various heights and depths.

Delta-T Devices supplied the main data logger, and the soil and air temperature sensors. The main data logger was a model DL2e. The soil and air temperature sensors were 2 kΩ thermistors, and the soil sensors were buried in a stainless steel sheath, which was in turn buried in the walls at different

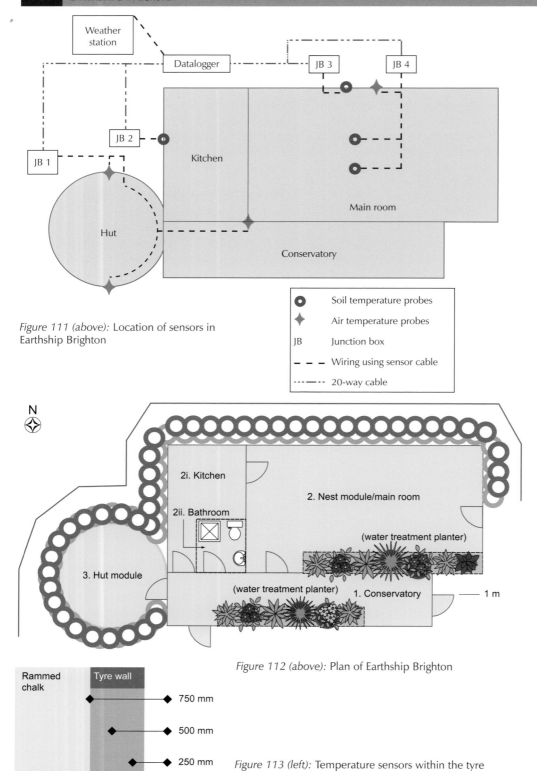

Figure 111 (above): Location of sensors in Earthship Brighton

⊙	Soil temperature probes
✦	Air temperature probes
JB	Junction box
– – –	Wiring using sensor cable
–··–··–	20-way cable

Figure 112 (above): Plan of Earthship Brighton

Figure 113 (left): Temperature sensors within the tyre wall

depths (Figure 113). There were two banks of nine soil sensors, on channels 4 to 12 in the kitchen and 13 to 21 in the main room, buried in the wall in a grid formation at three levels – low (0.63 m), mid (1.26 m) and high (1.89 m) – and then at three corresponding depths – shallow (0.25 m), mid (0.50 m) and deep (0.70 m). The wall sensors were probably slightly deeper than this, because a final layer of mud, approximately 0.025 m thick, was applied to the tyre walls after installation. The soil sensors operate over a range of -20°C to +80°C, with an error factor of ±0.2°C, and have a response time of 6 s[170]. The air temperature sensors operate over a range of -20°C to 60°C, with an error factor of ±0.1°C, and have the same response time. The two mini data loggers were Dickson temperature and humidity loggers[171]. Table A1 in the Appendix summarises the sensors in Earthship Brighton.

Subject to the limitations described above, the data was downloaded from the data loggers once a month, and imported into Microsoft Excel for manipulation and analysis. The quantity of sensors and the frequency of readings meant that a large volume of data was produced. To produce a range of results that highlight the thermal performance of Earthship Brighton, the raw data was treated in a variety of ways. The treatment processes are outlined below.

Data treatment 1: Daily means method

Using macros programmed in Visual Basic, the raw data from the main data logger (sensors 2 to 30) were reduced to hourly readings and averaged to give a daily mean average. The daily mean averages for all these sensors from November 2004 to February 2007 were then compiled to show the basic performance of Earthship Brighton, as a backdrop for closer analysis of the different seasons and the thermal characteristics of the two earthship modules.

The two groups of nine sensors in the thermal mass of the kitchen and main room were averaged, and then balanced in proportion to the volume of thermal mass in each room of the nest module to give a more accurate reflection of the temperature throughout the mass, rather than just take the mean average of all 18 sensors. The hut module also has 58 m³ of thermal mass in its walls, but this was discounted, as there were no soil sensors in the walls.

Results: Comparison of thermal performance of Earthship Brighton with external conditions

The passive solar heating strategy for the earthship is to provide thermal stability through large volumes of thermal mass through the course of the year. Figure 114 presents the daily mean indoor ambient temperature, the balanced average of the thermal mass temperature, external air temperature and external soil temperature, to give a broad overview over the whole period monitored.

The daily mean indoor air temperature is the mean of the temperatures in the conservatory, nest and hut modules. The thermal mass average for the nest module was calculated by taking the average of the two groups of sensors (nine in the kitchen and nine in the main room), and then balancing this using the volume of thermal mass in both rooms. This is significant because of the layout of Earthship Brighton, with the thermal mass in the kitchen receiving less solar gain than that in the main room. For this calculation the thermal mass in the floor has been discounted, as it is not isolated with insulation.

The results in Figure 114 indicate that the thermal performance of Earthship Brighton is cyclic on an annual scale, with peaks around the autumn equinox in September and troughs six months later, around the spring equinox in March. The results reported here will be referred to as the first and second heating and cooling cycles, as there are two peaks and troughs in each annual cycle. Each annual cycle comprises a heating phase and a cooling phase. The first cycle, as discussed below, also includes the pre-cycle period, included to show the trend of cooling from the point where monitoring began in November 2004. The first cycle has a definite peak, whereas the second has two peaks, with the first in July 2006 being slightly warmer that the second around the autumn equinox in mid-September.

The graph also demonstrates the broad trend of a close correlation between the thermal performance of the earthship modules, the thermal mass of the walls, and the external conditions: it follows closely the trend of the seasonal external air temperature. Another trend is that over the whole monitoring period the peak of the internal air and thermal mass temperature rose slightly, although

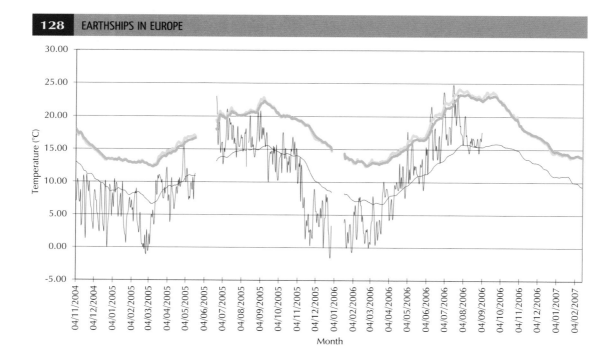

Figure 114: Daily mean indoor ambient temperature, balanced average of the thermal mass temperature, external air temperature and external soil temperature

the lack of data for 2007 makes it unclear whether this is a long-term or short-term trend. According to NASA Goddard Institute for Space Studies (GISS), 2005 was a warmer year than 2006[172].

The internal ambient air temperature is more stable than that of the external environment, which fluctuates over a wider range. This is to be expected. Both the internal and external soil temperatures are stable, although the difference between them is not uniform, and varies throughout the year. Also, during the heating phase of the annual cycles, the average internal ambient air temperature is higher than the balanced average nest thermal mass temperature, whereas during the cooling phase the temperature of the balanced thermal mass is higher than the ambient air temperature. This indicates that there is a flow of thermal energy between the walls of the earthship and the internal air space, providing heating through thermal storage from the warmer part of the cycle.

Results: First heating and cooling cycle, 4 November 2004 to 20 March 2006

The first heating and cooling cycle starts in March 2005, but includes the four months of a pre-cycle period. This is included because the external weather station was removed in September 2006, but it also demonstrates the cyclic nature of the thermal performance. Figure 115 shows the ambient air temperature of the nest and hut modules and the balanced thermal mass of the nest module against external air temperature, and Figure 116 traces the same variables against external soil temperature.

The internal ambient air temperature is more stable than external conditions, although it spends a lot of time below the thermal comfort threshold of 17°C. This will be explored later on. There are two periods of summer overheating as well, although as the data is not cross-referenced against an occupation log it is difficult to know whether the earthship was in use during these days, with the natural ventilation system in operation.

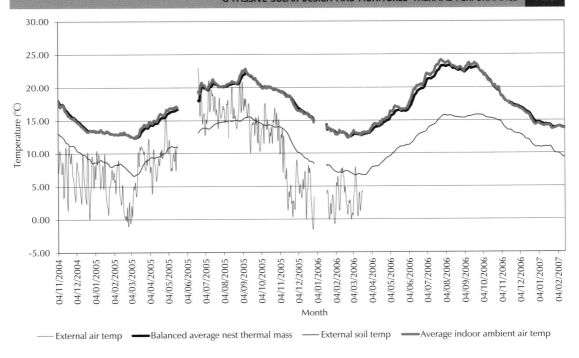

Figure 115: Daily mean of the nest and hut modules and the balanced thermal mass against external air temperature for the first heating and cooling cycle

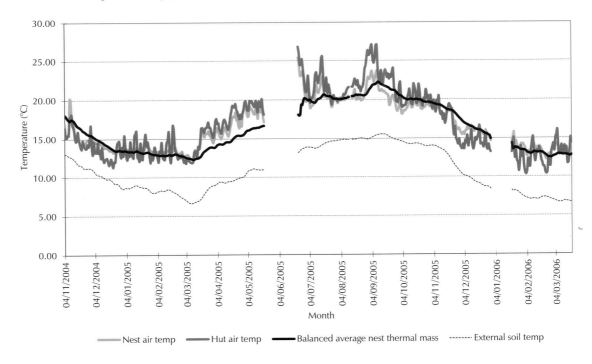

Figure 116: Daily mean of the nest and hut modules and the earth rammed-tyre walls against external earth temperature for the first heating and cooling cycle

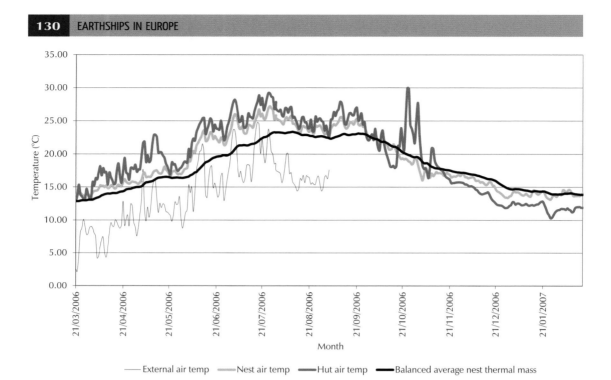

Figure 117: Daily mean of the nest and hut modules and the balanced thermal mass against external air temperature for the second heating and cooling cycle

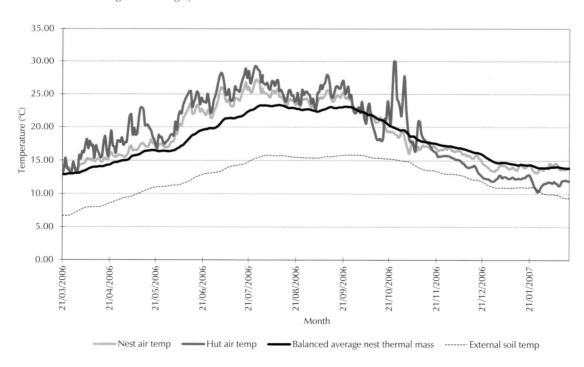

Figure 118: Daily mean of the nest and hut modules and the earth rammed-tyre walls against external earth temperature

The measurements of ambient air temperature show that the hut module, which contains less thermal mass than the nest, warms more quickly during the heating season and cools more rapidly during the cooling season: as a smaller space, it has a faster response to external conditions. Also, the thermal exchange between the thermal mass of the earthship and the internal ambient air temperature during the heating and cooling phase is shown in more detail.

From November 2004 to March 2006, following the first full heating and cooling cycle, the daily balanced mean of the 18 internal soil sensors demonstrates that the thermal mass reached its maximum temperature of 22.22°C on 11 September 2005, and a minimum of 12.33°C on 11 March 2005. It maintained a plateau over 20°C for 78 days between 12 July and 8 October, and although there is data missing from 21 May to 22 June and for 13 and 14 August, the assumption is that the thermal mass remained at over 20°C during the whole period. At the same time, the internal ambient air temperature of the nest module reached a maximum of 35.92°C and a minimum of 11.68°C. Here only the ambient air temperature of the nest module is reported, as the entire thermal mass sensors are located in this module. The maximum and minimum external air temperatures during this period were 29.13°C and -5.45°C, while the external soil temperature reached a maximum of 15.57°C and a minimum of 6.61°C.

Results: Second heating and cooling cycle, 21 March 2006 to 16 February 2007

The second heating and cooling cycle was from March 2006 to February 2007, but was incomplete by a month at the end of the period because of data collection issues. During this cycle the maximum thermal mass temperature was 23.39°C on 29 July 2006, and the minimum daily mean of 12.48°C was on 21 March 2006. The thermal mass reached a plateau over 20°C for 115 days between 30 June and 23 October. On 16 February 2007, the last monitored day, the daily mean was 13.84°C. If the performance of the thermal mass followed the trend of the previous cycle, then data from that period would have shown that the temperature dropped further, and reached a minimum in mid-March.

The internal ambient air temperature of the nest during this period reached a maximum of 29.09°C and a minimum of 12.91°C. The maximum and minimum external air temperatures during this period were 33.54°C and -0.63°C, while the maximum and minimum external soil temperatures were 15.88°C and 6.69°C. The external air temperature data is not available from 4 September onwards, so the maximum and minimum values do not include autumn and winter 2006. Figure 117 shows the daily mean of the nest and hut modules and the balanced thermal mass against external air temperature, and Figure 118 plots the same variables against external soil temperature for this cycle.

The same trends as previously noted are displayed by these results, which indicate the phenomenon of a thermal store or 'battery' charging up over the spring and summer period and discharging its heat back into the building throughout the autumn and winter period to provide a more stable indoor environment. Figures 115 to 118 all demonstrate that the ambient air temperature is higher than that of the thermal mass from March to September, and then the thermal mass is warmer than the ambient air between September and March. This indicates a flow of thermal energy either to or from the air to the walls. The peak in the ambient air temperature in October 2006 was caused by a gas heater being used to dry the walls between applications of mud plaster during the last phase of construction. Otherwise, the pattern of the hut module heating and cooling more rapidly than the nest module is again demonstrated in these graphs.

Results: Thermal mass, difference in thermal performance between walls and floor

Figures 114 to 118 show the thermal performance of the thermal mass in the walls, but there is thermal mass in the floor as well, although it is not isolated by insulation. Figure 119 compares the thermal performance of the daily mean of the balanced thermal mass of the earth rammed-tyre walls with the daily mean thermal mass of the floor against the external earth temperature over the monitored period. The thermal mass of the floor was warmer than the walls from 4 November 2004 to 14 January 2005, 29 June 2005 to 21 January 2006, and

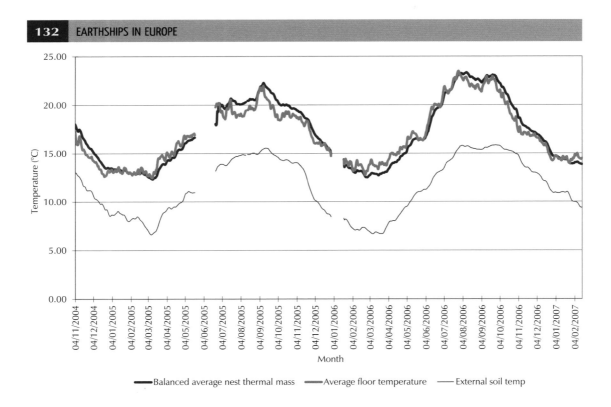

Figure 119: Daily mean of the thermal mass of the walls and floor against external earth temperature

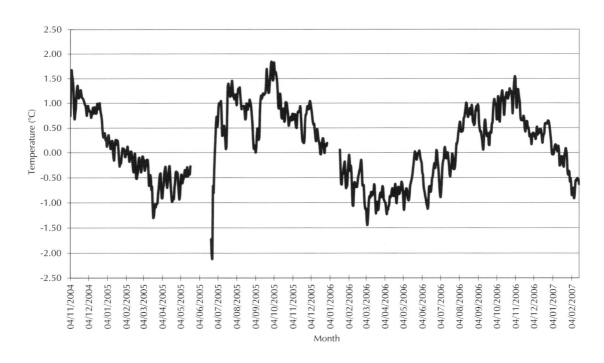

Figure 120: Temperature difference between thermal mass in the walls and thermal mass in the floor in nest module

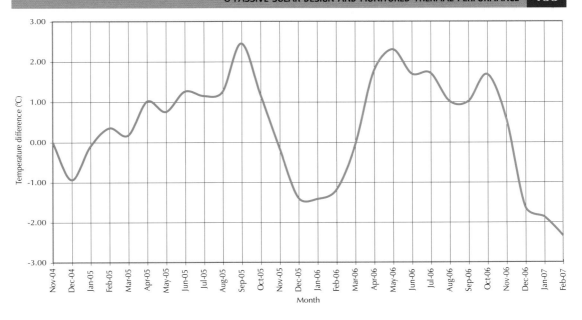

Figure 121: Temperature difference of ambient air temperature between monthly mean hut and nest modules

30 July 2006 to 14 January 2007; it was cooler the rest of the time. This could possibly be due to the lower angle of the sun at these times, meaning a higher incidence of solar radiation on this surface than at other times of the year. However, if this were the case we might be expected to see this effect either side of the winter solstice, which didn't happen.

On average, over the whole period the floor was 0.16°C warmer than the thermal mass of the walls, but there was significant variation, with it being 2.11°C warmer on 25 June 2005 and 1.84°C cooler on 30 September 2005. Figure 120 presents the temperature difference between the two areas of thermal mass over the whole period. The cooler floor will have implications for the perception of thermal comfort for users of the building, particularly as they will feel conductive losses acutely through this surface. It will also impact on the mean radiant temperature.

Results: Difference between internal and external soil temperature

Figure 121 shows the difference in internal and external soil temperature between the external soil sensor and the balanced average mass. This graph is produced from hourly readings over the monitored period. The smallest difference was 3.22°C in January 2007, and the largest was 7.82°C on 29 July 2006. There is an overall upward trend of the internal soil temperature getting warmer from November to October 2006, with a sudden decline until January 2007, and then the internal soil appears to be storing heat again.

Data treatment 2: Minimum, maximum and monthly mean method

The raw data from the main data logger was manipulated to give minimum, maximum and average monthly mean averages over the monitored period. The raw data was left in 10 minute readings to provide a wider sweep of data from which to draw averages.

Results

The overall trend is that the earthship follows the annual heating and cooling cycle of the seasons, but how effective is it at providing a stable indoor environment?

The results indicate that although, on a daily basis, the internal environment of the nest and hut modules is reasonably stable, there are wide

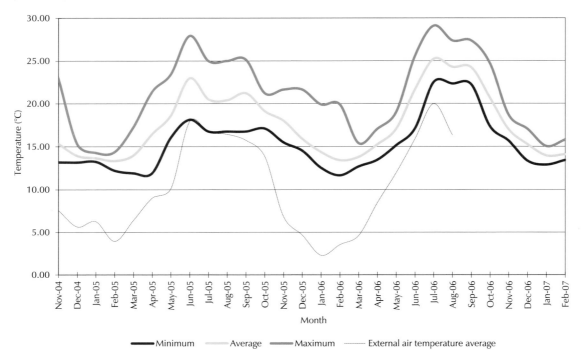

Figure 122: Monthly mean of minimum, maximum and average ambient air temperatures for nest module

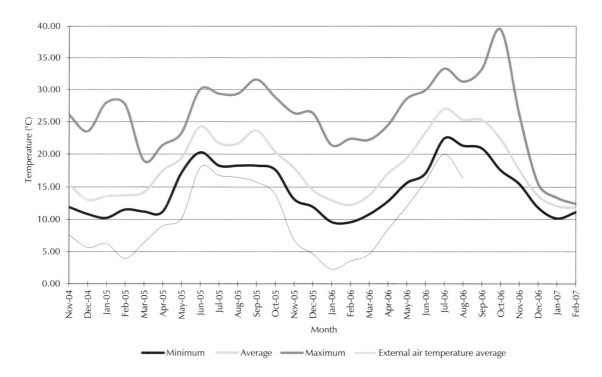

Figure 123: Monthly mean of minimum, maximum and average ambient air temperatures for hut module

variations in temperature. During the monitored period the minimum ambient air temperature in the nest module was 11.68°C in April 2005, and the maximum was 29.09°C in July 2006. The lowest monthly mean temperature was 13.33°C in February 2005, and the highest monthly mean was 25.02°C in July 2006.

In the hut module, the minimum ambient air temperature was 9.57°C in February 2006 and the maximum was 33.26°C in July 2006. The corresponding monthly means of minimum and maximum daily temperatures were 11.74°C in February 2007 and 26.91°C in July 2006. In the hut the actual highest recorded temperature was 39.43°C, but this was during the last phase of construction in October 2006, when a gas heater was used to dry the walls between applications of clay plaster.

Figures 122 and 123 present the monthly mean of the minimum, maximum and mean of ambient air temperatures for Earthship Brighton's nest and hut modules.

Data treatment 3: Incident radiation and internal temperature method

Hourly data was plotted for solar radiation (sensor 28), external air temperature (sensor 27), main room wall temperature (sensor 22), nest ambient air temperature (sensor 31) and hut ambient air temperature (sensor 33).

Results

The resulting graphs demonstrate the earthship's response to solar radiation over a sample of typical weeks and days. Figure 124 shows the internal thermal responses of the conservatory hut and nest modules against the external variables of soil temperature, ambient air temperature and irradiance over a typical winter week in February 2005. It can be seen that on sunny days (7, 8, 13 and 14 February) the hut and conservatory responded quickly to increased levels of irradiance, with air temperature increases of up to 3°C, whereas the nest, with more thermal mass, responded more slowly, with an increase of 0.5°C.

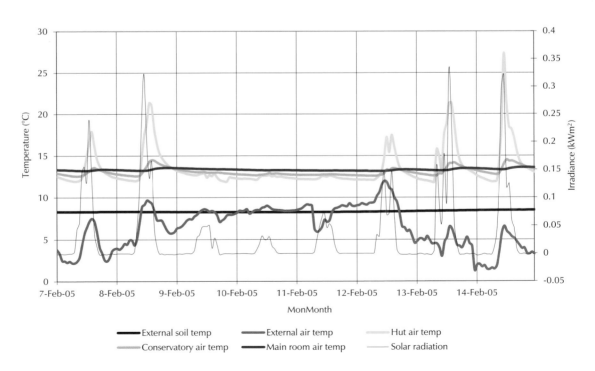

Figure 124: Hourly data for ambient air temperature of conservatory, hut and nest modules, external air temperature, soil temperature and irradiance, 7 to 14 February 2005

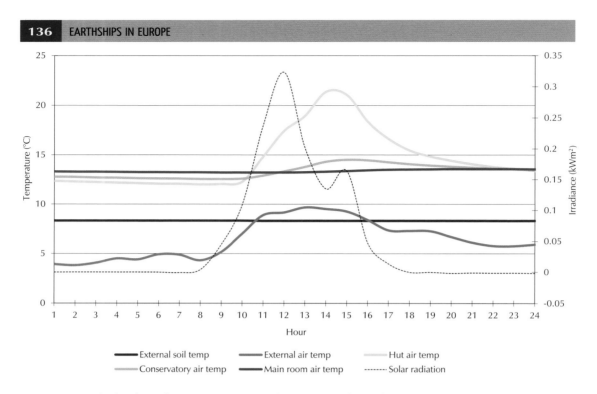

Figure 125: Hourly data for ambient air temperature of conservatory, hut and nest modules, external air temperature, soil temperature and irradiance, 8 February 2005

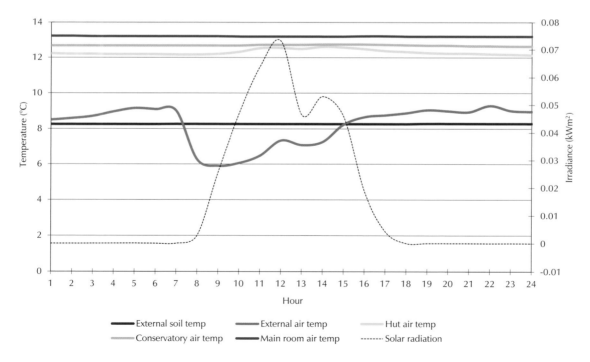

Figure 126: Hourly data for ambient air temperature of conservatory, hut and nest modules, external air temperature, soil temperature and irradiance, 11 February 2005

The nest module retained more heat throughout the whole week, though, and provided a slightly higher ambient air temperature than the hut module, although both modules were stable compared with the fluctuations in external air temperature. During the overcast days of 9, 10 and 11 February, indoor conditions were reliant on the warmth radiated by the thermal mass.

Figure 125 focuses on the detail of 8 February, with high winter levels of irradiance, and Figure 126 shows an occluded day. Figure 127 shows the same variables plotted for a sunny summer week during July 2006, with the peaks further indicating a strong correlation between module ambient air temperate and levels of beam irradiance. Figure 128 shows a day with high levels of irradiance.

The graphs suggest that the earthship responds favourably to increased levels of direct beam irradiance, but not of diffuse radiation. This is one of the differences between the New Mexico and UK climates, and will have a bearing on improving the design for temperate climates.

Data treatment 4: Thermal comfort analysis method

The raw data from the main data logger and the mini data loggers were reduced to hourly readings using macros programmed in VBA and then combined into a single dataset. The sensors used in this method are outlined in Table 23.

Table 23: Thermal comfort analysis method sensors	
Sensor	**Variable measured**
3	Conservatory air temperature
22	Nest module wall temperature
23	Nest module ground temperature
31	Nest module ambient air temperature
32	Nest module relative humidity
33	Hut module ambient air temperature
34	Hut module relative humidity

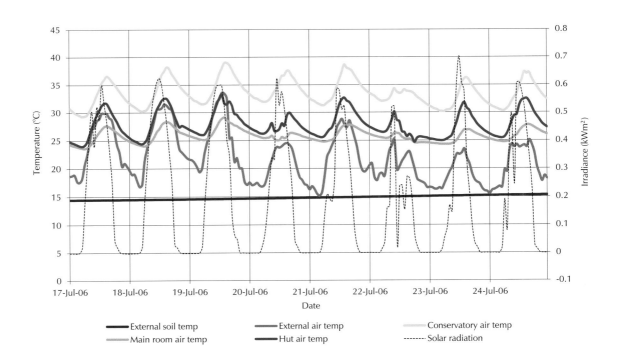

Figure 127: Hourly data for ambient air temperature of conservatory, hut and nest modules, external air temperature, soil temperature and irradiance, 17 to 24 July 2006

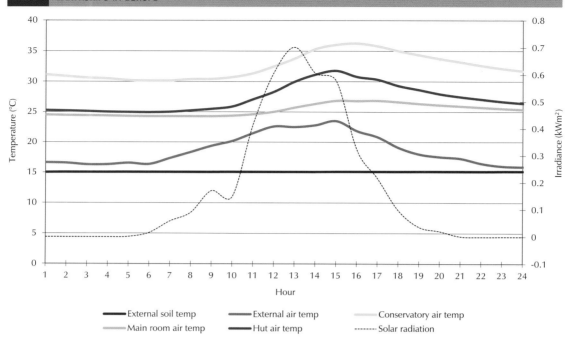

Figure 128: Hourly data for ambient air temperature of conservatory, hut and nest modules, external air temperature, soil temperature and irradiance, 23 July 2006

The dataset was divided into four seasons, with the solstices and equinoxes forming the boundaries. The data was then analysed using a bespoke software tool. The graphs produced from this tool initially show the results for dry resultant temperature and relative humidity separately, but then the two parameters are combined. For the conservatory, only the ambient air temperature was available, as data for mean radiant temperature and relative humidity were not collected. The set of parameters entered was a dry resultant temperature of 17°C to 25°C and a relative humidity of 40% to 70%. These parameters are wide in range, but follow temperatures similar to those at which thermostats are set in housing in the UK[173]. The thermal comfort parameter of convection was not included, in line with *Environmental Guide, CIBSE Guide A*, which states that internal air movement can be disregarded when it is less than 1 m/s[163]. Although the rate of air movement was not monitored, it was assumed that it was below this threshold.

The results are presented in Figures 129 to 135 showing the time in hours for which the rooms were

below the minimum value, between the values, and above the maximum values of the chosen parameters for each season. The dry resultant temperature t_{res} was realised by a combination of ambient air temperature and mean radiant temperature, which is usually expressed with the equation:

$$t_{res} = \frac{t_r + t_{ai}}{2}$$

where t_r is the mean radiant temperature. This is usually a combination of all the surface temperatures. In the nest module it was measured with a black globe radiant sensor (sensor 30), and in the hut module it was measured with sensor 28 after the mini data logger (sensor 33) was installed. The dry bulb temperature, t_{ai}, was measured by the mini data loggers: sensor 31 in the nest, and sensor 33 in the hut.

Results

The results from the previous three data treatments show the indoor climate in terms of ambient air temperature and thermal mass temperature, but for how much of the time would Earthship Brighton be considered to be thermally comfortable? All graphs in this section were produced using a thermal comfort data analysis tool built in Excel. Figures 129 to 131 show the amount of time that the nest module spent between the parameters of a dry resultant temperature of 17°C to 25°C and a relative humidity between 40% and 70%.

Figures 129 and 130 show the conditions of thermal comfort separately, to highlight the detail of each parameter, and Figure 129 combines them. Figure 129 shows that, generally, in autumn and winter the nest module was below the minimum threshold almost all the time, except in autumn

2005, when it was in range for 1568 hours. The first and last seasons on the graph are shorter periods of data, with the autumn monitoring beginning on 4 November 2004 and the winter monitoring ending on 16 February 2007. Spring 2005 and 2006 were also below the minimum of 17°C for 1093 and 929 hours, and were within range for 1115 and 1170 hours respectively. Spring 2006 saw overheating for 109 hours. The summers of 2005 and 2006 saw overheating for 226 and 779 hours, but the nest was within range for 1942 and 1429 hours. Autumn 2005 was within range for 1568 hours, and was below the minimum for the remaining 610 hours.

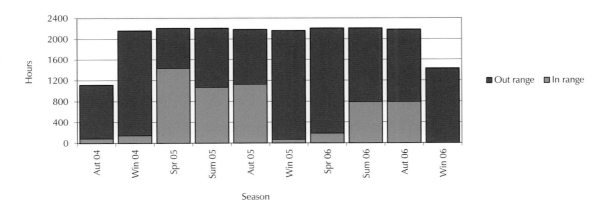

Figure 129: Dry resultant temperature of the nest module between 17°C and 25°C, expressed in hours

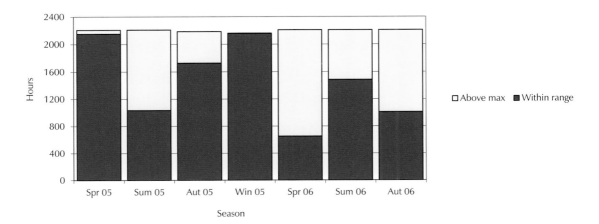

Figure 130: Relative humidity of the nest module between 40% and 70%, expressed in hours

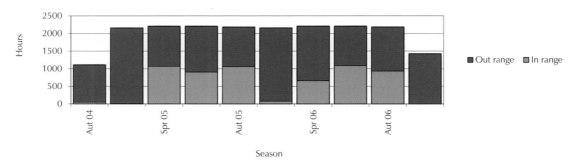

Figure 131: Combined dry resultant temperature between 17°C and 25°C and relative humidity between 40% and 70% in the nest module, expressed in hours

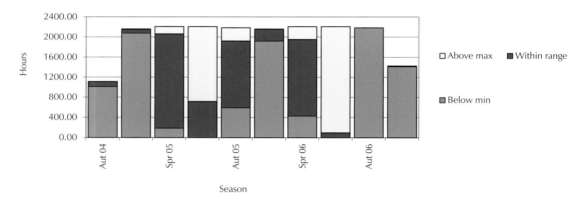

Figure 132: Ambient air temperature of the conservatory between 17°C and 25°C, expressed in hours

Figure 128 shows that the nest module had a very high relative humidity for most of the year, with only winter 2005 being within the 'safe' range of 40% to 70%. The nest module did not drop below the minimum threshold throughout the whole monitoring period. This is probably to do with the high levels of moisture produced by the greywater planters, which prevented relative humidity dropping to an uncomfortably low level. If Earthship Brighton was a house there could be problems with such a high level of humidity, especially in winter, when the only way to ventilate to prevent mould is to open the windows, and therefore lose heat as well as moisture. This issue is discussed in more detail in chapter 9. The levels of relative humidity are similar in the hut module, and this is reported below. Spring 2005, spring 2006 and summer 2006 were all over 70% relative humidity for 50% of the time. Figure 130 shows that the nest module was out of the range of specified conditions during winter, but was in range around 45% of the time during spring, autumn and summer.

Figure 132 demonstrates the ambient air temperature of the conservatory, the room that receives the most solar gain in Earthship Brighton, that has the least thermal mass, and which has large expanses of glass on two sides. The conservatory was designed to be a thermal buffer for the nest module and not really occupied as a usable room, but is included here as it is an interior space. During autumn and winter the conservatory was below 17°C for most of the time, but during summer it overheated for most of the time. Spring 2005, autumn 2005 and spring 2006 were within the range of 17°C to 25°C for 1876, 1327 and 1522 hours respectively. There are no relative humidity or mean radiant temperature data available for the conservatory, so ambient air temperature alone is used as an indicator of thermal comfort. This obviously has limitations.

The next series of graphs (Figures 133 to 135) demonstrate the amount of time that the hut module spent between the parameters of 17°C to 25°C and 40% to 70% relative humidity. The graphs are presented in the same order as for the nest module as reported above: first dry resultant temperature and relative humidity reported separately, and then combined. The patterns are similar to the results for the nest module.

Figure 133 shows that in autumn and winter the hut module was below 17°C for virtually all of the time. As previously reported, the monitoring of Earthship Brighton began in November 2004, so the autumn 2004 season runs from 4 November to 20 December. Also, the monitoring period ended in February 2007, so the last winter season lacks data from 16 February to 20 March. This means that the warmer days of the autumn 2004 and winter 2006 seasons are not included in the data, which will affect the results.

In 2005 the hut module was within the 17°C to 25°C range for 1435, 1835 and 1453 hours during spring, summer and autumn respectively. The hut overheated for 373 hours and 49 hours during summer and autumn, and was below the minimum threshold for 770 hours and 682 hours during spring and autumn. In 2006 the hut was in range for 900 hours and 1302 hours in spring and summer; it overheated for 141 hours and 1308 hours during the same months, and was below the minimum for 766 hours during spring.

Figure 134 shows that the hut module had a very high relative humidity for most of the year, with only

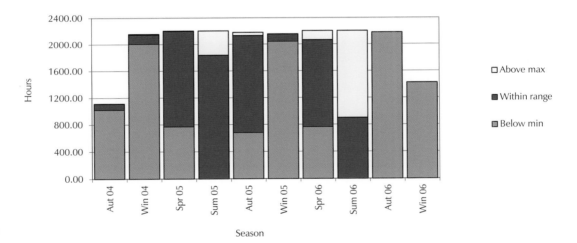

Figure 133: Dry resultant temperature of the hut module between 17°C and 25°C, expressed in hours

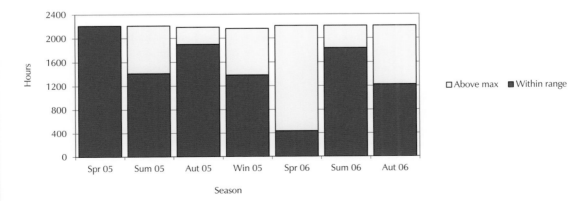

Figure 134: Relative humidity of the hut module between 40% and 70%, expressed in hours

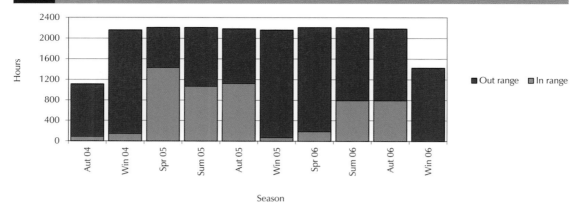

Figure 135: Combined dry resultant temperature between 17°C and 25°C and relative humidity between 40% and 70% in the hut module, expressed in hours

spring 2005 being constantly within the 40% to 70% range. Summer, autumn and winter 2005 were over 70% relative humidity for 796, 285 and 776 hours, and spring, summer and autumn 2006 were in range for 435, 1834 and 1224 hours respectively.

Figure 135 shows that the hut module of Earthship Brighton was out of the range of the specified thermal comfort conditions for most of winter, although it was within the parameters for around 50% of the time in spring, summer and autumn 2005, and for 36% and 37% in summer and autumn 2006.

SUMMARY OF FINDINGS

The results show that Earthship Brighton is functioning as a passive solar building and provides a thermally comfortable, stable environment for some of the year, but not during autumn and winter. Additional heating would be required during these seasons. There are factors that need to be taken into consideration when interpreting the results. For example, the building was unoccupied during the monitoring period, which means that there were very few incidental heat gains from cooking, lighting or body heat. Windows and doors weren't opened to increase ventilation during overheating in summer. An occupancy log wasn't recorded, so it's impossible to see how the building responded when people were actually using it. Finally, it would have been valuable to conduct some post-occupancy

evaluation to assess how people felt during their experience of using the earthship, to add a human dimension to the data.

The key points from the thermal monitoring of Earthship Brighton are as follows.
- The heating and cooling of the thermal mass in the walls are cyclic on an annual basis, and closely follow external conditions.
- The thermal mass in the walls gains heat on a gradient during spring and summer, and is warmest at the autumn equinox. It loses heat during autumn and winter, and is coolest at the spring equinox.
- During spring and summer the average internal ambient air temperature is higher than the balanced average nest thermal mass temperature, whereas during autumn and winter the balanced thermal mass is warmer than the ambient air. This indicates a flow of thermal energy between the walls of the earthship and the internal air space, providing some passive heating during cold periods.
- Over the whole monitoring period the annual peaks of internal air temperature and thermal mass temperature rise slightly, although there is a lack of data to indicate whether there is a trend of the thermal mass 'charging up'.
- The uninsulated floor in the nest module is, on average, 1°C warmer than the walls during spring and summer, but 1°C cooler during autumn and winter. This is probably due to solar gain on this surface during the

warmer parts of the year. The thermal mass in the hut wall and floor was not monitored for comparison.

- The hut module, which contains less thermal mass than the nest, warms more quickly during spring and summer, and cools more rapidly during the autumn and winter, indicating a faster response to external conditions.
- The earthship responds better to direct radiation than to diffuse radiation. This is a crucial difference between the New Mexico and UK climates, and will have a bearing on improving the design for European temperate climates.
- The nest module during autumn and winter is mostly below the minimum threshold for thermal comfort.
- The nest module has a very high relative humidity for most of the year, probably due to evaporation from the greywater planters. This could be a problem in colder climates, where the only way to prevent mould growth in winter would be to increase ventilation. This will have energy implications.
- The nest module overheats by a small amount in summer.

- The hut module was not thermally comfortable for most of winter, and is comfortable for only around 50% of spring, summer and autumn.
- The hut module overheats a lot in summer.

CONCLUSION

Although earthships have been built all over the world, the earthship concept was originally designed as a response to a specific climate. Currently there are very limited data reporting on how they perform in temperate climates, and there are no residential examples in Europe that have been consistently monitored. To successfully transfer the concept to Europe as a housing model, the current earthships that have been built need to be studied in depth and their thermal performance needs to be analysed to see whether they perform effectively. If they don't, then suitable design changes will be needed to improve thermal comfort in a temperate climate. The next and final chapter of this book makes several design recommendations based on these findings.

Rear entrance to the Happy Castle earthship at night
(Taos, New Mexico) © Kirsten Jacobsen

9 CONCLUSION: THE FUTURE OF EARTHSHIPS IN EUROPE

INTRODUCTION

'The inventors of the automobile perhaps had visions of faster, smoother vehicles rolling on wheels, such as the cars we have today; however, the best they could produce with their current industry and technology was the Model T. Likewise, our current technology today makes earthships barely functional, perhaps even crude, relative to the vision of the concept. It is only a step away from the dependent house, but it is a significant step. Future earthships will keep evolving toward that vision, as a Model T evolved into a 1990 Porsche.' Mike Reynolds[174]

The export of a US product – the earthship – to a European market seems to have suffered from some issues of translation. In 10 years there have been fewer than 10 earthships built in Europe, compared with the hundreds that now exist in the USA. And many of those that have begun construction have faced significant problems. Some, such as those at Greenhead Moss in Scotland and Växhuset in Sweden, have been abandoned mid-project after years of hard work (as a result of arson and lack of funds respectively). Others, such as Earthship Valencia, have taken many years to complete. And of those that have been finished, some, including Earthship Brighton and Earthship Zwolle, have not lived up to their full thermal performance potential – a basic requirement for earthships to fulfil their brief in reducing stress both on the planet and on the individual inhabitants.

Meanwhile, more ambitious plans for earthships in Europe, such as a multi-unit development in Brighton Marina, have been put to one side. There is plenty to celebrate as well, though – and this book is determinedly not about doom and gloom for European earthships. The pioneering builds across Europe have tested regulatory positions on several contentious points, such as building with waste, harvesting and treating potable water, and gaining planning permission for an unconventional structure. They have created precedents, built expertise, made mistakes and learned lessons that should all be useful for future earthship builders in Europe. Projects such as Earthship Brighton have provoked large-scale media coverage that has increased awareness of issues such as energy, waste and water use. Reports from occupants of residential builds such as the Groundhouse and Earthship Valencia have been very positive: they love what they have built.

Yet the fact that there have been so few completed projects suggests that earthships are living up to their reputation as a fringe type of building. For a variety of reasons they seem unlikely to be built in any great quantity in the foreseeable future – certainly not as mainstream housing, but not even by many self-builders. This may have something to do not just with the practical reasons that this chapter will examine in more detail, but also with the fact that they are distinctively American in many ways. Much of the USA's twentieth-century culture was built around the mythology of the motor car and the open road: the drive-thru, Kerouac's *On the Road*, out-of-town shopping malls, road movies such as *Thelma and Louise*, *Easy Rider*, *Wild at Heart* and *Fear and Loathing in Las Vegas*, and the cultural significance of highways such as Route 66, which have been at the heart of literature, cinema and popular music. The freedom to drive is regarded almost as a civil right on a par with the right to bear arms – one of the reasons why the USA has extremely low petrol prices relative to many other developed nations. And the earthship, first built out of old car tyres in a part of remote New Mexico accessible only by road, is also an homage – of sorts – to the motorcar. Mike Reynolds, a rugged, counter-culture, outlaw American individualist in the tradition of Henry David Thoreau,

Hunter S Thompson, Ken Kesey and Bill Hicks, makes an interesting analogy between earthships and cars:

'The automobile was an invention and a vision; however, this vision was limited. The inventors did not envision the planet filled with millions of cars emitting carbon monoxide, or cities filled with traffic jams, making life so unhealthy one could barely walk down the sidewalk. The car has evolved to the point where it could be the wrong thing now, due to the fumes, noise, pollution, the dependency on oil, and the stress it puts on the planet. The concept of moving along in a capsule may be fine, but there needs to be a new kind of vessel. The concept of a gasoline-fueled vessel must be evolved beyond the dependency on gasoline, the emission of pollutants and the noise. Likewise, the house must be developed into a new kind of vessel.'
Mike Reynolds[174]

Earthships are as much about autonomy and self-sufficiency as they are about a green lifestyle. Perhaps the individualistic self-sufficiency movement is weaker in Europe, where there is in general a lesser car culture, a more substantial public transport infrastructure, and a more developed welfare state. Arguably one of the most successful European earthships – near Valencia, in Spain – was built by people who were interested primarily not in reducing their carbon emissions, but in self-sufficiency and escaping from what they saw as the onerous financial system. This 'cultural baggage' – the issue of translation between the USA and Europe – might be one of the reasons why so few earthships have been built in Europe. This is a speculative point, certainly, but one that seems reasonable and germane to make.

We invited Mike Reynolds to participate in the writing of this book, but he declined to talk to the authors. This is a pity, as it was always our hope to spark off a constructive dialogue about the future of earthships in Europe, and this would have benefited from a contribution by their inventor – and still the most active global practitioner of earthship building. Nonetheless, in this chapter we summarise the findings we've presented in this book, and make recommendations as to how earthships can be improved, particularly in European climates. Ultimately we answer the question as to whether earthships will remain a marginal activity in Europe,

pursued by a few brave pioneers, or whether the pioneer spirit will at some point seep into the mainstream.

SUMMARY OF FINDINGS

The first edition of this book focused on what earthships could potentially teach the industry sectors of architecture and housebuilding in the UK as they began to face up to the challenges of responding to climate change by designing and building more ecologically sound housing. This edition, by contrast, has focused much more on earthships themselves, and the geographical scope has broadened to take in all of Europe. In part, we chose this new focus because it seems that the stated aspirations of earthships are not always being achieved. People building earthships do not always end up living the dream they set out to find. That is not always the fault of the building, but it does seem reasonable to investigate what has gone wrong. There is also a risk of earthships being entirely superseded as a form of environmental architecture by more rigorously designed and tested approaches such as Passivhaus[175]. If people genuinely want effective thermal performance with minimal heating bills and low carbon emissions, then it's likely that, unless earthships evolve, they can find other, better buildings to achieve this. But that's clearly not the only reason why people are attracted to earthships.

One of the main themes apparent in most of Mike Reynolds' writing is that of evolution. He has consistently stated, as in the above quote, in which he makes a comparison with cars, that the earthship concept needs to evolve. He says that by giving individual homeowners the tools to tweak their own building so that it performs at an optimum level, the potential for evolution is greater than when decision making is centralised. By compiling the experiences of earthship builders in Europe, as well as publishing data and analysis on thermal performance, airtightness and other measurements, we hope to contribute to developing the earthship concept in some small way, and give potential European earthship builders of the future the tools and knowledge to make their buildings the best they can possibly be, by learning lessons from the projects that have been built so far.

THE EUROPEAN EARTHSHIPS

The qualitative data taken from six main case studies of European builds is limited by being relatively small in number – although there are only a couple of other earthships that would have been interesting to include in detail (Zwolle and Skerray), and we were unable to get detailed accounts of either build. The main thing we wanted to present was simply the real stories and experiences of the people who had undertaken the experiment of building earthships in Europe. As such, the book is not so much data as pure narrative. This section summarises what we consider to be notable points of interest and key themes, rather than presenting a scientific analysis.

Of the six featured builds, four were private (ie residential family homes) and two were public (visitor/information centres). The two public builds (Earthship Brighton and Earthship Fife) took place in the UK; two of the residential builds were in Spain and two were in France. We also looked in brief at other builds, either in progress or abandoned, in Belgium, England, Estonia, Holland, Jersey, Scotland and Sweden.

One obvious finding is that many earthships have taken a long time to build in Europe: Earthship Valencia took seven years from start to finish; Earthship Almeria (unfinished) has taken more than four years to date; Earthship Greenhead Moss took 18 months, and was then abandoned after an arson attack; and Earthship Brighton took three years. It is difficult to assess whether this is a problem or not, as there are many issues that affect how long any building takes to get built. Dave Buchanan and Laura Davies in Almeria seem happy to go at their own pace, and have no apparent desire to speed up the process. Earthship Valencia and Earthship Brighton both took a long time primarily because of cash flow issues. And Earthship France and the Groundhouse both showed that earthships can be built speedily in Europe: Earthship France required only 26 weeks onsite and the Groundhouse took two years. No European projects have been particularly hindered by bureaucratic delays.

Project budgets have varied enormously, with relatively expensive builds for Earthship France and Earthship Brighton (£188,000 and £330,000 respectively) comparing unfavourably with those in Valencia, Fife and Almeria at €63,000, £50,000 and €17,000 (the last is anticipated rather than actual budget) respectively[176].

EUROPEAN THERMAL PERFORMANCE FINDINGS

Five of the six builds have been constructed relatively conventionally, following the main principles established in New Mexico, and either using plans drawn up by Mike Reynolds himself or using his books as their main guide. But the Groundhouse made a provocative departure from some of those principles. In particular, it is connected to the mains electrical and water systems, rather than being autonomous in these respects. It also has an insulated floor with underfloor heating, in contrast to the others, which have all followed Mike Reynolds' prescription of remaining in direct contact with the earth. This measure was taken to try to eliminate the heat loss that seems inevitable with an uninsulated floor, which may have contributed to thermal performance below expectations in builds in temperate climates, including Earthships France, Brighton and Zwolle. Gillian Trott suggested various improvements that might be made to Earthship France to improve its thermal performance, including having porches at both entrances to the building, and a greenhouse to act as thermal buffers. It is difficult to establish how effective Daren Howarth's measures at the Groundhouse have been in terms of thermal performance, as there has been no rigorous monitoring, although anecdotal reports suggest that the building has maintained a consistently comfortable temperature. Other measures may have reduced the building's thermal performance, though, such as having an 'operable' front face that can open up in the summer (increased risk of draughts), and no greenhouse at the front of the building.

More extensive thermal monitoring in Brighton, as detailed in chapter 8, points to significant shortcomings with thermal performance, although with the caveat that there has not been anyone living in the property, and therefore there has been none of the background heat that would be associated with activities such as cooking. On the other hand, it gives an insight into how an earthship might operate as a free-running, zero-energy building.

Earthship Valencia has suffered occasionally in the hot Spanish summers from the opposite problem to that which has troubled some of the northern European earthships – overheating. Oscar Briz and Lisa-Jane Roberts have mitigated this by installing exterior fabric sunshades. Further south in Spain, Dave Buchanan and Laura Davies plan to use a *brise soleil* – creeping plants that are in leaf in the hotter months, trained on an overhanging trellis – to achieve the same effect.

Thermal performance is the single most critical aspect of earthships. Reducing the space heating requirement is the biggest factor in cutting running costs to a minimum, so if the thermal performance is not adequate, extra energy has to be pumped into the house in order to heat its occupants – a key criterion of what Mike Reynolds called a 'dependent home'. This inevitably has both carbon and financial implications. But there are other costs that may create problems for the concept of reducing financial stress on the occupants. Maintenance costs are lower than in a conventional home but they still exist: earthships are not houses with zero bills.

Despite the problems that are recorded here, the people who have built earthships in Europe are generally proud of them, and are impressed by what the buildings do. Gillian Trott said that Earthship France is a 'fantastic building', and that she has been impressed by the very low maintenance costs. Oscar Briz and Lisa-Jane Roberts describe living off-grid as being 'miraculous', and although they have run out of electricity once, they feel they have now mastered the art of tailoring their consumption to the amount

Figure 136: Earthship Valencia with blinds © Lisa-Jane Roberts and Oscar Briz

they are able to generate. Daren Howarth writes in the book he wrote about the experience of building the Groundhouse that 'Our home has been great to live in.' Kevin McCloud, presenter of Channel 4 TV show Grand Designs, wrote that:

'The magical most powerful force in our lives ... comes from within us and our collective ability to organise, invent, create and transform inhospitable corners of the universe into places that lift the soul. The Groundhouse and its garden is one such corner.' Kevin McCloud[177]

Meanwhile, Earthship Brighton and Earthship Fife have attracted tens of thousands of visitors between them, providing tours, information, training courses and workshops on themes relating to green building and sustainable living[178].

SUMMARY OF DATA FINDINGS FOR EARTHSHIP BRIGHTON AND WIDER IMPLICATIONS

Detailed climate monitoring, U-value calculations and the only known airtightness test on an earthship have so far taken place at Earthship Brighton only, and one of our key recommendations is that monitoring and evaluation of earthships needs to take place more widely, to help increase understanding of how they are performing. This is crucial to enable the concept to evolve; it needs to be rigorously tested so that its claims and aspirations can be independently scrutinised. Only anecdotal findings are available for all the other earthships across Europe – indeed, for those in all other parts of the world as well – and the information is both mixed and to some extent unreliable, because there is no described methodology.

The data from Earthship Brighton also has obvious limitations when assessing the earthship design concept in general; the conditions are specific both in terms of the build itself, and also in terms of the climate, but it is the most in-depth information available. A further significant limitation of the Earthship Brighton example is that it is not residential, and therefore does not benefit from a variety of human inputs or 'incidental heat gains', such as cooking, the use of other appliances that generate heat, and the body warmth of occupants.

However, we believe that the similarities in design between the earthships that closely follow the Reynolds' plans, and commonalities in some climate types, such as the temperate climates of Scotland (Earthship Fife), Earthship Brighton, Normandy (Earthship France), Brittany (the Groundhouse), and Holland (Earthship Zwolle), as shown in the Nicol graphs in chapter 7 (Figures 78, 81, 85 and 95), mean that recommendations can be made beyond just looking at Earthship Brighton in isolation. The Köppen climate classification for the Spanish builds is mid-latitude desert, which is considerably different from marine west coast, but closely resembles the original climate type in which earthships were first designed in New Mexico, although with less harsh winters. Therefore it is more difficult to make any meaningful connections between the Earthship Brighton results and the anecdotal reports received relating to their performance. Unfortunately there is no direct performance data for either of the Spanish builds.

Anecdotal reports detailed in this book from Earthship France and Earthship Zwolle have indicated that they have both suffered from thermal comfort that has fallen below expectations, and damp issues in winter. This is in line with the findings from Earthship Brighton, which indicated that the internal temperature in the main nest module fell below minimum comfort levels for most of the time in autumn and winter, and that humidity levels were consistently high throughout the year. This demonstrates that in a temperate climate the earthship in its current guise is not a zero-energy building, and that a backup heating system is essential. In winter the increased ventilation required to deal with the high indoor humidity and prevent the concomitant damp problems would have significant thermal consequences; this is discussed below. The hut module in Earthship Brighton was not thermally comfortable for most of the winter, and is comfortable for only around 50% of spring, summer and autumn. It also overheats during the summer months. The nest module experienced only marginal overheating during summer, probably of a level that would have been offset if it had been inhabited and windows had been opened.

Thermal mass in passive solar buildings is most effective when the heat gains it is designed to store and deliver as a heat source in colder times are kept within an airtight building envelope. This prevents infiltration (draughts) from cooler ambient air dissipating the heat that has been collected. At Earthship Brighton the infiltration rate was measured by an air leakage or permeability test by Air Leakage Testing Ltd, which conducted a test on Earthship Brighton on 18 December 2008. The test was the standard test, conducted under conventions outlined in Building Regulations 2006 Part L: Conservation of Fuel and Power[179]. The test involved replacing one of the doors with a fan and cover, and then pressurising the building up to 50 Pa. Under current Building Regulations the minimum standard for air leakage in new-build housing is 10 ach (air changes per hour) at 50 Pa. The air leakage rate at Earthship Brighton was 8.43 ach at 50 Pa. Although this is within UK Building Regulation limits, it is actually a very poor result for a low-energy building. For comparison, the

requirement for Passivhaus buildings is a maximum of 0.6 ach. In the UK, to ensure a good indoor air quality, the Energy Saving Trust recommends a maximum level of 5 ach for naturally ventilated buildings (such the earthship), or 3 ach for mechanically ventilated homes[180].

BUILDING WITH WASTE FINDINGS

Building with what is legally classified as waste across Europe (tyres) remains potentially problematic, depending on how legislation is interpreted at a local level. In Belgium, earthship builders have been forced to build with bags rather than tyres. In England (but not, it seems, in Scotland, where the SEPA take a more pragmatic view), the Environment Agency has been anxious to avoid setting what it sees as precedents by granting permits for building with tyres. Instead it has been issuing exemptions from the requirement to have a permit. But as the number of tyre-wall buildings increases, there are more and more precedents across Europe for building with waste. There needs to be more definitive work done on whether building with tyres is an entirely benign activity. At present, the balance of probability suggests that it is, but some in situ and laboratory-based air quality monitoring would mean this could become a definitive statement – a great weapon in all earthship builders' armoury. If more work is done on airtightness in earthships (as we recommend below), then laying this ghost to rest will become increasingly important, as there is more potential for a build-up of VOCs through lower rates of background infiltration.

Gaining planning permission and complying with Building Regulations have been largely unproblematic for earthships across Europe. There have been other legislation issues. In Brighton the WOM is being redesigned to comply with legislation on water quality; this is discussed below. In summary, the case studies of existing earthships across Europe should open up the possibilities for building in new countries that don't yet have earthships. In those countries where precedents for gaining planning permission have already been achieved, new builders should expect to gain planning permission on the same terms as if they were building any other structure.

Figure 137: Blower door test at Earthship Brighton
© Mischa Hewitt

POWER FINDINGS

All of the European earthships have extensive onsite renewable energy systems, harvesting power from solar, wind and water. Most are off-grid, store electricity in batteries, and have Earthship Biotecture designed power organising modules. How effective these systems are, time will tell. One project has challenged the idea that earthships need to be entirely autonomous of all centralised services: The Groundhouse has dual systems for electricity, space heating, hot water and mains water supply, meaning that if anything goes wrong with its onsite renewable energy systems, then it has mains backup. It also allows the occupants to sell back to the grid any electricity they generate but do not use, creating income and – in theory, at least – a stronger financial case. Self-sufficiency may not always be the most sustainable option; batteries, and the energy implications of water self-sufficiency, sometimes mean that the infrastructure route may be the greenest. It seems sensible to make pragmatic decisions rather than to dogmatically follow the traditional 'one size fits all' earthship route. This may mean working out at the beginning of a project whether autonomy or sustainability is the highest priority; they don't always mean the same thing.

WATER FINDINGS

All the European earthships have rainwater harvesting, greywater and blackwater recycling facilities. The details of the systems vary, but all projects are rural, meaning that they are sited on fairly large plots and have room for onsite waste water treatment. Once urban earthship projects are developed, such as the Lizard project in Brighton, it will be interesting to see whether the theme of land-hungry waste water treatment systems will continue.

Most of the European earthships have Earthship Biotecture WOM systems. The systems can be described as experimental and should therefore be monitored closely, not only to prove their long-term viability, but also to show that they provide wholesome water to occupants. As discussed in chapter 6, consistent monitoring of water systems over the next couple of years would allow more robust design for the next generation of European earthships.

DESIGN RECOMMENDATIONS

This section outlines the design recommendations, based on our research and reflecting European best practice. The focus is on improving the thermal performance of earthships in temperate climates. What follows is a set of design guidelines that aims to reduce thermal losses from conduction and convection by upgrading the external building fabric, re-detailing the external elements to remove thermal bridges where possible, reducing the air leakage rate, adding an efficient auxiliary heating system, and possibly introducing a mechanical ventilation with heat recovery (MVHR) system. A more comprehensive set of design guidelines covering all areas of building sustainability is not included here, including the specification of all building services, material choices and other factors. The earthship is a concept, not an energy standard, nor a specific built form, nor an architectural style – and yet the manifestation is always the same. Let's evolve the concept more rapidly!

Well-insulated structure

Each earthship design should be specifically tailored to suit the climate it's being built in, but a rule of thumb should be that all the external fabric of the earthship should have a minimum U-value of 0.15 W/m²K. This includes the ground floor, external walls (both earth sheltered and timber frame), and roofs. This will reduce conductive and convective losses through the structure, and is especially important for all elements that are in contact with the ground. In a temperate climate, 'connection to the earth' is a constant source of thermal loss rather than being beneficial for passive cooling, as might be the case in climates where cooling is a significant factor, such as in the Mediterranean or New Mexico. As well as the opaque fabric, the glazing should be upgraded as well. On the south elevation, where solar gain is the main consideration, the windows and doors should be high-specification double glazing. On other elevations triple glazing should be specified, ideally with a U-value less than 0.8 W/m²K. This glazing regime will allow the maximum flow of solar energy through the south glazing, while accepting the thermal losses associated with double instead of triple glazing. In any case, all glazing should have a g-value (solar transmission) of at least 60%, to avoid increased electrical demand during daytime due to a low daylight factor. On all other façades the important thing is to minimise thermal losses. In addition, the glazing should be detailed so that there is an overlap of the insulation over the frame, reducing heat loss and air movement at these junctions. The addition of a greenhouse, while acting as a 'thermal buffer' on the front of an earthship, will reduce the direct energy flow.

Minimising thermal bridges

The external fabric should be designed to limit and, if possible, eliminate thermal bridges: that is, the fabric should have a continuous uninterrupted insulation layer around it. This will isolate any thermal mass within the structure, and improve its performance. Also, any repeating thermal bridging patterns should be avoided where possible. This guideline is especially important for all elements that are in contact with the earth to reduce this source of constant thermal loss, as the external earth temperature at Earthship Brighton demonstrates. Therefore floor slabs should be insulated with at least 200 mm of insulation. This guideline would also involve evaluating and redesigning the timber and glass front façade to include insulation, as discussed above. This guideline is a development of the previous guideline to encapsulate the whole envelope and is demonstrated in Figures 138 to 140.

Airtightness and detailing

The earthship should be detailed to be airtight to the maximum rate of 3 ach at 50 Pa if reliance is on natural ventilation, or for this rate to be much lower if mechanical ventilation is specified – ideally down to 0.6 ach at 50 Pa. This would include a continuous, airtight barrier around the whole structure, with an airtight junction where all services could be rationalised where they enter or exit the building. This would significantly reduce convective losses, but if greywater planters are included, then to maintain good indoor air quality in winter, to avoid opening windows a different ventilation strategy from the traditional earthship model would be required (see guideline below). At the moment the tyre walls are airtight, but the junction between the tyre wall and the timber frame is weak. This, and the front timber frame, would need careful attention.

Ventilation system

Ideally the earthship should have an MVHR system installed to reduce heat loss through ventilation during the colder parts of the year, and to improve indoor air quality. The high humidity levels observed in monitoring in Earthship Brighton, and anecdotally in Earthships France and Zwolle, suggest that this is an urgent requirement in temperate climates, to avoid damp and mould growth – and even more so if significant improvements in airtightness are achieved. This requirement would be less if the internal greywater planters were removed.

The current natural ventilation system could be left in place for summer ventilation, and at other times when people want to open the windows. Therefore the earthship's ventilation system would be mixed mode, although natural and mechanical ventilation cannot be used at the same time. Skylights would need to be redesigned to reduce infiltration at these points, and they would also need to adhere to the fabric U-values as outlined above. This guideline is a radical departure from conventional earthship wisdom, where no attention to airtightness is currently observed. In addition, the provision of mechanical ventilation would have an energy impact that would need to be factored into the design of the electrical systems.

Auxiliary heating system

The earthship should have a biomass backup heating system to provide a thermally comfortable environment in winter and other cooler parts of the year. Ideally, biomass would be sourced from locally sourced coppice. Other fuels could be considered, such as LPG or mains gas, but these would have implications for the autonomous nature of the earthship. This guideline has been informed by the results from Earthship Brighton's thermal performance and other published academic papers. The auxiliary system could also supply domestic hot water in winter.

IMPLICATIONS

The above recommendations all have implications, and this section will look at these and potential benefits by considering the increased financial cost of installation, changes to the construction process, and finally the reduction of summer overheating.

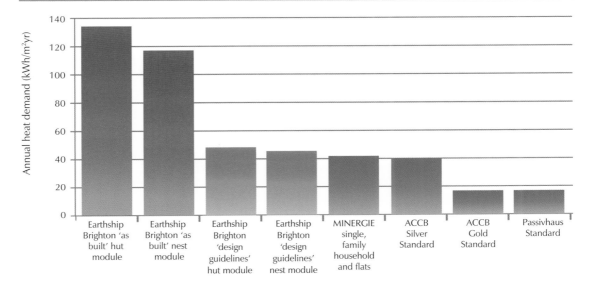

Figure 138: Comparison of Earthship Brighton computer models and European low-energy standards for space heating requirements

All the design guidelines have been modelled using computer software, but all of them reflect European best-practice low-energy design. Figure 138 shows the results for space heating requirements from the modelling, using both 'as built' and design guidelines models for Earthship Brighton, and then compares them with various European low-energy standards. The assumption behind the model is that residents use heating for a few hours each day at a set point of 17°C. As can be seen, if energy is used to heat an earthship, then thanks to all the typical features discussed earlier in the book (a connection to the earth, a small amount of insulation in the walls, an uninsulated floor slab, a low level of airtightness, and lack of attention to thermal bridges), the amount of energy required on an annual basis for space heating is far above European best-practice energy standards. If the design guidelines outlined above are adopted, then the energy requirement is halved, but it is still around three times the amount of energy required for buildings designed to the Passivhaus standard. Detailed modelling and optimisation of the earthship using the latest design tools, such as the Passivhaus Planning Package, could enable it to reach this level of energy use[181]. For example, the design guidelines computer model was not tested using the thermal-

bridge-free envelope design guidelines. Of course, there are limitations with any model, but once the need for auxiliary heating is accepted, as various academic papers and the results in the last section have indicated, then the amount of heat required for acceptable thermal comfort becomes paramount. As the earthship is not zero energy, there is a clear and pressing need for this to be addressed.

Increased financial cost of installation

The design guidelines should offer the benefit of increased levels of thermal comfort with reduced operational costs. Once built, the earthship should be cheaper to run, although the design guidelines model results in Figure 138 indicate that the annual heat requirement is still fairly high compared with other forms of low-energy housing. A full cost benefit analysis would be useful to ascertain how long it would take for the passive measures to effectively pay for themselves, compared with a conventional house. There is some debate as to how quickly the capital costs of such features are offset by reduced operational costs[182].

All the design guidelines would have slightly increased upfront capital costs during construction, because of upgrades to the building fabric: the use

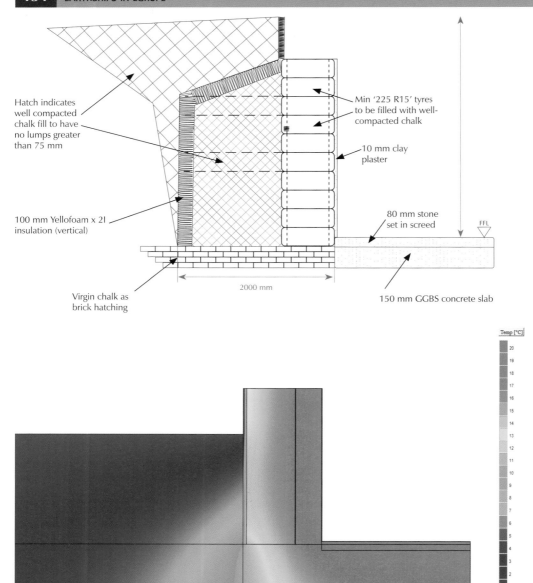

Hatch indicates well compacted chalk fill to have no lumps greater than 75 mm

Min '225 R15' tyres to be filled with well-compacted chalk

10 mm clay plaster

80 mm stone set in screed

FFL

100 mm Yellofoam x 2I insulation (vertical)

Virgin chalk as brick hatching

2000 mm

150 mm GGBS concrete slab

Temp [°C]

20
19
18
17
16
15
14
13
12
11
10
9
8
7
6
5
4
3
2
1
0

Figure 139: Wall to floor junction as built

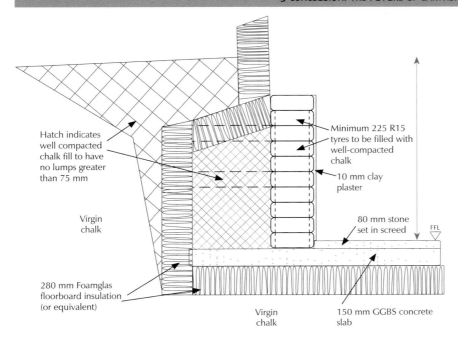

Hatch indicates well compacted chalk fill to have no lumps greater than 75 mm

Minimum 225 R15 tyres to be filled with well-compacted chalk

10 mm clay plaster

Virgin chalk

80 mm stone set in screed

FFL

280 mm Foamglas floorboard insulation (or equivalent)

Virgin chalk

150 mm GGBS concrete slab

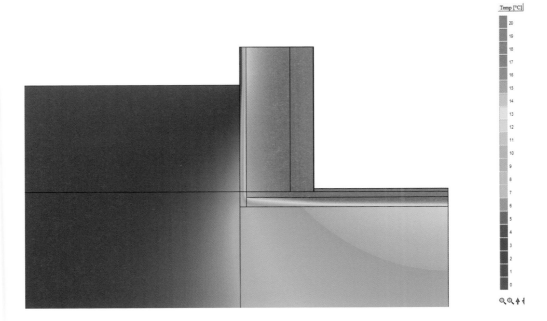

Temp [°C]

Figure 140: Wall to floor junction enhanced

of more insulation in all the elements, and also the introduction of an air control membrane, tapes and ducting in certain places. The use of these materials onsite would take more time, care and attention to detail, and the package of measures, taken together, would mean that the level of building skill required to build an earthship might be beyond that of a self-builder. It would also increase the level of embodied energy of the materials used in the construction, although this would be offset by reduced operation energy.

The biomass heating system and MVHR would have an increased capital cost as well, all to be balanced against the improved levels of thermal comfort and lower operational costs, as highlighted above. In some low-energy systems the increased cost of building fabric materials is offset by the removal of the need for an auxiliary heating system[181].

Construction process

With the increased complexity of detailing, some of the material choices may change. At present most of the earthship is built onsite by hand, although some components, such as engineered trusses, can be manufactured offsite[183]. It may well be that an increasing number of components could be made offsite in factory-controlled conditions, including the windows and doors as complete units, other joinery items, and even the walls, if the tyre walls were replaced by another system such as structurally insulated panels or precast concrete insulated panels. This would clearly change one of the current readily identifiable key features of an earthship – that is, its reuse of car tyres as a recycled material. But if offsite construction techniques were adopted, the build cost would be lower, as the process would be faster and involve less onsite labour[184].

Reduction of summer overheating

Thermal modelling results suggest that the risk of summer overheating is fairly minimal, but the recorded thermal performance data indicates that it is already a problem in Earthship Brighton. As thermal losses are reduced through the building design being upgraded it could become a bigger issue, owing to slower movement of the heat contained in the air, which would be absorbed into the heavyweight structure. To accommodate climate change, shading devices such as louvres or a *brise soleil* may need to be considered in all European earthships to reduce solar gain during the summer months. These are already being used in the Spanish earthships. Night-time cooling may be required as well. More detailed, climate-specific thermal analysis is required, especially given the context of long-term predictions for climate change, such as annual temperatures over Europe increasing at a rate of between 0.1°C and 0.4°C per decade[185]. Some reports state that heavyweight buildings will perform more favourably with predicted increased external temperatures, so the extensive thermal mass of the earthship may be a useful future-proofing feature[186].

This set of design guidelines, as outlined, is a refinement of the earthship concept that goes further than any earthships that have been built in Europe so far. However, it is also just a starting point, and covers only the thermal performance of the earthship. If earthships are to form a serious part of the low-energy building debate in Europe, and provide a thermally comfortable environment, then adoption of the guidelines is mandatory. If the guidelines are not followed, then earthships will be one of the evolutionary branches that are a dead end.

CONCLUSION: THE FUTURE OF EARTHSHIPS IN EUROPE

We have tried to show in this book that earthships are not just 'ecological' buildings. They are also several other things – but, most importantly, they are autonomous, self-sufficient buildings. The two things are not necessarily the same. And it seems that, in temperate European climates at least, the earthship is failing to achieve the thermal performance necessary to mean that it is an effective, sustainable, low-carbon building. If earthships are going to be taken seriously as sustainable buildings they need to be subject to rigorous independent monitoring and evaluation to drive significant design improvements such as those recommended in this book. If they do not evolve, they probably will not die, but they will remain 'outlaw' buildings, on the fringes of architecture – or perhaps they will be the refuges of the last survivors in a post-industrial, post-apocalyptic future.

Whereas in the first edition of this book we suggested that mainstream housebuilding had a lot to learn from earthships, it is increasingly the case that this is a two-way street, and earthships could be improved by learning from some of the more rigorous standards being applied in housebuilding at the moment, such as the German Passivhaus or Swiss 'Minergie'[187]. Earthships present a compelling vision of integrating buildings holistically into landscapes. They are designed by a visionary man, who has inspired many people around the world into action. We commend all of this. We also contend that, in order to deliver this vision in Europe, they need to be built with a more professional approach, and with more attention to the significant details that we have outlined. The only argument against this is that professionalising the building process of earthships also risks taking the process out of the residents' hands. Self-empowerment and self-sufficiency are important parts of the earthship concept. So too is the celebration of rugged individualism and survival on the margins of society. But, to a greater or lesser degree, improved detailing can still be achieved by self-builders without compromising the values embodied in earthships.

This paradox also demonstrates the profound problems at the heart of any idea that earthships will ever become a form of mass housing. The design and philosophy are oriented around individuals taking control of their own lives and building their own dwellings. As we have demonstrated, earthships contest many of the core notions of what constitutes architecture; they are a protest against numerous conventional ways of doing things. This is one of the main things that appeal to many earthship builders. Mass production destroys this attraction – like a protest movement having to form a government. But there are also more practical reasons why earthships as mass housing seems unlikely – problems such as the fact that earthships are low-density, the materials supply chain is completely different from the established construction supply chain, and there is a different skills set that is not yet established in Europe. The more likely scenario is an increasing number of developments across Europe, such as BedZED in south London or One Brighton in Brighton, that take many principles manifest in earthships and apply them using modern, conventional, professional building techniques to create high-density, low-carbon, urban housing. But in their undiluted form, it seems most likely that earthships in Europe will remain 'grand designs' for a few resolute and determined self-builders, drawn by the powerful vision of the 'earthship dream'. In the foreword to the first edition of this book, the author and broadcaster Kevin McCloud wrote that:

'Experimental projects are essential. The rest of the triangle feeds off the crackling brilliance of edgy invention. Sustainable development would not be possible on a large scale if there were no straw bale houses, no cob construction and no Superadobe Earthships. So I salute this survey of the experimental and the innovative, of "first adopters" and adventurers who inform the wider world with their exploits. They are the heroes of the construction world and this book is a fitting tribute.' Kevin McCloud[3]

We wish luck to all those people who plan to join the pioneering trail and build their own earthship. It does not seem an extreme position to want to live either an environmentally-friendly life or one free from the most egregious aspects of the financial system, or both together, yet earthships remain tagged as an alternative brand that appeals to a small minority. And that is as much a comment on society in general as it is on earthships in particular. The brave new world offered by earthships can only now be grasped by those brave enough to reach for it in the first place. And so far, in Europe at least, those people can be counted on two hands. Of course, earthships are utopian and idealistic, and are made out of finely spun dreams as much as of tyres rammed with earth – but that's precisely why people should try to make them work: build them better, yes, interrogate their effectiveness – but carry on dreaming too. As Eleanor Roosevelt said: 'The future belongs to those who believe in the beauty of their dreams.' Amen to that, and vive la earthship!

APPENDIX

Sensor	Sensor type	Location	Frequency (minutes)	Vertical height (metres)	Sensor depth ex. probe (metres)
1	N/A	N/A	N/A	N/a	N/a
2	Air temperature	Between hut wall and glass	10	N/a	N/a
3	Air temperature	On wall of conservatory	10	N/a	N/a
4	Soil temperature	Kitchen	60	1.89	0.25
5	Soil temperature	Kitchen	60	1.89	0.51
6	Soil temperature	Kitchen	60	1.89	0.79
7	Soil temperature	Kitchen	60	1.26	0.25
8	Soil temperature	Kitchen	60	1.26	0.51
9	Soil temperature	Kitchen	60	1.26	0.79
10	Soil temperature	Kitchen	60	0.63	0.25
11	Soil temperature	Kitchen	60	0.63	0.51
12	Soil temperature	Kitchen	60	0.63	0.79
13	Soil temperature	Main room	60	1.89	0.11
14	Soil temperature	Main room	60	1.89	0.51
15	Soil temperature	Main room	60	1.89	0.73
16	Soil temperature	Main room	60	1.26	0.11
17	Soil temperature	Main room	60	1.26	0.51
18	Soil temperature	Main room	60	1.26	0.73
19	Soil temperature	Main room	60	0.63	0.11
20	Soil temperature	Main room	60	0.63	0.51
21	Soil temperature	Main room	60	0.63	0.73
22	Wall temperature	Main room wall temperature	10	N/a	N/a
23	Soil temperature	Main room – ground	60	N/a	N/a
24	Soil temperature	Main room – ground	60	N/a	N/a
25	N/A	N/A	N/A	N/a	N/a
26	Soil temperature	Weather station – ground	5	N/a	N/a
27	Air temperature	Weather station	5	N/a	N/a

Table A1: Earthship Brighton sensor summary

Table A1: Earthship Brighton sensor summary (contd)

Sensor	Sensor type	Location	Frequency (minutes)	Vertical height (metres)	Sensor depth ex. probe (metres)
28	Solar radiation	Weather station	5	N/A	N/A
29	Wall temperature	Hut wall	10	N/A	N/A
30	Radiant temperature	Main room wall	10	N/A	N/A
31*	Nest air temperature	Shelf in main roof	10	2.0	N/A
32*	Nest relative humidity	Shelf in main roof	10	2.0	N/A
33*	Hut air temperature	Balustrade in hut	10	1.2	N/A
34*	Hut relative humidity	Balustrade in hut	10	1.2	N/A

* Sensors 31, 32, 33 and 34 are each one mini data logger with two channels. One channel monitors ambient air temperature and the other relative humidity.

REFERENCES AND NOTES

1   Department for Communities and Local Government. The Code for Sustainable Homes. Wetherby, Communities and Local Government Publications, 2006.

2   Climate Change Act 2008. London, The National Archives, 2008.

3   Hewitt M and Telfer K. Earthships: Building a zero carbon future for homes. Bracknell, BRE IHS Press, 2007.

4   Ibid, p 16.

5   For example, in the UK see Blair D. Average household faces fuel poverty by 2015. Financial Times, 10 October 2011.

6   See chapter 7 for full details of interviews with European earthship builders.

7   Telfer K. Earth mover. The Architects' Journal, 19 June 2003, 18–19.

8   Reynolds M E. Earthship. Volume 1: How to build your own. Taos, New Mexico, Solar Survival Press, 1990. p 19.

9   Ibid, p 74.

10   http://nysc.eas.cornell.edu/newyork_c20.html.

11   Reynolds M. A coming of wizards: A manual of human potential. Taos, New Mexico, The High Mesa Foundation, 1989.

12   Conversation with author, 2006.

13   Reynolds M E. Earthship. Volume 1: How to build your own. Taos, New Mexico, Solar Survival Press, 1990. p 44.

14   www.youtube.com/watch?v=3tFJa2aHgN4.

15   www.garbagewarrior.com.

16   Shukman H. New age New Mexico. Observer, 19 March 2006.

17   Department for Business, Innovation and Skills. Estimate of CO_2 emissions that the construction industry can influence. Crown, London, Autumn 2010.

18   www.passivhaus.org.uk.

19   www.oneplanetvision.org/one-planet-living/opl-framework.

20   Thompson H S. The great shark hunt: Strange tales from a strange time. Gonzo Papers, Vol. 1. New York, Summit Books, 1979. p 49.

21   http://eebu.earthshipeurope.org.

22   Johnston L. September 2011. www.earthship.net/begin-here-articles/1042-larry-johnston-eco-friendly-earthship-homes-are-out-of-this-world.

23   Reynolds M E. Earthship. Volume 1: How to build your own. Introduction. Taos, New Mexico, Solar Survival Press, 1990.

24   Ibid, p 9.

25   Ibid, p 8.

26   CIUT FM Radio. The green majority interview with Mike Reynolds. Toronto, Canada, March 7, 2008. Can be found at: http://besustainable.com/greenmajority/2008/03/07/tgm-75.

27   Reynolds M E. Earthship. Volume 2: Systems and Components. Taos, New Mexico, Solar Survival Press, 1990.

28   www.telegraph.co.uk/news/worldnews/europe/6227454/EU-energy-security-is-in-the-pipeline.html.

29   Crossing Continents. http://news.bbc.co.uk/1/hi/programmes/crossing_continents/141812.stm.

30   Biotecture (2011) Earthship Biotecture website, Taos, New Mexico, US. Available at: www.earthship.com/Communities/communities.html.

31   Lawrence, E. et al. The greater world earthship community and earthship water, waste and energy systems. University of Oregon, Washington, US, 2006. Available at: http://design.uoregon.edu/nywc/arch/studio/arch484/2006/484s06cases/Earthships.pdf.

32   Reynolds M E. Earthship. Volume 1: How to build your own. Taos, New Mexico, Solar Survival Press, 1990. p 4.

33   For example, see http://epa.gov/climatechange/effects/extreme.html.

34   www.fuel-poverty.org/files/WP7_D26-1_en.pdf.

35 Hyett P. Awful warnings on the pressing need for sustainable cities. The Architects' Journal, 8 July, 1999.

36 Reynolds M E. Earthship. Volume 1: How to build your own. Taos, New Mexico, Solar Survival Press, 1990, p 8.

37 See chapter 7 for a description of the interviews conducted with European earthship builders.

38 Boyle G (ed.). Renewable energy. Oxford, Oxford University Press, 2004, p 12.

39 Desai P and King P. One planet living: A guide to enjoying life on our one planet. Bristol, Alastair Sawday Publishing, 2006.

40 Wines J. Green architecture: The art of architecture in the age of ecology. Köln, Taschen, 2000, p 237.

41 Wines J. Green architecture. 2000, p 39.

42 Sustainable Homes embodied energy in residential property development: A guide for registered social landlords. Teddington, Sustainable Homes, 1999.

43 CIRIA. Environmental impacts of materials. Volume A: Summary. London, CIRIA, 1995.

44 http://m.building.co.uk/data/sustainability-%E2%80%94-embodied-carbon/3097160.article.

45 www.letsrecycle.com/news/latest-news/waste-management/uk-leads-europe-on-tyre-recycling.

46 Reynolds M E. Earthship. Volume 1: How to build your own. Taos, New Mexico, Solar Survival Press, 1990, p 77.

47 TecEco, Glenorchy, Tasmania. www.tececo.com.

48 See the YouTube video 'Fishing in the Phoenix Earthship'. www.youtube.com/watch?v=j-OZrtnx1SQ.

49 Mazria E. The passive solar energy book. Emmaus, PA, Rodale Press, 1979.

50 Reynolds M E. Package Earthship detail booklet with plan options. Taos, New Mexico, Solar Survival Press, 2002.

51 Kachadorian J. The passive solar house: The complete guide to heating and cooling your home. White River Junction, VT, Chelsea Green Publishing Company, 2006.

52 Reynolds M E. Earthship. Volume 3: Evolution beyond economics. Taos, New Mexico, Solar Survival Press, 1993.

53 Cowie P. The earthship toolkit: Your guide to building a zero waste zero energy future. Kinghorn, Sustainable Communities Initiative, 2004.

54 Rawell Environmental. Rawell Environmental Ltd website, Hoylake, Wirral, UK, 2011.

55 Jones B. Information guide to straw bale building for self builders and the construction industry. Todmorden, Amazon Nails, 2001.

56 Halliday S. Earthship Fife: Building control and monitoring issues final report. Edinburgh, Gaia Research, 2003.

57 Rowe M. Dumped on. The Guardian, London, 15 May 2002. Available online at www.guardian.co.uk/society/2002/may/15/environment.waste.

58 Reynolds M E. Comfort in any climate. Taos, New Mexico, Solar Survival Press, 2000, p 58.

59 Claytec, Boisheim, Germany. www.claytec.com.

60 Reynolds M E. Earthship. Volume 1: How to build your own. Taos, New Mexico, Solar Survival Press, 1990. p 18.

61 Council Directive 1999/31/EC of 26 April 1999 on the landfill of waste.

62 European Tyre & Rubber Manufacturers' Association. End of life tyres: A valuable resource with growing potential. Brussels 2010. Can be accessed online at: www.etrma.org/pdf/20101220%20Brochure%20ELT_2010_final%20version.pdf.

63 Crossing Continents, BBC Radio 4, London, BBC, 1998.

64 Reynolds M E. Earthship. Volume 1: How to build your own. Taos, New Mexico, Solar Survival Press, 1990, p 77.

65 Ibid, p 78.

66 www.odyssee-indicators.org/reports/household/households.pdf.

67 Lyall S. Specifiers' choice: Earthship Brighton. AJ Specification, 2006.

68 The Waste Management Licensing Regulations. London, The National Archives, 1994.

69 Environment Agency regulatory position statement relating to the Schumacher earthship (EA ref. RPS 069, July 2010).

70 Cowie P and Kemp S. The earthship toolkit. 2nd edn Kinghorn, Sustainable Communities Initiative, 2007.

71 Letter sent by the Environment Agency to the directors of the company building the earthship – the Low Carbon Network Ltd (LCN) – in February 2003.

72   The Environment Council. Required exemptions to waste management licensing for tyre recovery. London, 2004.

73   This situation was revealed through an email conversation between Schumacher College and the Environment Agency in 2010, copied to the authors.

74   www.wrap.org.uk/downloads/mini_PAAS108_approved_25april07.c686017a.3779.pdf.

75   Quote from a telephone conversation with Clive Humphries, Senior Advisor: Environment and Business at the Environment Agency, 18 November 2011.

76   Environment Agency. Tyres in the environment. Bristol, Environment Agency, 1998.

77   Cowie P and Kemp S. The earthship toolkit. 2nd edn. Kinghorn, Sustainable Communities Initiative, 2007, p 57.

78   Evans M S. Tyre compounding for improved performance. Shrewsbury, Rapra Technology Limited, 2004.

79   World Health Organization. Indoor air quality: Organic pollutants. Copenhagen, World Health Organization, Regional Office for Europe, 1989.

80   California Department of Public Health. Indoor Air Quality Programme. www.cal-iaq.org/separator/voc/voc-questions.

81   Earthship Biotecture. Taos, New Mexico. www.earthship.net/offgassing.

82   National Institute for Occupation Safety. National Institute for Occupation Safety and Health pocket guide to chemical hazards. Publication no. 2005–149. Cincinnati, OH, DHHS (NIOSH) Publications, 2007, p 52.

83   Ibid, p 311.

84   Etyres, Cambridge. www.etyres.co.uk/tyre-construction.

85   www.iso.org/iso/iso_catalogue/catalogue_tc/catalogue_detail.htm?csnumber=38203.

86   Earthship Biotecture website. Earthship Biotecture, Taos, New Mexico, USA. Accessed 7 April 2008, www.earthship.net/modules.php?name=News&file=article&sid=21.

87   Great Britain. Her Majesty's Courts Service website (2008), Her Majesty's Courts Service. www.hrcompanion.co.uk/component/k2/item/678-coxall-v-goodyear-great-britain-limited-court-of-appeal.

88   Hall K (ed). The green building bible. Volume 1. Llandysul, 3rd edn. Green Building Press, 2006, p 163.

89   Great Britain. Parliament, House of Commons Hansard Website (2012). Hansard, London, Available at: www.publications.parliament.uk/pa/cm198990/cmhansrd/1990-07-26/Debate-4.html.

90   Brighton & Hove Wood Recycling Project. www.woodrecycling.org.uk.

91   Boyle G (ed.). Renewable energy. Oxford, Oxford University Press, 2004, p 31.

92   Clarke A and Grant N. Biomass: A burning issue. Lllandysul, Association of Environment Conscious Building, 2010.

93   Boyle G (ed.). Renewable energy. Oxford, Oxford University Press, 2004. Footnote 20.

94   Piggott H. Windpower workshop: Building your own wind turbine. Machynlleth, Centre for Alternative Technology Publications, 2000.

95   Energy Saving Trust. Location, location, location: Domestic small-scale wind field trial report. London: Energy Saving Trust, 2009.

96   Phillips R, Blackmore P, Anderson J, Clift M, Aguilo-Rullan A and Pester S. Micro wind turbines in urban environments: An assessment. Bracknell, IHS BRE Press, 2007.

97   Boyle G (ed.). Renewable energy. Oxford, Oxford University Press, 2004. p 12.

98   Boyle G (ed.). Renewable energy. Oxford, Oxford University Press, 2004.

99   European Commission. Photovoltaic Geographical Information System (PVGIS) website, Ispra, Italy. Available online at http://re.jrc.ec.europa.eu/pvgis.

100   Olivier D. Less is more. Proceedings of the AECB Conference, University of Nottingham, 16–17 September 2011. Lllandysul, AECB, 2011, unpublished.

101   Reynolds M. Water from the sky. Taos, New Mexico, Solar Survival Press, 2005, p22.

102   Reynolds M. Presentation to Green Party councillors at Brighton Town Hall on 26 June 2006; also conversation with the authors.

103   Henley J. The no money man. The Guardian, London, 25 January 2010. Available online at www.guardian.co.uk/environment/video/2010/jan/25/mark-boyle-no-money-man.

104   Reynolds M. Water from the sky. Taos, New Mexico, Solar Survival Press, 2005.

105   Pearce F. When the rivers run dry: What happens when our water runs out? London, Eden Project Books, 2006.

106 BBC. Europe drought: France pledges 1 bn euros for farmers, 10 June 2011. Available online at www.bbc.co.uk/news/world-europe-13725016.

107 Nash, E. Spain's drought: a glimpse of our future? 24 May 2008, London, UK, 2011. Available online at www.independent.co.uk/news/world/europe/spains-drought-a-glimpse-of-our-future-833587.html.

108 BBC. Homes forced to get water meters, 1 March 2006. Available online at http://news.bbc.co.uk/1/hi/4759960.stm.

109 Environment Agency. Water resources and abstraction. Available online at www.environment-agency.gov.uk/cy/ymchwil/llyfrgell/data/34375.aspx.

110 WWF. Living planet report. Gland, Switzerland, WWF International.

111 Watkins K. Human development report 2006. Beyond scarcity: Power, poverty and the global water crisis. New York, United Nations Development Programme, 2006.

112 Reed B and Reed B. Technical notes on drinking water, sanitation and hygiene in emergencies. Geneva, World Health Organization, 2011.

113 Environment Agency. Save water. Available online at www.environment-agency.gov.uk/homeandleisure/beinggreen/117266.aspx.

114 Waterwise. www.waterwise.org.

115 Thorton J. Rainwater harvesting systems: are they a green solution to water shortages? Green Building Magazine, 2008, 17 (4) 40–43.

116 ech$_2$o. Conversation with author, 2007.

117 Rainfall data from Meteonorm. www.meteonorm.com.

118 Reynolds M. Water from the sky. Taos, New Mexico, Solar Survival Press, 2005, p 29.

119 Ecoplay, Doncaster, UK. www.ecoplay-systems.com.

120 Reynolds M. Water from the sky. Taos, New Mexico, Solar Survival Press, 2005, p 11.

121 Vortex Fine Filter, from WISY, Hitzkirchen, Germany. Available online at www.wisy.de/eng/eng/wff1xx.htm.

122 Parsloe C. CIBSE knowledge series: Reclaimed water. London, The Chartered Institute of Building Services Engineers, 2005.

123 The reduced figures are calculated from 150 l/person/day, minus toilet flushing and outdoor usage.

124 Kruis N J and Heun M K. Analysis of the performance of earthship housing in various global climates. Proceedings of the ASME 2007 Energy Sustainability Conference. Long Beach, CA, 27–30 June 2007, pp 431–440.

125 Earthship Biotecture water organizing module. Earthship Biotecture, Taos, New Mexico. Available online at http://earthship.net/buildings/836.

126 The Water Supply (Water Quality) Regulations 2000. London, HMSO.

127 WHO. Guidelines for drinking water quality. Volume 1: Recommendations. 3rd edn. Geneva, World Health Organization, 2004.

128 Directive 98/83/EC. The Drinking Water Directive. Brussels, European Parliament and Council of the European Union, 1998.

129 www.legislation.gov.uk/uksi/2009/3101/pdfs/uksi_20093101_en.pdf. p 3.

130 Leggett D J, Brown R, Stanfield G, Brewer D and Holliday E. Rainwater and greywater use in buildings: Decision making for water conservation. CIRIA PR80. London, Construction Industry Research and Information Association, 2001.

131 Nicol J F and Humphreys M A. Adaptive thermal comfort and sustainable thermal standards for buildings. Oxford, Oxford Centre for Sustainable Development, 2000.

132 Roaf S. Ecohouse 2: A design guide. Oxford, Architectural Press, 2007.

133 Cowie P and Kemp S. The earthship toolkit: Your guide to building a zero waste zero energy future. Kinghorn, Sustainable Communities Initiative, 2007, 2nd edn. p 2.

134 Ibid, p 45.

135 Ibid, p 47.

136 Ibid, p 57.

137 www.homebuilding.co.uk/feature/how-much-will-your-project-cost-part-one.

138 Telfer K. Super green European breaks. Guardian, London, 26 April 2008. Available to view online at: www.guardian.co.uk/travel/2008/apr/26/top100flightfreeholidays.green.

139 Howarth D and Nortje A. Groundhouse build + cook: Diary of a natural home. Brighton, Bliksem, 2010, p 17.

140 http://earthship.es/planning.

141 www.sunseed.org.uk.

142 www.sakuvald.ee/43113.

143 www.greenheadmoss.org.uk/id14.html.

144 http://bristolgreenhouse.co.uk/tyrewalls.html.

145 www.earthshipbelgium.be/en/articles/projects/257-project-earthresidence.html?start=2.

146 Pearson D. In search of natural architecture. London, Gaia Books, 2005.

147 Butti K and Perlin J. A golden thread: 2500 years of solar architecture and history. London, Marion Boyars Publishers, 1980.

148 Frum D. How we got here: The '70s. New York, Basic Books, 2000, p 318.

149 Post Carbon Institute, Santa Rosa, California. www.energybulletin.net/primer.php.

150 Whittier J. New Mexico passive solar home temperature survey. Albuquerque, New Mexico Solar Energy Institute, 1987.

151 Reynolds M. Comfort in any climate. Taos, New Mexico, Solar Survival Press, 2000.

152 Holladay M. Solar versus superinsulation: a 30-year-old debate. Green Building Advisor website, Newtown, Connecticut. Available online at www.greenbuildingadvisor.com/book/export/html/18187.

153 Shurcliff W. Super insulated houses and double envelope houses. Andover, Massachusetts, Brick House Publishing, 1981.

154 Holladay M. Forgotten pioneers of energy efficiency. Green Building Advisor website, Newtown, Connecticut. Available online at www.greenbuildingadvisor.com/book/export/html/12869.

155 Lebens R (ed). Passive solar architecture in Europe: The results of the First European Passive Solar Competition – 1980. London, Architectural Press, 1980.

156 Boyle G (ed.). Renewable energy. Oxford, Oxford University Press, 2004.

157 Reynolds M E. Earthship. Volume 1: How to build your own. Taos, New Mexico, Solar Survival Press, 1990, p 38.

158 NASA GISS. 2009: Second warmest year on record; end of warmest decade. NASA GISS, Washington, DC, 2009. Available online at www.giss.nasa.gov/research/news/20100121.Touch The Earth Ranch website, Colorado. www.touchtheearthranch.com/Rhome.htm.

159 Herald's Earthship Adventure. Available on www.genrefluent.com/earthshi.htm.

160 Trott K. Conversation with author, 2 June 2009.

161 Howarth D and Nortje A. Groundhouse build + cook: Diary of a natural home. Brighton, Bliksem, 2010, pp 17, 19.

162 Oscar and Lisa's Earthship Build website, Valencia, Spain. Available on http://oscarlisabuild.blogspot.com/2009/01/winter-in-earthship.html.

163 Butcher K (ed). Environmental design: CIBSE guide A. London, Yale Press, 2006.

164 Leaman A and Bordass B. Are users more tolerant of 'green' buildings? Building Research and Information, 2007, 35 (6) 662–673.

165 Grindley P and Hutchinson M. The thermal behaviours of an earthship. Renewable Energy, 1996 8 (1–4) 154–159.

166 Ip K and Miller A. The Brighton Earthship: Evaluating the thermal performance. Brighton, University of Brighton, 2005.

167 Butcher K (ed). Environmental design: CIBSE guide A. London, Yale Press, 2006.

168 Miller A, Ip K, Lam M and Shaw K. The predicted and observed thermal performance of the Brighton 'Earthship In: World Sustainable Building Conference, 27 September 2005, Tokyo, Japan.

169 Miller, A and Ip K. Thermal storage – an evaluation of the thermal performance of the Brighton Earthship In: World Sustainable Building Conference, 2–25 Sept 2008, Melbourne, Australia.

170 Delta T Devices, Cambridge, UK. www.delta-t.co.uk.

171 Dickson, Addison, Illinois. www.dicksondata.com.

172 NASA website. www.nasa.gov/centers/goddard/news/topstory/2006/2006_warm.html.

173 Energy Saving Trust. www.energysavingtrust.org.uk/In-your-home/Heating-and-hot-water/Thermostats-and-controls.

174 Reynolds M. Earthship. Volume 1: How to build your own. Taos, New Mexico, 1990, p 23.

175 PHI, Darmstadt, Germany. Available online on www.passiv.de.

176 The Earthship Fife toolkit states that materials were £26,034, and the estimated value of voluntary labour was £20,000–24,000.

177 Howarth D and Nortje A. Groundhouse build + cook: Diary of a natural home. Brighton, Bliksem, 2010. p 9.

178 See www.lowcarbon.co.uk/earthship-brighton and www.sci-scotland.org.uk/earthship_centre.shtml.

179 Department for Communities and Local Government (DCLG). The Building Regulations 2006 (England and Wales). Approved Document L1A: Conservation of fuel and power (New dwellings) (2006 edition). London, DCLG, 2006. Available online at www.planningportal.gov.uk/uploads/br/BR_PDF_ADL1A_2006.pdf.

180 Energy Saving Trust. Energy efficient ventilation in dwellings: A guide for specifiers. London, Energy Saving Trust, 2006.

181 PHI, Darmstadt, Germany. Available at www.passivhaustagung.de/Passive_House_E/PHPP.html.

182 Audenaerta A, De Cleynb SH and Vankerckhoveb, B. Economic analysis of passive houses and low-energy houses compared with standard houses. Energy Policy, 2007, vol. 36, pp 47–55.

183 Hewitt M and Telfer K. Earthships: Building a zero carbon future for homes. Bracknell, BRE IHS Press, 2007.

184 Bågenholm C, Yates A and McAllister I. Prefabricated housing in the UK: A summary paper. Watford, BRE.

185 IPCC. Climate scenarios for the future. Geneva, Intergovernmental Panel on Climate Change. Available at www.ipcc.ch/ipccreports/tar/wg2/index.php?idp=495.

186 Twinn C and Hacker J. UK housing and climate change: Heavyweight versus lightweight construction. London, Ove Arup and Partners Ltd, 2005.

187 Minergie, Bern, Germany. Available at www.minergie.com/home_en.html.

188 Hewitt M and Telfer K. Earthships: Building a zero carbon future for homes. Bracknell, BRE IHS Press, 2007, p x.

All URLs accessed 25 October 2011. The publisher accepts no responsibility for the persistence or accuracy of URLs referred to in this publication, and does not guarantee that any content on such websites is, or will remain, accurate or appropriate.

INDEX